JOHN WESLEY'S
JOURNAL

Also available in the Spiritual Lives series

JOHN WESLEY'S
JOURNAL

Abridged by
Percy Livingstone Parker

with an introduction by
Hugh Price Hughes, MA

and an appreciation of the Journal by
Augustine Birrell, KC

Edited by Robert Backhouse

Hodder & Stoughton
LONDON SYDNEY AUCKLAND

This selection first published 1902

This edition first published in Great Britain 1993

10 9 8 7 6 5 4 3 2

British Library Cataloguing in Publication Data
A record for this book is available from the British Library

ISBN 0 340 57774 6

Printed and bound in Great Britain by
Cox & Wyman Ltd, Reading, Berks.

Hodder and Stoughton
A division of Hodder Headline PLC
338 Euston Road
London NW1 3BH

Contents

Introduction to the 1993 Edition

John Wesley's original, unedited *Journal* extended to some twenty-six volumes. Wesley himself reduced these to four volumes. Percy Livingstone Parker made selections from these four volumes for his own abridgement. This 1993 edition is an abridgement of Percy Livingstone Parker's large single volume of Wesley's *Journal*. It retains Hugh Price Hughes' Introduction as well as Augustine Birrell's Appreciation, both of which appeared in the 1902 edition of Parker's single volume of the *Journal*. These provide valuable insight into the life and work of Wesley and into the writing of his *Journal*.

Robert Backhouse
Crostwight, 1992

Editor's Note

When John Wesley prepared his *Journal* for publication he prefaced it with the following account of its origin:

It was in pursuance of an advice given by Bishop Taylor, in his *Rule for Holy Living and Dying*, that, about fifteen years ago, I began to take a more exact account than I had done before, of the manner wherein I spent my time, writing down how I had employed every hour.

This I continued to do, wherever I was, till the time of my leaving England for Georgia. The variety of scenes which I then passed through induced me to transcribe, from time to time, the more material parts of my diary, adding here and there such little reflections as occurred to my mind.

Of this Journal thus occasionally compiled, the following is a short extract: it not being my design to relate all those particulars which I wrote for my own use only, and which would answer no valuable end to others, however important they were to me.

Rev John Telford, one of Wesley's biographers, says:

The earlier parts of the Journal were published in the interest of Methodism, that the calumny and slander then rife might be silenced by a plain narrative of the facts as to its founding, and its purpose. The complete Journals, still preserved in twenty-six bound volumes, have never been printed. Copious extracts were made by John Wesley himself, and issued in twenty-one parts, the successive instalments being eagerly expected by a host of readers.

The published *Journal* makes four volumes, each about the size of the present book. But though I have had to curtail it by three-quarters I have tried to retain the atmosphere of tremendous activity which is one of its most remarkable features.

Mr Birrell, in his Appreciation, has focused in a very striking way upon the interest, actuality, and charm of Wesley's *Journal,* and all I have had to do was to select those portions which best illustrate them.

The wonder is that it has not been done before. Edward FitzGerald once wrote to Professor Norton: 'Had I any interest with publishers I would get them to reprint parts of it,' for he was a great lover of the *Journal.*

Writing to another friend about Wesley's *Journal,* FitzGerald said:

> If you don't know it, do know it. It is curious to think of this diary running coevally with Walpole's letters—diary—the two men born and dying too within a few miles of one another, and with such different lives to record. And it is remarkable to read pure, unaffected, undying English, while Addison and Johnson are tainted with a style which all the world imitated.

Macaulay's estimate of Wesley may also be recalled. Wesley, he said, was

> a man whose eloquence and logical acuteness might have made him eminent in literature, whose genius for government was not inferior to that of Richelieu, and who, whatever his errors may have been, devoted all his powers in defiance of obloquy and derision, to what he sincerely considered as the highest good of his species.

Wesley is one of the most strenuous ethical figures in history, and literature has no other such record of personal endeavour as that contained in these pages. To make that record accessible to everyone is the object of this edition.

Introduction to the 1902 Edition

He who desires to understand the real history of the English people during the seventeenth, eighteenth and nineteenth centuries should read most carefully three books: George Fox's *Journal*, John Wesley's *Journal*, and John Henry Newman's *Apologia Pro Vita Sua*.

As Lord Hugh Cecil has recently said in a memorable speech, the religious question cannot be ignored. It is *the* question; in the deepest sense it is the only question. It has always determined the course of history everywhere. In all ages the sceptical literary class has tried ignore it, as the Roman historians, poets, and philosophers ignored Christianity until the time when Christianity became triumphant and dominant throughout the Roman Empire.

But, however much ignored or boycotted by literary men, the growth or decline of religion ultimately settles everything. Has not Carlyle said that George Fox making his own clothes is the most remarkable event in our history? George Fox was the very incarnation of that individualism which has played, and will yet play, so great a part in the making of modern England. If you want to understand 'the dissidence of Dissent and the Protestantism of the Protestant religion', read the *Journal* of George Fox.

Then came John Wesley and his 'helpers'. They were the first preachers since the days of the Franciscan friars in the Middle Ages who ever reached the working classes. In England, as in France, Germany, and everywhere else, the Reformation was essentially a middle class movement. It never captured either the upper classes or the working classes. That explains its limitations.

As Dr Rigg has shown, Wesley's itineraries were deliberately planned to bring him into direct contact neither with the aristocracy nor with the dependent or poverty-stricken poor, but with the industrious self-supporting workmen in town and country. The ultimate result was that the man in the street became Methodist in his conception of Christianity, whatever his personal conduct and character might be. A profound French critic said, fifty years ago, that modern England was Methodist, and the remark applied equally to the United States and to our colonies. The doctrines of the Evangelical Revival permeated the English-speaking world.

Then Newman appeared on the scene and a tremendous change began. The Anglican Church revived, and revived in Newman's direction. We witness today on every side the vast results of the Newman era. Many of these results are beneficial in the extreme; others cannot be welcome to those who belong to the schools of George Fox and John Wesley.

The whole future of the British Empire depends upon this question of questions—will George Fox and John Wesley on the one hand, or John Henry Newman on the other, ultimately prevail? And the best way to arrive at the true inwardness of the issue is to read, ponder, and inwardly digest Wesley's *Journal* and Newman's *Apologia*.

It is a great advantage that Mr Parker has secured permission to republish Mr Augustine Birrell's Appreciation. That brilliant writer demonstrates that there is no book in existence that gives you so exact and vivid a description of the eighteenth century in England as Wesley's *Journal*. It is an incalculably more varied and complete account of the condition of the people of England than Boswell's *Johnson*.

As Mr Birrell says, Wesley was himself 'the greatest force of the eighteenth century in England. No man lived nearer the centre than John Wesley. Neither Clive nor Pitt, neither Mansfield nor Johnson. No single figure influenced so many minds, no single voice touched so many hearts. No other man did such a life's work for England.' Wesley has demonstrated that a true prophet of God has more influence than all the politicians and soldiers and millionaires put together. He is the incalculable and unexpected element that is always putting all the devices of the clever to naught.

I do not understand what Mr Birrell means by saying that 'as a writer Wesley has not achieved distinction. He was no Athanasius, no Augustine; he was ever a preacher.' It is true that Wesley's main business was not to define metaphysical theology, but to cultivate friendly relations with Christians of all schools, and to save living men from sin. But he gave a death-blow to the destructive dogma of limited salvation with which the names of Augustine and Calvin will be for ever associated.

No doubt, like Oliver Cromwell, Wesley was essentially a 'man of action', and he deliberately sacrificed the niceties of literary taste to the greater task of making Englishmen on both sides of the Atlantic real Christians. Even so, the style of some of his more literary productions is a model of lucidity and grace.

But my main point here is to echo Mr Birrell's final statement, that 'we can learn better from Wesley's *Journal* than from anywhere else what manner of man Wesley was, and the character of the times during which he lived and moved and had his being.' My co-religionists and all who love the most characteristic qualities of modern English life are under a deep debt of obligation to my friend Mr Parker and his publishers for giving them an opportunity of studying the eventful eighteenth century of English history at its centre and fountain-head.

The fact that this edition of the work has been

condensed is no drawback. The *Journal*, as originally published, was itself condensed by Wesley. The Wesleyan Book Room has in its possession large unpublished portions of the manuscript, much of which will be included in the standard edition which the Wesleyan Methodist Editor has now in hand; but for popular purposes Mr Parker's edition will answer all important ends, and will give Englishmen for the first time an opportunity of reading in a handy form one of the most important, instructive, and entertaining books ever published in the English language.

Of course Mr Parker alone is responsible for the selection of the portions of the *Journal* which appear in this volume.

Hugh Price Hughes
Adelboden, May 30, 1902

An Appreciation of John Wesley's Journal

John Wesley, born as he was in 1703 and dying as he did in 1791, covers as nearly as mortal man may, the whole of the eighteenth century, of which he was one of the most typical and certainly the most strenuous figure.

He began his published *Journal* on October 14, 1735, and its last entry is under date Sunday, October 24, 1790, when in the morning he explained to a numerous congregation in Spitalfields Church 'The Whole Armour of God', and in the afternoon enforced to a still larger audience in St Paul's, Shadwell, the great truth, 'One thing is needful', the last words of the *Journal* being: 'I hope many, even then, resolved to choose the better part.'

Between these two Octobers there lies the most amazing record of human exertion ever penned or endured.

I do not know whether I am likely to have among my readers anyone who has ever contested an English or Scottish county in a parliamentary election since household suffrage. If I have, that tired soul will know how severe is the strain of its three weeks, and how impossible it seemed at the end of the first week that you should be able to keep it going for another fortnight, and how when the last night arrived you felt that had the strife been accidentally prolonged another seven days you must have perished by the wayside.

21

Contesting the three kingdoms

Well, John Wesley contested the three kingdoms for the cause of Christ during a campaign which lasted forty years.

He did it for the most part on horseback. He paid more turnpikes than any man who ever bestrode a beast. Eight thousand miles was his annual record for many a long year, during each of which he seldom preached less frequently than five hundred times. Had he but preserved his bills at all the inns where he lodged, they would have made by themselves a history of prices. And throughout it all he never knew what depression of spirits meant—though he had much to try him, suits in chancery and a jealous wife.

In the course of this unparalleled context Wesley visited again and again the most out of the way districts—the remotest corners of England—places which today lie far removed even from the searcher after the picturesque.

In 1899, when the map of England looks like a gridiron of railways, none but the sturdiest of pedestrians, the most determined of cyclists can retrace the steps of Wesley and his horse, and stand by the rocks and the natural amphitheatres in Cornwall and Northumberland, in Lancashire and Berkshire, where he preached his gospel to the heathen.

Exertion so prolonged, enthusiasm so sustained, argues a remarkable man, while the organisation he created, the system he founded, the view of life he promulgated, is still a great fact among us. No other name than Wesley's lies embalmed as his does. Yet he is not a popular figure. Our standard historians have dismissed him curtly. The fact is, Wesley puts your ordinary historian out of conceit with himself.

How much easier to weave into your page the gossip of Horace Walpole, to enliven it with a heartless jest of George Selwyn's, to make it blush with sad stories of the extravagance of Fox, to embroider it with the rhetoric of Burke, to humanise it with the talk of Johnson, to discuss the rise and fall of administrations, the growth and decay of the constitution, than to follow John Wesley into the streets of Bristol, or on to the bleak moors near Burslem, when he met, face to face in all their violence, all their ignorance, and all their generosity the living men, women, and children who made up the nation.

A book of plots, plays and novels

It has perhaps also to be admitted that to found great organisations is to build your tomb—a splendid tomb, it may be, a veritable sarcophagus, but none the less a tomb. John Wesley's chapels lie a little heavily on John Wesley. Even so do the glories of Rome make us forgetful of the grave in Syria.

It has been said that Wesley's character lacks charm, that mighty antiseptic. It is not easy to define charm, which is not a catalogue of qualities, but a mixture. Let no one deny charm to Wesley who has not read his *Journal*. Southey's *Life* is a dull, almost a stupid book which happily there is no need to read. Read the *Journal*, which is a book full of plots and plays and novels, which quivers with life and is crammed full of character.

Wesley's family stock

John Wesley came of a stock which had been much harassed and put about by our unhappy religious difficulties. Politics, business, and religion are the three things Englishmen are said to worry themselves about. The Wesleys early took up with religion. John Wesley's great-grandfather and grandfather were both ejected from their livings in 1662, and the grandfather was so bullied and oppressed by the Five Mile Act that he early gave up the ghost. Whereupon his remains were refused what is called Christian burial, though a holier and more primitive man never drew breath. This poor, persecuted spirit left two sons according to the flesh, Matthew and Samuel; and Samuel it was who in his turn became the father of John and Charles Wesley.

Samuel Wesley, though minded to share the lot, hard though that lot was, of his progenitors, had the moderation of mind, the Christian conservatism which ever marked the family, and being sent to a dissenting college became disgusted with the ferocity and bigotry he happened there to encounter. Those were the days of the Calf's Head Club and feastings on the 29th of January, graceless meals for which Samuel Wesley had no stomach. His turn was for the things that are 'quiet, wise, and good'. He departed from the Dissenting seminary and in 1685 entered himself as a poor scholar at Exeter College, Oxford. He brought £2 6s. with him, and as for prospects, he had none. Exeter received him.

During the eighteenth century our two universities, famous despite their faults, were always open to the poor scholar who was ready to subscribe, not to boat clubs or cricket clubs, but to the Thirty-nine Articles. Three archbishops of Canterbury during the eighteenth century were the sons of small tradesmen. There was, in fact, much less snobbery and money-worship during the century when the British empire was being won than during the century when it is being talked about.

Samuel Wesley was allowed to remain at Oxford, where he supported himself by devices known to his tribe, and when he left the university to be ordained he had clear in his pouch, after discharging his few debts, £10 15s. He had thus made £8 9s. out of his university, and had his education, as it were, thrown in for nothing. He soon obtained a curacy in London and married a daughter of the well-known ejected clergyman Dr Annesley, about whom you may read in another eighteenth-century book, *The Life and Errors of John Dunton*.

Wesley's mother

The mother of the Wesleys was a remarkable woman, though cast in a mould not much to our minds nowadays. She had nineteen children, and greatly prided herself on having taught them, one after another, by frequent chastisements to, what do you think? to cry softly. She had theories of education and strength of will, and of arm too, to carry them out.

She knew Latin and Greek, and though a stern, forbidding, almost an unfeeling, parent, she was successful in winning and retaining not only the respect but the affection of such of her huge family as lived to grow up. But out of the nineteen, thirteen early succumbed. Infant mortality was one of the great facts of the eighteenth century whose Rachels had to learn to cry softly over their dead babies. The mother of the Wesleys thought more of her children's souls than of their bodies.

A domestic squall

The revolution of 1688 threatened to disturb the early married life of Samuel Wesley and his spouse.

The husband wrote a pamphlet in which he defended revolution principles, but the wife secretly adhered to the old cause; nor was it until a year before Dutch William's death that the rector made the discovery that the wife of his bosom, who had sworn to obey him and regard him as her over-lord, was not in the habit of saying Amen to his fervent prayers on behalf of his suffering sovereign. An explanation was demanded and the truth extracted, namely, that in the opinion of the rector's wife her true king lived over the water. The rector at once refused to live with Mrs Wesley any longer until she recanted. This she refused to do, and for a twelvemonth the couple dwelt apart, when William III having the good sense to die, a reconciliation became possible. If John Wesley was occasionally a little pig-headed, need one wonder?

The story of the fire at Epworth Rectory and the miraculous escape of the infant John was once a tale as well known as Alfred in the neat-herd's hut, and pictures of it still hang up in many a collier's home.

John Wesley received a sound classical education at Charterhouse and Christ Church, and remained all his life very much the scholar and the gentleman. No company was too good for John Wesley, and nobody knew better than he did that had he cared to carry his powerful intelligence, his flawless constitution, and his infinite capacity for taking pains into any of the markets of the world, he must have earned for himself place, fame, and fortune.

Coming, however, as he did of a theological stock, having a saint for a father and a notable devout woman for a mother, Wesley from his early days learned to regard religion as the business of his life, just as the younger Pitt came to regard the House of Commons as the future theatre of his actions.

'My Jack is Fellow of Lincoln'

After a good deal of heart-searching and theological talk with his mother, Wesley was ordained a deacon by the excellent Potter, afterward Primate, but then (1725) Bishop of Oxford. In the following year Wesley was elected a Fellow of Lincoln, to the great delight of his father. 'Whatever I am,' said the good old man, 'my Jack is Fellow of Lincoln.'

Wesley's motive never eludes us. In his early manhood, after being greatly affected by Jeremy Taylor's *Holy Living and Dying* and the *Imitation of Christ*, and by Law's *Serious Call* and *Christian Perfection*, he met 'a serious man' who said to him, 'Sir, you wish to serve God and go to heaven. Remember you cannot serve him alone. You must therefore find companions or make them. The Bible knows nothing of solitary religion.'

He was very confident, this serious man, and Wesley never forgot his message. 'You must find companions or make them. The Bible knows nothing of solitary religion.' These words for ever sounded in Wesley's ears, determining his theology, which rejected the stern individualism of Calvin, and fashioning his whole polity, his famous class meetings and generally gregarious methods.

> There to him it was given
> Many to save with himself.

We may continue the quotation and apply to Wesley the words of Mr Arnold's memorial to his father:

> Languor was not in his heart,
> Weakness was not in his word,
> Weariness not on his brow.

If you ask what is the impression left upon the reader of the *Journal* as to the condition of England question, the answer will vary very much with the tenderness of the reader's conscience and with the extent of his acquaintance with the general behaviour of mankind at all times and in all places.

No sentimentalist

Wesley himself is no alarmist, no sentimentalist, he never gushes, seldom exaggerates, and always writes on an easy level. Naturally enough he clings to the supernatural and is always disposed to believe in the bona fides of ghosts and the diabolical origin of strange noises, but outside this realm of speculation, Wesley describes things as he saw them. In the first published words of his friend, Dr Johnson, 'he meets with no basilisks that destroy with their eyes, his crocodiles devour their prey without tears, and his cataracts fall from the rocks without deafening the neighbouring inhabitants.'

Wesley's humour is of the species donnish, and his modes and methods quietly persistent.

Wesley's humour

'On Thursday May 20 [1742], I set out. The next afternoon I stopped a little at Newport Pagnell and then rode on till I overtook a serious man with whom I immediately fell into conversation. He presently gave me to know what his opinions were, therefore I said nothing to contradict them. But that did not content him. He was quite uneasy to know "whether I held the doctrines of the decrees as he did"; but I told him over and over "We had better keep to practical things lest we should be angry at one another." And so we did for two miles till he caught me unawares and dragged me into the dispute before I knew where I was. He then grew warmer and warmer; told me I was rotten at heart and supposed I was one of John Wesley's followers. I told him "No. I am John Wesley himself." Upon which he would gladly have run away outright. But being the better mounted of the two I kept close to his side and endeavoured to show him his heart till we came into the street of Northampton.'

What a picture have we here of a fine May morning in 1742, the unhappy Calvinist trying to shake off the Arminian Wesley! But he cannot do it! *John Wesley is the better mounted of the two,* and so they scamper together into Northampton.

The England described in the *Journal* is an England still full of theology; all kinds of queer folk abound; strange subjects are discussed in odd places. There was drunkenness and cock-fighting, no doubt, but there were also deists, mystics, Swedenborgians, antinomians, necessitarians, anabaptists, Quakers, nascent heresies, and slow-dying delusions. Villages were divided into rival groups, which fiercely argued the nicest points in the aptest language. Nowadays in one's rambles a man is as likely to encounter a grey badger as a black Calvinist.

England in Wesley's day

The clergy of the established church were jealous of Wesley's interference in their parishes, nor was this unnatural—he was not a Nonconformist but a brother churchman. What right had he to be so peripatetic? But Wesley seldom records any instance of gross clerical misconduct. Of one drunken parson he does indeed tell us, and he speaks disapprovingly of another whom he found one very hot day consuming a pot of beer in a lone alehouse. I am bound to confess I have never had any but kindly feelings toward that thirsty ecclesiastic. What, I wonder, was he thinking of as Wesley rode by!

When Wesley, with that dauntless courage of his, a courage which never forsook him, which he wore on every occasion with the delightful ease of a soldier, pushed his way into fierce districts, amid rough miners dwelling in their own village communities almost outside the law, what most strikes one with admiration, not less in Wesley's *Journal* than in George Fox's (a kindred though earlier volume), is the essential fitness for freedom of our rudest populations. They were coarse and brutal and savage, but rarely did they fail to recognise the high character and lofty motives of the dignified mortal who had travelled so far to speak to them.

The mobs he met

Wesley was occasionally hustled, and once or twice pelted with mud and stones, but at no time were his sufferings at the hands of the mob to be compared with the indignities it was long the fashion to heap upon the heads of parliamentary candidates. The mob knew and appreciated the difference between a Bubb Doddington and a John Wesley.

I do not think any ordinary Englishman will be much horrified at the demeanour of the populace. If there was disturbance it was usually quelled. At Norwich two soldiers who disturbed a congregation were seized and carried before their commanding officer, who ordered them to be soundly whipped. In Wesley's opinion they richly deserved all they got. He was no sentimentalist, although an enthusiast.

Where the reader of the *Journal* will be shocked is when his attention is called to the public side of the country—to the state of the gaols—to Newgate, to Bethlehem, to the criminal code—to the brutality of so many of the judges, and the harshness of the magistrates, to the supineness of the bishops, to the extinction in high places of the missionary spirit—in short, to the heavy slumber of humanity.

Wesley was full of compassion, of a compassion wholly free from hysterics and like exaltative. In public affairs his was the composed zeal of a Howard. His efforts to penetrate the dark places were long in vain. He says in his dry way: 'They won't let me go to Bedlam because they say I make the inmates mad, or into Newgate because I make them wicked.' The reader of the *Journal* will be at no loss to see what these sapient magistrates meant.

Wesley was a terribly exciting preacher, quiet though his manner was. He pushed matters home without flinching. He made people cry out and fall down, nor did it surprise him that they should.

Ever a preacher

If you want to get into the eighteenth century, to feel its pulses throb beneath your finger, be content sometimes to leave the letters of Horace Walpole unturned, resist the drowsy temptation to waste your time over the learned triflers who sleep in the seventeen volumes of Nichols, nay even deny yourself your annual reading of Boswell or your biennial retreat with Sterne, and ride up and down the country with the greatest force of the eighteenth century in England.

No man lived nearer the centre than John Wesley. Neither Clive nor Pitt, neither Mansfield nor Johnson. You cannot cut him out of our national life. No single figure influenced so many minds, no single voice touched so many hearts. No other man did such a life's work for England.

As a writer he has not achieved distinction, he was no Athanasius, no Augustine, he was ever a preacher and an organiser, a labourer in the service of humanity; but happily for us his *Journals* remain, and from them we can learn better than from anywhere else what manner of man he was, and the character of the times during which he lived and moved and had his being.

Augustine Birrell

Important Wesley Dates

Wesley born	June 17 (Old Style), 1703
Epworth parsonage burned	1709
Goes to Charterhouse School	1714
Enters Christ Church, Oxford	1720
Ordained deacon; first sermon preached at S. Leigh	1725
Elected Fellow of Lincoln College	1726
Leaves Oxford to assist his father; Holy Club started	1727
Ordained priest	1728
Returns to Oxford as Tutor	1729
Goes to Georgia; published *Journal* begins	1735
Returns to England	1738
Meets Peter Böhler	February 7 (O.S.), 1738
Wesley's 'heart was strangely warmed'	May 24 (O.S.), 1738
Wesley begins open air preaching	1739
Foundery (the cradle of Methodism) taken	1739
First Methodist preaching-place built at Bristol	1739
Lay preachers employed	1741
Methodist classes established at Bristol	1742
First Conference (London)	1744
Wesley married	1751
City Road chapel built	1778
Wesley's wife dies	1781
Wesley's last field preaching (at Winchelsea)	October 6, 1790
Last entry in his Journal	October 24, 1790
Last sermon in City Road	February 22, 1791
His last sermon (Leatherhead)	February 23, 1791
His last letter (to Wilberforce)	February 24, 1791
Returns to City Road house to die	February 25, 1791
Wesley dies in his eighty-eighth year	March 2, 1791

Wesley's Journal

The first entry in Wesley's Journal is that of October 14, 1735. But the following letter, which Wesley published with the first edition of his *Journal*, precedes it, as it describes the incidents which led to the formation of the Holy Club and to the social activities from which, as the *Journal* shows, Methodism has evolved.

The letter was written from Oxford in 1732 to Mr Morgan, whose son is mentioned. It runs thus:

Wesley begins his work

In November 1729, at which time I came to reside at Oxford, your son [Mr Morgan], my brother, myself, and one more, agreed to spend three or four evenings in a week together. Our design was to read over the classics, which we had before read in private, on common nights, and on Sunday some book in divinity. In the summer following, Mr M. told me he had called at the gaol, to see a man who was condemned for killing his wife; and that, from the talk he had with one of the debtors, he verily believed it would do much good if anyone would be at the pains of now and then speaking with them.

This he so frequently repeated, that on August 24, 1730, my brother and I walked with him to the castle. We were so well satisfied with our conversation there, that we agreed to go there once or twice a week; which we had not done long before he desired me to go with him to see a poor woman in the town, who was sick. In this employment too, when we came to reflect upon it, we believed it would be worth while to spend an hour or two in a week; provided the minister of the parish, in which such person was, were not against it. But that we might not depend wholly on our own judgements, I wrote an account to my father of our whole design, begging that he, who had lived seventy years in the world, and seen as much of it as most private men have ever done, would advise us whether we had yet gone too far, and whether we should now stand still, or go forward.

Origin of the Holy Club

In pursuance of [his] directions, I immediately went to Mr Gerard, the Bishop of Oxford's chaplain, who was likewise the person that took care of the prisoners when any were condemned to die (at other times they were left to their own care): I proposed to him our design of serving them as far as we could, and my own intention to preach there once a month, if the bishop approved of it. He much commended our design, and said he would answer for the bishop's approbation, to whom he would take the first opportunity of mentioning it. It was not long before he informed me he had done so, and that his lordship not only gave his permission, but was greatly pleased with the undertaking, and hoped it would have the desired success.

Soon after, a gentleman of Merton College, who was one of our little company, which now consisted of five persons, acquainted us that he had been much rallied the day before for being a member of the Holy Club; and that it was become a common topic of mirth at his college, where they had found out several of our customs, to which we ourselves were strangers. Upon this I consulted my father again. . . .

Upon [his] encouragement we still continued to meet

together as usual; and to confirm one another as well as we could in our resolutions, to receive communion as often as we had opportunity (which is here once a week); and do what service we could to our acquaintance, the prisoners, and two or three poor families in the town.

Wesley sails for America

1735. Tuesday October 14. Our end in leaving our native country was not to avoid want (God having given us plenty of temporal blessings), nor to gain the dung or dross of riches or honour; but only this—to save our souls; to live wholly to the glory of God. In the afternoon we found the *Simmonds* off Gravesend, and immediately went on board.

Friday 17. I began to learn German, in order to converse with the Germans, twenty-six of whom we had on board. On Sunday, the weather being fair and calm, we had the morning service on quarter-deck. I now first preached extempore, and then administered the Lord's supper to six or seven communicants.

Monday 20. Believing that denying ourselves, even in the smallest instances, might, by the blessing of God, be helpful to us, we wholly left off the use of flesh and wine, and confined ourselves to vegetable food—chiefly rice and biscuits.

Life on board

Tuesday 21. We now began to be a little regular. Our common way of living was this: From four in morning till five each of us used private prayer. From five to seven we read the Bible together, carefully comparing it (that we might not lean to our own understandings) with the writings of the earliest ages. At seven we breakfasted. At eight were the public prayers. From nine to twelve I usually learned German, and Mr Delamotte, Greek. My brother wrote sermons, and Mr Ingham instructed the children. At twelve we met to give an account to one another what we had done since our last meeting, and what we designed to do before our next. About one we dined.

The time from dinner to four we spent in reading to those whom each of us had taken in charge, or in speaking to them separately, as need required. At four were the evening prayers, when either the second lesson was explained (as it always was in the morning) or the children were catechised and instructed before the congregation. From five to six I read in our cabin to two or three of the passengers (of whom there were about eighty English on board), and each of my brethren to a few more in theirs.

At seven I joined with the Germans in their public service, while Mr Ingham was reading between the decks to as many as desired to hear. At eight we met again to exhort and instruct one another. Between nine and ten we went to bed, where neither the roaring of the sea nor the motion of the ship could take away the refreshing sleep which God gave us.

Memorable Atlantic storms

1736. Sunday January 25. At noon our third storm began. At four it was more violent than before. At seven I went to the Germans. I had long before observed the great seriousness of their behaviour. Of their humility they had given a continual proof, by performing those servile offices for the other passengers, which none of the English would undertake; for which they desired, and would receive, no pay, saying it was good for their proud hearts, and their loving saviour had done more for them. And every day had given them an occasion of showing a meekness, which no injury could move. If they were pushed, struck, or thrown down, they rose again and went away; but no complaint was found in their mouth. There was now an opportunity of seeing whether they were delivered from the spirit of fear, as well as from that of pride, anger and revenge.

In the midst of the psalm with which their service began, the sea broke over, split the mainsail in pieces, covered the ship, and poured in between the decks, as if the great deep had already swallowed us up. A terrible screaming began among the English. The Germans calmly sung on. I asked one of them afterwards, 'Was you not afraid?' He replied, mildly, 'No; our women and children are not afraid to die.'

Sunday February 1. We spoke with a ship of Carolina; and *Wednesday 4* came within soundings. About noon, the trees were visible from the masts, and in the afternoon from the main deck. In the evening lesson were these words: 'A great door for effective work has opened to me.' Oh, let no one shut it!

Thursday 5. Between two and three in the afternoon, God brought us all safe into the Savannah river. We cast anchor near Tybee Island, where the groves of pines, running along the shore, made an agreeable prospect, showing, as it were, the bloom of spring in the depth of winter.

Wesley arrives in Georgia

Friday 6. About eight in the morning, we first set foot on American ground. It was a small uninhabited island, over against Tybee. Mr Oglethorpe led us to a rising ground, where we all kneeled down to give thanks. He then took boat for Savannah. When the rest of the people had come on shore, we called our little flock together to prayers.

Saturday 7. Mr Oglethorpe returned from Savannah with Mr Spangenberg, one of the pastors of the Germans. I soon found what spirit he was of; and asked his advice with regard to my own conduct. He said, 'My brother, I must first ask you one or two questions. Have you the witness within yourself? Does the Spirit of God bear witness with your spirit, that you are a child of God?' I was surprised, and knew not what to answer. He observed it, and asked, 'Do you know Jesus Christ?' I paused, and said, 'I know he is the saviour of the world.' 'True,' replied he; 'but do you know he has saved you?' I answered, 'I hope he has died to save me.' He only added, 'Do you know yourself?' I said, 'I do.' But I fear they were vain words.

Saturday 14. About one, Tomo Chachi, his nephew Thleeanouhee, his wife Sinauky, with two more women and two or three Indian children, came on board. As soon as we came in, they all rose and shook us by the hand; and Tomo Chachi (one Mr Musgrove interpreted) spoke as follows:

'I am glad you are come. When I was in England, I desired that some would speak the great word to me and my nation then desired to hear it; but now we are all in confusion. Yet I am glad you are come. I will go up and speak to the wise men of our nation; and I hope they will hear. But we would not be made Christians as the Spaniards make Christians: we would be taught, before we are baptised.'

I answered, 'There is but one, he who sits in heaven, who is able to teach man wisdom. Though we are come so far, we know not whether he will please to teach you by us or no. If he teaches you, you will learn wisdom, but we can do nothing.' We then withdrew.

Begins his ministry at Savannah

Sunday March 7. I entered upon my ministry at Savannah, by preaching on the epistle for the day, being the thirteenth chapter of 1 Corinthians. In the second lesson (Luke 18) was our Lord's prediction of the treatment which he himself (and, consequently, his followers) was to meet with from the world. 'I tell you the truth, no one who has left home or wife or brothers or parents or children for the sake of the kingdom of God will fail to receive many times as much in this age and, in the age to come, eternal life.'

Tuesday 30. Mr Ingham, coming from Frederica, brought me letters, pressing me to go there. The next day Mr Delamotte and I began to see if life might not as well be sustained by one sort as by variety of food. We chose to make the experiment with bread; and were never more vigorous and healthy than while we tasted nothing else.

'I waked under water'

Sunday April 4. About four in the afternoon I set out for Frederica, in a pettiawga—a sort of flat-bottomed barge. The next evening we anchored near Skidoway Island, where the water, at flood, was twelve or fourteen foot deep. I wrapped myself up from head to foot, in a large cloak, to keep off the sand flies, and lay down on the quarter-deck. Between one and two I waked under water, being so fast asleep that I did not find where I was till my mouth was full of it. Having left my cloak, I know not how, upon deck, I swam round to the other side of the pettiawga, where a boat was tied, and climbed up by the rope without any hurt more than wetting my clothes.

Saturday 17. Not finding, as yet, any door open for pursuing our main design, we considered in what manner we might be most useful to the little flock at Savannah. And we agreed: 1. To advise the more serious among them to form themselves into a sort of little society, and to meet once or twice a week, in order to reprove, instruct, and exhort one another. 2. To select out of these a smaller number for a more intimate union with each other, which might be forwarded partly by our conversing singly with each, and partly by inviting them all together to our house; and this, accordingly, we determined to do every Sunday in the afternoon.

Tuesday 22. Observing much coldness in M. ——'s behaviour, I asked him the reason of it. He answered, 'I like nothing you do. All your sermons are satires upon particular persons, therefore I will never hear more; and

all the people are of my mind, for we won't hear ourselves
abused.

'Beside, they say, they are Protestants. But as for you,
they cannot tell what religion you are of. They never heard
such a religion before. They do not know what to make of
it. And then your private behaviour: all the quarrels that
have been here since you came, have been because of you.
Indeed there is neither man nor woman in the town, who
minds a word you say. And so you may preach long
enough; but nobody will come to hear you.'

He was too warm for hearing an answer. So I had nothing to do but to thank him for his openness, and walk
away.

Fearless of rains and dews

Monday August 2. I set out for the Lieutenant-Governor's
seat, about thirty miles from Charlestown, to deliver Mr
Oglethorpe's letters. Finding Mr Oglethorpe was gone, I
stayed only a day at Savannah; and leaving Mr Ingham
and Delamotte there, set out on Tuesday morning for Frederica. In walking to Thunderbolt I was in so heavy a
shower that all my clothes were as wet as if I had gone
through the river. On which occasion I cannot but observe
that popular error, concerning the hurtfulness of the rains
and dews of America. I have been thoroughly wet with
these rains more than once; yet without any harm at all.
And I have lain many nights in the open air, and received
all the dews that fell; and so, I believe, might anyone if his
constitution was not impaired by the softness of a genteel
education.

Desires to go among the Indians

Tuesday November 23. Mr Oglethorpe sailed for England,
leaving Mr Ingham, Mr Delamotte, and me at Savannah;
but with less prospect of preaching to the Indians than we

had the first day we set foot in America. 'You cannot leave Savannah without a minister.'

To this indeed my plain answer was: 'I know not that I am under any obligation to the contrary. I never promised to stay here one month. I openly declared both before, at, and ever since my coming here, that I neither would nor could take charge of the English any longer than till I could go among the Indians.' If it was said, 'But did not the trustees of Georgia appoint you to be minister of Savannah?' I replied: 'They did; but it was not done by my solicitation: it was done without either my desire or my knowledge. Therefore I cannot conceive that appointment to lay me under any obligation of continuing there any longer than I expressly declared at the time I consented to accept that appointment.'

But though I had no other obligation not to leave Savannah now, yet that of love I could not break through: I could not resist the importunate request of the more serious parishioners to watch over their souls yet a little longer, till someone came who might supply my place. And this I the more willingly did, because the time was not come to preach the gospel of peace to the heathens, all their nations being in such a ferment, and Paustoobee and Mingo Mattaw having told me in as many words, in my own house, 'Now our enemies are all about us, and we can do nothing but fight; but if beloved ones should ever give us to be at peace, then we would hear the great word.'

Wednesday December 22. Mr Delamotte and I, with a guide, set out to talk to the Cowpen. When we had walked two or three hours, our guide told us plainly he did not know where we were. However, believing it could not be far off, we thought it best to go on. In an hour or two we came to a cypress-swamp, which lay directly across our way: there was not time to walk back to Savannah before night, so we walked through it, the water being about breast high.

By the time we had gone a mile beyond it, we had

completely left any path; and it being now past sunset, we sat down, intending to make a fire, and to stay there till morning; but finding our tinder wet, we were at a stand. I advised to walk on still; but my companions, being faint and weary, were for lying down, which we accordingly did about six o'clock; the ground was as wet as our clothes, which, it being a sharp frost, were soon froze together; however, I slept till six in the morning. There fell a heavy dew in the night, which covered us over as white as snow. Within an hour after sunrise, we came to a plantation; and in the evening, without any hurt, to Savannah.

Begins to learn Spanish

1737. Monday April 4. I began learning Spanish, in order to converse with my Jewish parishioners; some of whom seem nearer the mind that was in Christ than many of those who call him Lord.

Sunday July 3. Immediately after the holy communion, I mentioned to Mrs Williamson (Mr Causton's niece) some things which I thought reprovable in her behaviour. At this she appeared extremely angry; said she did not expect such usage from me; and at the turn of the street through which we were walking home, went abruptly away. The next day Mrs Causton endeavoured to excuse her; told me she was exceedingly grieved for what had passed the day before, and desired me to tell her in writing what I disliked; which I accordingly did the day following.

But first I sent Mr Causton the following note:

Sir,—To this hour you have shown yourself my friend; I ever have and ever shall acknowledge it. And it is my earnest desire that he who has hitherto given me this blessing, would continue it still.

But this cannot be, unless you will allow me one request, which is not so easy as it appears: do not condemn me for doing, in the execution of my office, what I think it my duty to do.

If you can prevail upon yourself to allow me this, even when I act without respect of persons, I am persuaded there will never be, at least not long, any misunderstanding between us. For even those who seek it shall, I trust, find no occasion against me, 'unless it concerns the law of my God'.

I am, &c.

July 5, 1737

Wednesday 6. Mr Causton came to my house with Mr Bailiff Parker and Mr Recorder, and warmly asked how I could possibly think he should condemn me for executing any part of my office. I said short, 'Sir, what if I should think it the duty of my office to repel one of your family from the holy communion?' He replied, 'If you repel me or my wife, I shall require a legal reason. But I shall trouble myself about none else. Let them look to themselves.'

Warrant for Wesley's arrest

Sunday August 7. I repelled Mrs Williamson from the holy communion. And *Monday, 8,* Mr Recorder, of Savannah, issued the warrant following:

Georgia. Savannah ss.

To all Constables, Tithingmen, and others, whom these may concern: You, and each of you, are hereby required to take the body of John Wesley, Clerk:

And bring him before one of the Bailiffs of the said town to answer the complaint of William Williamson and Sophia, his wife, for defaming the said Sophia, and refusing to administer to her the sacrament of the Lord's supper in a public congregation without cause; by which the said William Williamson is damaged one thousand pounds sterling; and for so doing, this is your warrant, certifying what you are to do in the premises. Given under my hand and seal the 8th day of August, Anno. Dom. 1737.   *Tho. Christie*

Thursday 11. Mr Causton came to my house, and,

among many other sharp words, said: 'Make an end of this
matter; you had better. My niece to be treated like this! I
have drawn the sword, and I will never sheath it till I have
satisfaction.'

Soon after, he added: 'Give the reasons of your repelling
her before the whole congregation.' I answered: 'Sir, if you
insist upon it, I will; and so you may be pleased to tell her.'
He said, 'Write to her, and tell her so yourself.' I said, 'I
will'; and after he went I wrote as follows:

To Mrs Sophia Williamson

At Mr Causton's request, I write once more. The rules
whereby I proceed are these:

'So many as intend to be partakers of the holy communion,
shall signify their names to the curate, at least some time the
day before.' This you did not do.

'And if any of these have done any wrong to his neighbours,
by word or deed, so that the congregation be therby offended,
the curate shall advertise him that in any wise he presume not
to come to the Lord's table until he hath openly declared himself to have truly repented.'

If you offer yourself at the Lord's table on Sunday, I will
advertise you (as I have done more than once) wherein you
have done wrong. And when you have openly declared yourself to have truly repented, I will administer to you the mys-
teries of God.

John Wesley

Mr Causton declared to many persons that Mr Wesley
had repelled Sophy from the holy communion purely out
of revenge, because he had made proposals of marriage to
her which she rejected, and married Mr Williamson.

Tuesday 16. Mrs Williamson swore to and signed an
affidavit insinuating much more than it asserted; but
asserting that Mr Wesley had many times proposed marriage
to her, all which proposals she had rejected. Mr Causton
gave a long and earnest charge, 'to beware of spiritual
tyranny, and to oppose the new, illegal authority which

was usurped over their consciences'. A list of grievances the grand jury altered in some particulars, and on Thursday, September 1, delivered it again to the court.

Friday September 2. The sense of the minority of the grand jurors themselves (for they were by no means unanimous) concerning these presentments may appear from the following paper, which they transmitted to the trustees:

To the Honourable the Trustees for Georgia

Whereas two presentments have been made: the one of August 23, the other of August 31, by the grand jury for the town and county of Savannah, in Georgia, against John Wesley, Clerk.

We, whose names are underwritten, being members of the said grand jury, do humbly beg leave to signify our dislike of the said presentments; being, by many and divers circumstances, thoroughly persuaded in ourselves that the whole charge against Mr Wesley is an artifice of Mr Causton's, designed rather to blacken the character of Mr Wesley, than to free the colony from religious tyranny, as he was pleased, in his charge to us, to term it. But as these circumstances will be too tedious to trouble your Honours with, we shall only beg leave to give the reasons of our dissent from the particular bills. . . .

Why Wesley left Georgia

Friday October 7. I consulted my friends, whether God did not call me to return to England. The reason for which I left it had now no force; there being no possibility yet of instructing the Indians; neither had I, as yet, found or heard of any Indians on the continent of America, who had the least desire of being instructed. And as to Savannah, having never engaged myself, either by word or letter, to stay there a day longer than I should judge convenient, nor ever taken charge of the people any otherwise than as in my passage to the heathens, I looked upon myself to be fully discharged from it by abandoning that plan. Besides, there was a probability of doing more service to that unhappy people in England than I could do in Georgia, by representing, without fear or favour, to the trustees the real state the colony was in. After deeply considering these things, they were unanimous that I ought to go; but not yet. So I laid the thoughts of it aside for the present; being persuaded that when the time was come, God would make the way plain before me.

Friday December 2. In the afternoon, the magistrates published an order requiring all the officers and sentinels to prevent my going out of the province; and forbidding any person to assist me so to do. Being now only a prisoner at large, in a place where I knew by experience, every day would give fresh opportunity to procure evidence of words I never said, and actions I never did, I saw clearly the hour was come for leaving this place: and as soon as evening prayers were over, about eight o'clock, the tide then serving, I shook off the dust of my feet, and left Georgia, after having preached the gospel there (not as I thought, but as I was able) one year and nearly nine months.

Farewell to America

Thursday 22. I took leave of America (though, if it please God, not for ever), going on board the *Samuel*, Captain Percy, with a young gentleman who had been a few months in Carolina, one of my parishioners of Savannah, and a Frenchman, late of Purrysburg, who had escaped from there by the skin of his teeth.

Monday 26. I began instructing a negro lad in the principles of Christianity. The next day I resolved to break off living delicately, and return to my old simplicity of diet; and after I did so, neither my stomach nor my head much complained of the motion of the ship.

1738. Sunday January 1. All in the ship, except the captain and steersman, were present both at the morning and evening service, and appeared as deeply attentive as even the poor people of Frederica did, while the word of God was new to their ears.

Monday 2. Being sorrowful and very heavy (though I could give no particular reasons for it), and utterly unwilling to speak close to any of my little flock (about twenty persons), I was in doubt whether my neglect of them was not one cause of my own heaviness. In the evening, therefore, I began instructing the cabin-boy; after which I was much easier.

I went several times the following days, with a design to speak to the sailors, but could not. I mean, I was quite averse from speaking; I could not see how to make an occasion, and it seemed quite absurd to speak without. Is not this what men commonly mean by, 'I could not speak'? And is this a sufficient cause of silence, or no? Is it a prohibition from the good spirit, or a temptation from nature, or the evil one?

The voyage to England

Friday 13. It blew a proper hurricane; which beginning at south-west, then went west, north-west, north, and, in a quarter of an hour, round by the east to the south-west point again. At the same time the sea running, as they term it, mountain-high, and that from many different points at once, the ship would not obey the helm; nor indeed could the steersman, through the violent rain, see the compass. So he was forced to let her run before the wind, and in half an hour the stress of the storm was over.

Tuesday 24. We spoke with two ships, outward-bound, from whom we had the welcome news of our being only one hundred and sixty leagues short of Land's End. My mind was now full of thought; part of which I wrote down as follows:

I went to America, to convert the Indians; but oh, who shall convert me? who, what is he that will deliver me from this evil heart of mischief? I have a fair summer religion. I can talk well; nay, and believe myself, while no danger is near; but let death look me in the face, and my spirit is troubled. Nor can I say, 'To die is gain!'

> I have a sin of fear, that when I've spun
> My last thread, I shall perish on the shore!

I think, verily, if the gospel be true, I am safe: for I not only have given, and do give, all my goods to feed the poor; I not only give my body to be burned, drowned, or whatever God shall appoint for me; but I follow after charity (though not as I ought, yet as I can), if haply I may attain it. I now believe the gospel is true. 'I show my faith by my works,' by staking my all upon it. I would do the same again and again a thousand times, if the choice were still to make.

Whoever sees me, sees I would be a Christian. Therefore 'are my ways not like other men's ways'. There I have been, I am, I am content to be 'a by-word, a proverb of reproach'. But in a storm I think, 'What, if the gospel be not true? Then you are of all men most foolish. For what cause have you given up your goods, your ease, your friends, your reputation, your country, your life? For what cause are you wandering over the face of the earth? A dream, a cunningly devised fable!'

Oh, who will deliver me from this fear of death? What shall I do? Where shall I fly from it? Should I fight against it by thinking, or by not thinking of it? A wise man advised me some time ago, 'Be still and go on.' Perhaps this is best, to look upon it as my cross; when it comes, to let it humble me, and quicken all my good resolutions, especially that of praying without ceasing; and at other times, to take no thought about it, but quietly to go on 'in the work of the Lord'.

Lands at Deal

Sunday 29. We saw English land once more; which, about noon, appeared to be the Lizard Point. We ran by it with a fair wind; and at noon, the next day, made the west end of the Isle of Wight.

Toward evening was a calm; but in the night a strong north wind brought us safe into the Downs. The day before, Mr Whitefield had sailed out, neither of us then knowing anything of the other. At four in the morning we took boat, and in half an hour landed at Deal: it being *Wednesday February 1*.

It is now two years and almost four months since I left my native country, and in order to teach the Georgian Indians the nature of Christianity: but what have I learned myself in the meantime? Why (what I the least of all suspected), that I who went to America to convert others, was never myself converted to God. 'I am not mad,' though I thus speak; but 'I speak the words of truth and soberness'; if perhaps some of those who still dream may awake, and see that as I am, so are they.

In London again

Friday February 3.   In the evening I came once more to London, from which I had been absent two years and near four months.

Many reasons I have to bless God, though the plan I went with did not take effect, for my having been carried into that strange land, contrary to all my preceding resolutions. By this I trust he has in some measure 'humbled me and tested me, and shown me what was in my heart'. By this I have been taught to 'beware of men'. By this I have come to know for sure that if 'in all our ways we acknowledge God, he will', where reason fails, 'direct our path' by chance, or by the other means which he knows. By this I am delivered from the fear of the sea, which I had both dreaded and abhorred from my youth.

By this God has given me to know many of his servants; particularly those of the Church of Herrnhut. By this my passage is opened to the writings of men in the German,

Spanish and Italian languages. I hope, too, some good may come to others by this. All in Georgia have heard the word of God. Some have believed, and begun to run well. A few steps have been taken towards publishing the good news both to the African and American heathens.

Saturday 4. I was desired to preach at St John the Evangelist's. I did so on those strong words: 'If anyone is in Christ, he is a new creature.' I was afterwards informed that many of the best in the parish were so offended that I was not to preach there any more.

Wesley meets Peter Böhler

Tuesday 7. (A day much to be remembered.) At the house of Mr Weinantz, a Dutch merchant, I met Peter Böhler, Schulius Richter, and Wensel Neiser, just then landed from Germany. Finding they had no acquaintance in England, I offered to procure them a lodging, and did so near Mr Hutton's, where I then was. And from this time I did not willingly lose any opportunity of conversing with them while I stayed in London.

Wednesday 8. I went to see the Board of Trustees, and gave them a short but plain account of the state of the colony: an account, I fear, not a little differing from those which they had frequently received before, and for which I have reason to believe some of them have not forgiven me to this day.

Sunday 12. I preached at St Andrew's, Holborn, on: 'If I give all I possess to the poor and surrender my body to the flames, but have not love, I gain nothing.' Oh, hard sayings! Who can hear them? Here too, it seems, I am to preach no more.

Friday 17. I set out for Oxford with Peter Böhler, where we were kindly received by Mr Sanrey, the only one now remaining of many who, at our embarking for America, were used to 'take sweet counsel together' and rejoice in 'bearing the reproach of Christ'.

Saturday 18. We went to Stanton Harcourt. The next day I preached once more at the castle, in Oxford, to a numerous and serious congregation.

All this time I conversed much with Peter Böhler, but I understood him not; and least of all when he said, 'My brother, my brother, that philosophy of yours must be purged away.'

Monday 20. I returned to London. On Tuesday I preached at Great St Helen's, on: 'If anyone would come after me, he must deny himself and take up his cross daily and follow me.'

Sunday 26. I preached at six, at St Lawrence's; at ten, in St Katharine Cree church; and in the afternoon at St John's, Wapping. I believe it pleased God to bless the first sermon most, because it gave more offence; being, indeed, an open defiance of that mystery of iniquity which the world calls 'prudence', grounded on those words of St Paul to the Galatians: 'Those who want to make a good impression outwardly are trying to compel you to be circumcised. The only reason they do this is to avoid being persecuted for the cross of Christ.'

Tuesday 28. I saw my mother once more. The next day I prepared for my journey to my brother at Tiverton. But on *Thursday* morning, *March 2*, a message that my brother Charles was dying at Oxford obliged me to set out for that place immediately.

Wesley's four resolutions

With regard to my own behaviour, I now renewed and wrote down my former resolutions.

1. To use absolute openness and unreserve with all I should converse with.

2. To labour after continual seriousness, not willingly indulging myself in any the least levity of behaviour, or in laughter; no, not for a moment.

3. To speak no word which does not tend to the glory of

God; in particular, not to talk of worldly things. Others
may, nay must. But what is that to you? And,

4. To take no pleasure which does not tend to the glory
of God; thanking God every moment for all I do take, and
therefore rejecting every sort and degree of it, which I feel
I cannot so thank him in and for.

Saturday March 4. I found my brother at Oxford, recovering from his pleurisy; and with him Peter Böhler; by
whom, in the hand of the great God, I was, on *Sunday 5,*
clearly convinced of unbelief, of the lack of that faith
whereby alone we are saved.

Immediately it struck into my mind: 'Leave off preaching. How can you preach to others, who have not faith yourself?' I asked Böhler whether he thought I should leave it
off or not. He answered, 'By no means.' I asked, 'But what
can I preach?' He said: 'Preach faith till you have it; and
then, because you have it, you will preach faith.'

Accordingly, *Monday 6,* I began preaching this new doctrine, though my soul started back from the work. The first
person to whom I offered salvation by faith alone, was a
prisoner under sentence of death. His name was Clifford.
Peter Böhler had many times desired me to speak to him
before. But I could not prevail on myself to do it; being still,
as I had been for many years, a zealous asserter of the
impossibility of death-bed repentance.

Tuesday 14. I set out for Manchester with Mr Kinchin,
Fellow of Corpus Christi, and Mr Fox, late a prisoner in the
city prison.

Companions on horseback

Friday 17. Early in the morning we left Manchester, taking
with us Mr Kinchin's brother, for whom we came, to be
entered at Oxford. We were fully determined to lose no
opportunity of awakening, instructing, or exhorting, any
whom we might meet within our journey. At Knutsford,
where we first stopped, all we spoke to thankfully received

the word of exhortation. But at Talk-on-the-hill, where we dined, she with whom we were was so much of a gentlewoman that for about an hour our labour seemed to be in vain. However, we spoke on. Upon a sudden, she looked as one just awaked out of a sleep. Every word sunk into her heart. Nor have I seen so entire a change both in the eyes, face, and manner of speaking, of anyone in so short a time.

About five, Mr Kinchin riding by a man and woman double-horsed, the man said, 'Sir, you ought to thank God it is a fair day; for if it rained, you would be sadly dirty with your little horse.' Mr Kinchin answered, 'True; and we ought to thank God for our life, and health, and food, and raiment, and all things.' He then rode on, Mr Fox following, the man said, 'Sir, my mistress would be glad to have some more talk with that gentleman.' We stayed, and when they came up, began to search one another's hearts. They came to us again in the evening, at our inn at Stone, where I explained to them and many of their acquaintance who were come together, that great truth—godliness has the promise both of this life and of that which is to come.

Thursday 23. I met Peter Böhler again, who now amazed me more and more, by the account he gave of the fruits of living faith—the holiness and happiness which he affirmed to attend it. The next morning I began the Greek Testament again, resolving to abide by 'the law and the testimony'; and being confident that God would hereby show me whether this doctrine was of God.

Preaches in Oxford Castle

Monday 27. Mr Kinchin went with me to the castle, where, after reading prayers, and preaching on 'Man is destined to die once,' we prayed with the condemned man, first in several forms of prayer, and then in such words as were given us in that hour. He kneeled down in much heaviness and confusion, having 'no rest in' his 'bones, by reason of' his 'sins'. After a while he rose up, and eagerly said, 'I am now ready to die. I know Christ has taken away my sins; and there is no more condemnation for me.' The same composed cheerfulness he showed when he was carried to execution; and in his last moments he was the same, enjoying a perfect peace, in confidence that he was 'accepted in the Beloved'.

Sunday April 2. Being Easter Day, I preached in our college chapel on 'A time is coming and has now come when the dead will hear the voice of the Son of God and those who hear will live.' I preached in the afternoon, first at the castle, and then at Carfax, on the same words. I see the promise; but it is afar off.

Believing it would be better for me to wait for the accomplishment of it in silence and retirement, on *Monday 3* I complied with Mr Kinchin's desire, and went to him at Dummer, in Hampshire. But I was not suffered to stay here long; being earnestly pressed to come up to London, if it were only for a few days. So I returned there on *Tuesday 18*.

Talks with Böhler

I asked P. Böhler again whether I ought not to refrain from teaching others. He said, 'No; do not hide in the earth the talent God has given you.' Accordingly, on *Tuesday 25,* I spoke clearly and fully at Blendon to Mr Delamotte's family, of the nature and fruits of faith. Mr Broughton's great objection was, he could never think that I had not faith, who had done and suffered such things. My brother was very angry, and told me I did not know what mischief I had done by talking thus. And, indeed, it did please God then to kindle a fire, which I trust shall never be extinguished.

On *Wednesday 26*, P. Böhler walked with me a few miles, and exhorted me not to stop short of the grace of God. At Gerrards Cross I plainly declared to those whom God gave into my hands, the faith as it is in Jesus: as I did next day to a young man I overtook on the road, and in the evening to our friends at Oxford. A strange doctrine, which some, who did not care to contradict, yet knew not what to make of; but one or two, who were thoroughly bruised by sin, willingly heard, and received it gladly.

In the day or two following, I was much confirmed in the 'truth that is after godliness', by hearing the experiences of Mr Hutchins, of Pembroke College, and Mrs Fox: two living witnesses that God can (at least, if he does not always) give that faith from which salvation comes in a moment, as lightning falling from heaven.

Monday May 1. The return of my brother's illness obliged me again to hasten to London. In the evening I found him at James Hutton's, better as to his health than I expected; but strongly averse from what he called 'the new faith'.

Wednesday 3. My brother had a long and detailed conversation with Peter Böhler. And it now pleased God to open his eyes, so that he also saw clearly what was the nature of the one true living faith, whereby alone, 'through grace, we are saved'.

Thursday 4. Peter Böhler left London, in order to embark for Carolina. O what a work God has begun since his coming into England! Such a work as shall never come to an end till heaven and earth pass away.

Sunday 7. I preached at St Lawrence's in the morning; and afterwards at St Katharine Cree. I was enabled to speak strong words at both; and was therefore the less surprised at being informed, I was not to preach any more in either of those churches.

Sunday 14. I preached in the morning at St Ann's, Aldersgate; and in the afternoon at the Savoy chapel, free salvation by faith in the blood of Christ. I was quickly told that at St Ann's, likewise, I am to preach no more.

Monday, Tuesday and *Wednesday* I had continual sorrow and heaviness in my heart.

Wednesday 24. I think it was about five this morning that I opened my Testament on those words, 'He has given us his very great and precious promises, so that through them you may participate in the divine nature' (2 Peter 1:4). Just as I went out, I opened it again on those words, 'You are not far from the kingdom of God'. In the afternoon I was asked to go to St Paul's. The anthem was 'Out of the deep have I called unto thee, O Lord: Lord, hear my voice. O let thine ears consider well the voice of my complaint. If thou, Lord, wilt be extreme to mark what is done amiss, O Lord, who may abide it? For there is mercy with thee; therefore shalt thou be feared. O Israel, trust in the Lord: for with the Lord there is mercy, and with him is plenteous redemption. And he shall redeem Israel from all his sins.'

'I felt my heart strangely warmed'

In the evening I went very unwillingly to a society in Aldersgate Street, where someone was reading Luther's preface to the Epistle to the Romans. About a quarter before nine, while he was describing the change which God works in the heart through faith in Christ, I felt my heart strangely warmed. I felt I did trust in Christ, Christ alone, for salvation; and an assurance was given me that he had taken away my sins, even mine, and saved me from the law of sin and death.

I began to pray with all my might for those who had in a more especial manner despitefully used me and persecuted me. I then testified openly to all there what I now first felt in my heart. But it was not long before the enemy suggested, 'This cannot be faith; for where is your joy?' Then was I taught that peace and victory over sin are essential to faith in the Captain of our salvation; but that, as to the transports of joy that usually attend the beginning of it, especially in those who have mourned deeply, God sometimes gives, sometimes withholds them, according to the counsels of his own will.

After my return home, I was much buffeted with temptations; but cried out, and they fled away. They returned again and again. I as often lifted up my eyes, and he 'sent me help from his holy place'. And I found the difference between this and my former state chiefly consisted in this. I was striving, yes, fighting with all my might under the law, as well as under grace. But then I was sometimes, if not often, conquered; now, I was always conqueror.

Thursday 25. The moment I awoke, 'Jesus, Master' was in my heart and in my mouth; and I found all my strength lay in keeping my eye fixed on him, and my soul waiting on him continually. Being again at St Paul's in the afternoon, I could taste the good word of God in the anthem, which began, 'My song shall be always of the loving kindness of the Lord: with my mouth will I ever be showing forth thy truth from one generation to another.' Yet the enemy injected a fear, 'If you believe, why is there not a more tangible change?' I answered (yet not I), 'That I do not know. But this I know, I now have peace with God. And I sin not today, and Jesus my Master has forbidden me to worry about tomorrow.'

Wednesday June 7. I determined, if God should permit, to retire for a short time into Germany. I had fully proposed, before I left Georgia, so to do, if it should please God to bring me back to Europe. And I now clearly saw the time was come. My weak mind could not bear to be thus sawn asunder. And I hoped the conversing with those holy men who were themselves living witnesses of the full power of faith, and yet able to bear with those that are weak, would be a means, under God, of so establishing my soul that I might go on from faith to faith and from strength to strength.

[The next three months Wesley spent in Germany visiting the Moravians.]

Sunday September 17 (London). I began again to declare in my own country the glad tidings of salvation, preaching three times, and afterwards expounding the holy scripture to a large group in the Minories. On *Monday* I rejoiced to meet with our little Society, which now consisted of thirty-two persons.

Wesley preaches in Newgate prison

The next day I went to the condemned felons in New-gate, and offered them free salvation. In the evening I went to a Society in Bear Yard, and preached repentance and remission of sins. The next evening I spoke the truth in love at a Society in Aldersgate Street: some contradicted at first, but not long; so that nothing but love appeared at our parting.

Sunday December 3 (Oxford). I began reading prayers at Bocardo prison, which had been long discontinued.

Tuesday 5. I began reading prayers and preaching in Gloucester Green workhouse; and on Thursday, in that belonging to St Thomas's parish. On both days I preached at the castle. At St Thomas's was a young woman, raving mad, screaming and tormenting herself continually. I had a strong desire to speak to her. The moment I began she was still. The tears ran down her cheeks all the time I was telling her, 'Jesus of Nazareth is able and willing to deliver you.'

Monday 11. Hearing Mr Whitefield was arrived from Georgia, I hastened to London from Oxford; and on *Tuesday 12* God gave us once more to take sweet counsel together.

1739. March 15. During my stay in London I was fully employed; between our own society in Fetter Lane, and many others, where I was continually desired to expound; so that I had no thought of leaving London, when I received, after several others, a letter from Mr Whitefield, and another from Mr Seward, entreating me in the most pressing manner to come to Bristol without delay. This I was not at all forward to do.

Wednesday 28. My journey was proposed to our society in Fetter Lane. But my brother Charles would scarcely bear the mention of it; till appealing to the oracles of God, he received those words as spoken to himself, and answered not again: 'Son of man, with one blow I am about to take away from you the delight of your eyes. Yet do not lament or weep or shed any tears.' Our other brethren, however, continuing the dispute, without any probability of their coming to one conclusion, we at length all agreed to decide it by lot. And by this it was determined I should go.

Wesley begins field-preaching

Thursday 29. I left London, and in the evening expounded to a small group at Basingstoke.

Saturday 31. In the evening I reached Bristol, and met Mr Whitefield there. I could scarcely reconcile myself at first to this strange way of preaching in the fields, of which he set me an example on Sunday; having been all my life (till very recently) so tenacious of every point relating to decency and order, that I should have thought the saving of souls almost a sin, if it had not been done in a church.

April 1. In the evening (Mr Whitefield being gone) I began expounding our Lord's sermon on the mount (one pretty remarkable precedent of field-preaching, though I suppose there were churches at that time also), to a little society which was accustomed to meet once or twice a week in Nicholas Street.

Monday 2. At four in the afternoon, I submitted to be more vile, and proclaimed in the highways the glad tidings of salvation, speaking from a little eminence in a ground adjoining the city, to about three thousand people. The scripture on which I spoke was this (is it possible anyone should be ignorant that it is fulfilled in every true minister of Christ?): 'The Spirit of the Lord is on me, because he has anointed me to preach good news to the poor. He has sent me to proclaim freedom for the prisoners and recovery of sight for the blind, to release the oppressed, to proclaim the year of the Lord's favour.'

Sunday 8. At seven in the morning I preached to about a thousand persons at Bristol, and afterwards to about fifteen hundred on the top of Hannam Mount in Kingswood. I called to them in the words of the evangelical prophet: 'Come, all you who are thirsty, come to the waters. Come, buy wine and milk without money and without cost.' About five thousand were in the afternoon at Rose Green (on the other side of Kingswood); among whom I stood and cried, in the name of the Lord, 'If any man is thirsty, let him come to me and drink. Whoever believes in me, as the Scripture has said, streams of living water will flow from within him.'

Monday May 7. I was preparing to set out for Pensford, having now had leave to preach in the church, when I received the following note:

> Sir,—Our minister, having been informed you are beside yourself, does not care you should preach in any of his churches.

I went, however; and on Priestdown, about half a mile from Pensford, preached Christ our 'wisdom, righteousness, sanctification, and redemption'.

The first Methodist building

Wednesday 9. We took possession of a piece of ground near St James's churchyard, in the Horse Fair, Bristol, where it was planned to build a room large enough to contain both the Societies of Nicholas and Baldwin Street, and such of their acquaintance as might desire to be present with them, at such times as the scripture was expounded. And on *Saturday 12* the first stone was laid with the voice of praise and thanksgiving.

I had not at first the least apprehension or plan of being personally engaged either in the expense of this work or in the direction of it, having appointed eleven feoffees, on whom I supposed these burdens would fall, of course; but I quickly found my mistake. First, with regard to the expense: for the whole undertaking would have stood still, had not I immediately taken upon myself the payment of all the workmen; so that before I knew where I was, I had contracted a debt of more than a hundred and fifty pounds. And this I was to discharge how I could; the subscriptions of both Societies not amounting to one quarter of the sum.

As to the direction of the work, I presently received letters from my friends in London, Mr Whitefield in particular, that neither he nor they would have anything to do with the building, neither contribute anything towards it, unless I would instantly discharge all feoffees and do everything in my name. Many reasons they gave for this; but one was enough, namely that such feoffees always would have it in their power to control me; and if I preached not as they liked, to turn me out of the room I had built. I accordingly yielded to their advice, and calling all the feoffees together, cancelled (no man opposing) the instrument made before, and took the whole management into my own hands. Money, it is true, I had not, nor any human prospect or probability of procuring it; but I knew 'the earth is the Lord's, and all that is in it,' and in his name set out, nothing doubting.

Sunday 13. My ordinary employment, in public, was now as follows: Every morning I read prayers and preached at Newgate. Every evening I expounded a portion of scripture at one or more of the Societies. On Monday, in the afternoon, I went away to preach, near Bristol; on Tuesday, at Bath and Two Mile Hill alternately; on Wednesday, at Baptist Mills; every other Thursday, near Pensford; every other Friday, in another part of Kingswood; on Saturday in the afternoon, and Sunday morning, in the bowling green (which lies near the middle of the city); on Sunday, at eleven, near Hannam Mount; at two, at Clifton; and at five on Rose Green. And hitherto, as my days, so my strength has been.

Wesley's living arguments

During this whole time I was almost continually asked, either by those who purposely came to Bristol to inquire concerning this strange work, or by my old or new correspondents, 'How can these things be?' And innumerable cautions were given me (generally grounded on gross misrepresentations of things), not to regard visions or dreams, or to fancy people had remission of sins because of their cries, or tears, or bare outward professions of belief. To one who had many times written to me on this subject, the sum of my answer was as follows:

'The questions between us turn chiefly, if not wholly, on matter of fact. You deny that God does now work these effects; at least, that he works them in this manner. I affirm both, because I have heard these things with my own ears, and have seen with my own eyes. I have seen (as far as a thing of this kind can be seen) very many persons changed in a moment from the spirit of fear, horror, despair, to the spirit of love, joy, and peace; and from sinful desire, till then reigning over them, to a pure desire of doing the will of God. These are matters of fact, whereof I have been, and almost daily am, an eye or ear witness.

'What I have to say touching visions or dreams, is this: I know several persons in whom this great change was wrought in a dream, or during a strong representation to the eye of their mind, of Christ either on the cross or in glory. This is the fact; let any judge of it as they please. And that such a change was then wrought appears (not from their shedding tears only, or falling into a fit, or crying out; these are not the fruits, as you seem to suppose, whereby I judge, but) from the whole tenor of their life, till then in many ways wicked; from that time holy, just, and good.

'I will show you him that was a lion till then, and is now a lamb; him that was a drunkard, and is now exemplarily sober; the whoremonger that was, who now abhors the very "garment spread by the flesh". These are my living arguments for what I assert, namely that God does now, as aforetime, give remission of sins and the gift of the Holy Spirit even to us and to our children; yes, and that always suddenly as far as I have known, and often in dreams or in the visions of God. If it be not so, I am found a false witness before God. For these things I do, and by his grace will testify.'

Beau Nash argues with Wesley

Tuesday June 5. There was great expectation at Bath of what a noted man was to do to me there; and I was much entreated not to preach, because no one knew what might happen. By this report I also gained a much larger audience, among whom were many of the rich and great. I told them plainly, the scripture had concluded them all under sin—high and low, rich and poor, one with another. Many of them seemed to be a little surprised, and were sinking apace into seriousness, when their champion appeared, and coming close to me, asked me by what authority I did these things.

I replied, 'By the authority of Jesus Christ, conveyed to me by the (now) Archbishop of Canterbury, when he laid hands upon me, and said, "Take thou authority to preach the gospel."' He said, 'This is contrary to Act of Parliament: this is a conventicle.' I answered, 'Sir, the conventicles mentioned in that Act (as the preamble shows) are seditious meetings; but this is not such; here is no shadow of sedition; therefore it is not contrary to that Act.' He replied, 'I say it is: and beside, your preaching frightens people out of their wits.'

'Sir, did you ever hear me preach?' 'No.' 'How, then, can you judge of what you never heard?' 'Sir, by common report.' 'Common report is not enough. Give me leave, Sir, to ask, Is not your name Nash?' 'My name is Nash.' 'Sir, I dare not judge of you by common report: I think it not enough to judge by.' Here he paused awhile, and, having recovered himself, said, 'I desire to know what this people comes here for'; at which someone replied, 'Sir, leave him to me: let an old woman answer him. You, Mr Nash, take care of your body; we take care of our souls; and for the food of our souls we come here.' He replied not a word, but walked away.

Monday 11. I received a pressing letter from London (as I had several others before), to come there as soon as possible; our brethren in Fetter Lane being in great confusion for want of my presence and advice.

Yet, during this whole time, I had many thoughts concerning the unusual manner of my ministering among them. But after frequently laying it before the Lord, and calmly weighing whatever objections I heard against it, I could not but adhere to what I had some time since written to a friend, who had freely spoken his sentiments concerning it. An extract of that letter I here subjoin that the matter may be placed in a clear light.

'All the world my parish'

You say, you cannot reconcile some parts of my behaviour with the character I have long supported. No, nor ever will. Therefore I have disclaimed that character on every possible occasion. I told all in our ship, all at Savannah, all at Frederica, and that over and over, in express terms, 'I am not a Christian; I only follow after, so that perhaps I may attain it.' . . .

If you ask on what principle I acted, it was this: a desire to be a Christian, and a conviction that whatever I judge conducive to being a Christian, that I am bound to do; wherever I judge I can best answer this purpose, it is my duty to go there. On this principle I set out for America; on this I visited the Moravian church; and on the same am I ready now (God being my helper) to go to Abyssinia or China or wherever it pleases God, by this conviction, to call me.

As to your advice that I should settle in college, I have no business there, having now no office, and no pupils. And whether the other branch of your proposal be expedient for me, namely to accept a cure of souls, it will be time enough to consider when one is offered to me.

But in the meantime you think I ought to sit still; because otherwise I should invade someone else's office, if I interfered with other people's business and intermeddled with souls that did not belong to me. You accordingly ask how it is that I assemble with Christians who are none of my charge, to sing psalms and pray and hear the scriptures expounded; and you think it hard to justify doing this in other men's parishes, upon catholic principles.

Permit me to speak plainly. If by catholic principles you mean any other than scriptural, they weigh nothing with me; I allow no other rule, whether of faith or practice, than the holy scriptures. But on scriptural principles, I do not think it hard to justify whatever I do. God in scripture commands me, according to my power, to instruct the ignorant, reform the wicked, confirm the virtuous. Man forbids me to do this in another's parish; that is, in effect, to do it at all; seeing I have now no parish of my own, nor probably ever shall. Whom then shall I hear, God or man? . . .

I look upon all the world as my parish; thus far I mean, that in whatever part of it I am, I judge it meet, right, and my bounden duty, to declare unto all that are willing to hear, the glad tidings of salvation. This is the work which I know God has called me to; and sure I am that his blessing attends it. Great encouragement have I, therefore, to be faithful in fulfilling the work he has given me to do. His servant I am, and as such am employed according to the plain direction of his word, 'As we have opportunity, let us do good to all people'; and his providence clearly concurs with his word; which has disengaged me from all things else, that I might singly attend on this very thing, 'and go about doing good'.

Susanna Wesley and her son

Wednesday 13. After receiving the holy communion at Islington, I had once more an opportunity of seeing my mother, whom I had not seen since my return from Germany.

I cannot but mention an odd circumstance here. I had

read her a paper in June last year, containing a short account of what had passed in my own soul, till within a few days of that time. She greatly approved it, and said she heartily blessed God, who had brought me to so just a way of thinking. While I was in Germany a copy of that paper was sent (without my knowledge) to one of my relations. He sent an account of it to my mother, whom I now found under strange fears concerning me, being convinced 'by an account taken from one of your own papers, that I had greatly erred from the faith'. I could not conceive what paper that should be; but, on inquiry, found it was the same I had read her myself. How hard it is to form a true judgement of any person or thing from the account of a prejudiced informant, be he ever so honest a man! For he who gave this information was one of unquestionable veracity, and yet by his sincere account of a writing which lay before his eyes, was the truth so totally disguised that my mother did not know that she had heard the paper from end to end, nor did I know that I had written it myself.

Thursday 14. I went with Mr Whitefield to Blackheath, where there were, I believe, twelve or fourteen thousand people. He a little surprised me by desiring me to preach in his stead; which I did (though nature recoiled) on my favourite subject, 'Christ Jesus, who has become for us wisdom from God—that is, our righteousness, holiness and redemption'.

I was greatly moved with compassion for the rich that were there, to whom I made a particular application. Some of them seemed to attend, while others drove away their coaches from so uncouth a preacher.

Sunday 17. I preached, at seven, in Upper Moorfields, to (I believe) six or seven thousand people, on 'Come, all you who are thirsty, come to the waters'.

At five I preached on Kennington Common, to about fifteen thousand people, on those words, 'Look at me, and be saved.'

Monday 18. I left London early in the morning, and the

next evening reached Bristol, and preached (as I had appointed, if God should permit) to a numerous congregation. My text now also was, 'Look at me and be saved.' Howell Harris called upon me an hour or two after. He said he had been much dissuaded from either hearing or seeing me, by many who said all manner of evil of me. 'But,' said he, 'as soon as I heard you preach, I quickly found what spirit you was of. And before you had done, I was so overpowered with joy and love, that I had much ado to walk home.'

Talks with Whitefield

Friday July 6. In the afternoon I was with Mr Whitefield, just come from London, with whom I went to Baptist Mills, where he preached concerning 'the Holy Spirit, which all who believe are to receive'; not without a just, though severe, censure of those who preach as if there were no Holy Spirit.

Saturday 7. I had an opportunity to talk with him of those outward signs which had so often accompanied the inward work of God. I found his objections were chiefly grounded on gross misrepresentations of matter of fact. But the next day he had an opportunity of informing himself better: for no sooner had he begun (in the application of his sermon) to invite all sinners to believe in Christ, than four persons sank down close to him, almost in the same moment. One of them lay without either sense or motion. A second trembled exceedingly. The third had strong convulsions all over his body, but made no noise, unless by groans. The fourth, equally convulsed, called upon God, with strong cries and tears. From this time, I trust, we shall all suffer God to carry on his own work in the way that pleases him.

Press-gang disturbs the sermon

Saturday 21. I began expounding, a second time, our Lord's sermon on the mount. In the morning, *Sunday 22,*

as I was explaining 'Blessed are the poor in spirit,' to about
three thousand people, we had a fair opportunity of showing all men what manner of spirit we were of: for in the
middle of the sermon the press-gang came, and seized on
one of the hearers (you who are learned in the law, what
becomes of Magna Carta, and of English liberty and property? Are not these mere sounds, while, on any pretence,
there is such a thing as a press-gang suffered in the land?),
all the rest standing still and none opening his mouth or
lifting up his hand to resist them.

Monday September 3 (London). I talked for some time
with my mother, who told me that till a short time ago she
had scarcely heard such a thing mentioned, as the having
forgiveness of sins now, or God's Spirit bearing witness
with our spirit: much less did she imagine that this was the
common privilege of all true believers. 'Therefore,' said
she, 'I never dared ask for it myself. But two or three
weeks ago, while my son Hall was pronouncing those
words, in delivering the cup to me, "The blood of our
Lord Jesus Christ, which was given for you," the words
struck through my heart, and I knew God for Christ's sake
had forgiven me all my sins.'

I asked whether her father (Dr Annesley) had not the
same faith; and whether she had not heard him preach it
to others. She answered, he had it himself; and declared, a
little before his death, that for more than forty years he
had no darkness, no fear, no doubt at all of his being 'accepted in the Beloved'. But that, nevertheless, she did not
remember having heard him preach, no, not once,
explicitly upon it: whence she supposed he also looked
upon it as the peculiar blessing of a few; not as promised
to all the people of God.

Sunday 9. I declared to about ten thousand, in Moorfields, what they must do to be saved. My mother went with
us, about five, to Kennington, where were supposed to be
twenty thousand people. I again insisted on that foundation of all our hope, 'Believe in the Lord Jesus, and you

will be saved.' From Kennington I went to a society at Lambeth. The house being filled, the rest stood in the garden. The deep attention they showed gave me a good hope that they will not all be forgetful hearers.

The new name of Methodism

Sunday 16. I preached at Moorfields to about ten thousand, and at Kennington Common to, I believe, about twenty thousand, on those words of the calmer Jews to St Paul, 'We want to hear what your views are, for we know that people everywhere are talking against this sect.' At both places I described the real difference between what is generally called Christianity and the true old Christianity, which, under the new name of Methodism, is now also everywhere spoken against.

An accident and a long sermon

Thursday 27. I went in the afternoon to a society at Deptford, and from there, at six, came to Turner's Hall: which holds (by computation) two thousand persons. The press both within and without was very great. In the beginning of the expounding, there being a large vault beneath, the main beam which supported the floor broke. The floor immediately sank, which occasioned much noise and confusion among the people. But two or three days before, a man had filled the vault with hogsheads of tobacco. So that the floor, after sinking a foot or two, rested upon them, and I went on without interruption.

Sunday October 7. About eleven I preached at Runwick, seven miles from Gloucester. The church was much crowded, though a thousand or upwards stayed in the churchyard. In the afternoon I explained further the same words, 'What must I do to be saved?' I believe some thousands were then present, more than had been in the morning.

Between five and six I called on all who were present (about three thousand) at Stanley, on a little green, near the town, to accept Christ, as their only 'wisdom from God—that is, our righteousness, holiness and redemption'. I was strengthened to speak as I never did before; and continued speaking about two hours: the darkness of the night, and a little lightning, not lessening the numbers, but increasing the seriousness, of the hearers. I concluded the day by expounding part of our Lord's sermon on the mount, to a small, serious company at Ebly.

Wesley in Wales

Monday 15. Upon a pressing invitation, some time since received, I set out for Wales. About four in the afternoon I preached on a little green, at the foot of the Devauden (a high hill, two or three miles beyond Chepstow), to three or four hundred plain people, on 'Christ Jesus, who has become for us wisdom from God—that is, our righteousness, holiness and redemption'. After the sermon, one who I trust is an old disciple of Christ, willingly received us into his house: to which many followed, so I showed them their need of a saviour, from these words, 'Blessed are the poor in spirit.' In the morning I described more fully the way to salvation—'Believe in the Lord Jesus, and you will be saved': and then, taking leave of my friendly host, before two came to Abergavenny.

I felt in myself a strong aversion to preaching here. However, I went to Mr W. (the person in whose ground Mr Whitefield preached), to desire the use of it. He said, with all his heart—if the minister was not willing to let me have the use of his church: after whose refusal (for I wrote a line to him immediately), he invited me to his house. About a thousand people stood patiently (though the frost was sharp, it being after sunset), while, from Acts 28:22, I simply described the plain, old religion of the Church of England, which is now almost everywhere spoken against, under the new name of Methodism.

Friday 19. I preached in the morning at Newport on 'What must I do to be saved?' to the most insensitive, ill-behaved people I have ever seen in Wales. One ancient man, during a great part of the sermon, cursed and swore almost incessantly; and towards the conclusion took up a great stone which he many times attempted to throw. But that he could not do.—Such are the champions, such the arms against field-preaching!

At four I preached at the Shire Hall of Cardiff again, where many gentry, I found, were present. Such freedom of speech I have seldom had as was given me in explaining those words, 'The kingdom of God is not a matter of eating and drinking, but righteousness, peace and joy in the Holy Spirit.' At six almost the whole town (I was informed) came together, to whom I explained the last six beatitudes: but my heart was so enlarged, I knew not how to give over, so that we continued three hours.

Saturday 20. I returned to Bristol. I have seen no part of England so pleasant for sixty or seventy miles together as those parts of Wales I have been in. And most of the inhabitants are indeed ripe for the gospel.

'A terrible sight'

Tuesday 23. In riding to Bradford I read over Mr Law's book on the new birth. Philosophical, speculative, precarious: Behmenish, void, and vain! 'Oh what a fall is there!' At eleven I preached at Bearfield to about three thousand on the spirit of nature, of bondage, and of adoption.

Returning in the evening, I was exceedingly pressed to go back to a young woman in Kingswood. (The fact I nakedly relate, and leave every man to his own judgement of it.) I went. She was nineteen or twenty years old; but, it seems, could not write or read. I found her on the bed, two or three persons holding her. It was a terrible sight. Anguish, horror, and despair, above all description, appeared in her pale face. The thousand distortions of her whole body showed how the dogs of hell were gnawing her heart. The shrieks intermixed were scarcely to be endured. But her stony eyes could not weep. She screamed out, as soon as words could find their way, 'I am damned, damned; lost for ever! Six days ago you might have helped me. But it is past. I am the devil's now. I have given myself to him. His I am. Him I must serve. With him I must go to hell. I will be his. I will serve him. I will go with him to hell. I cannot be saved. I will not be saved. I must, I will, I will be damned!' She then began praying to the devil. We began: 'Arm of the Lord, awake, awake!' She immediately sank down as asleep; but, as soon as we left off, broke out again, with inexpressible vehemence: 'Stony hearts, break! I am a warning to you. Break, break, poor stony hearts! Will you not break? What can be done for stony hearts? I am damned that you may be saved. Now break, now break, poor stony hearts! You need not be damned, though I must.' She then fixed her eyes on the corner of the ceiling, and said: 'There he is: ay, there he is! Come, good devil, come! Take me away. You said you would dash my brains out: come, do it quickly. I am yours. I will be yours. Come just now. Take me away.'

We interrupted her by calling again upon God, at which she sank down as before: and another young woman began to roar out as loud as she had done. My brother now came in, it being about nine o'clock. We continued in prayer till past eleven; when God in a moment spoke peace into the soul, first of the first tormented, and then of the other. And they both joined in singing praise to him who had 'silenced the foe and the avenger'.

'Yonder comes Wesley, galloping'

Saturday 27. I was sent for to Kingswood again, to one of those who had been so ill before. A violent rain began just as I set out, so that I was thoroughly wet in a few minutes.

Just at that time the woman (then three miles off) cried out, 'Yonder comes Wesley, galloping as fast as he can.' When I was come, I was quite cold and dead, and fitter for sleep than prayer. She burst out into a horrid laughter, and said, 'No power, no power; no faith, no faith. She is mine; her soul is mine. I have her, and will not let her go.'

We begged of God to increase our faith. Meanwhile her pangs increased more and more; so that one would have imagined, by the violence of the throes, her body must have been shattered to pieces. One who was clearly convinced this was no natural disorder, said, 'I think Satan is let loose. I fear he will not stop here.' And added, 'I command you, in the name of the Lord Jesus, to tell if you have commission to torment any other soul.' It was immediately answered, 'I have. L.C. and S.J.' (two who lived at some distance, and were then in perfect health).

We betook ourselves to prayer again; and ceased not till she began, about six o'clock, with a clear voice and composed, cheerful look: 'Praise God, from whom all blessings flow.'

Sunday 28. Returning in the evening, I called at Mrs J.'s in Kingswood. S.J. and L.C. were there. It was scarcely a quarter of an hour before L.C. fell into a strange agony; and presently after, S.J. The violent convulsions all over their bodies were too horrid to be borne, till one of them, in a tone not to be expressed, said: 'Where is your faith now? Come, go to prayers. I will pray with you. "Our Father, which art in heaven."' We took the advice, from whomsoever it came, and poured out our souls before God, till L.C.'s agonies so increased, that it seemed she was in the pangs of death. But in a moment God spoke: she knew his voice; and both her body and soul were healed.

We continued in prayer till near one, when S.J.'s voice was also changed, and she began strongly to call upon God. This she did for the greatest part of the night. In the morning we renewed our prayers, while she was crying continually, 'I burn! I burn! O what shall I do? I have a fire

within me. I cannot bear it. Lord Jesus! Help!'—Amen,
Lord Jesus! when your time comes.

The colliers of Kingswood

Tuesday November 27. I wrote to Mr D. (at his request) a
short account of what had been done in Kingswood, and of
our present undertaking there. The account was as follows:

Few persons have lived long in the west of England who have
not heard of the colliers of Kingswood; a people famous, from
the beginning till now, for neither fearing God nor regarding
man: so ignorant of the things of God, that they seemed but
one remove from the beasts that perish; and therefore utterly
without desire of instruction, as well as without the means of
it.

Many last winter used to tauntingly to say of Mr Whitefield,
'If he will convert the heathens, why does not he go to the colliers of Kingswood?' In spring he did so. And as there were
thousands who resorted to no place of public worship, he
went after them into their own wilderness, 'to seek and save
that which was lost'. When he was called away others went into
'the highways and hedges, to compel them to come in'. And,
by the grace of God, their labour was not in vain. The scene is
already changed. Kingswood does not now, as a year ago,
resound with drunkenness and uncleanness, and the idle
diversions that naturally lead to them. It is no longer full of
wars and fightings, of clamour and bitterness, of wrath and
envyings. Peace and love are there. Great numbers of the
people are mild, gentle, and easy to be entreated. They do not
'quarrel or cry out'; and hardly is their voice heard in the
streets; or, indeed, in their own wood; unless when they are at
their usual evening diversion—singing praise to God their
saviour.

That their children too might know the things which make
for their peace, it was some time since proposed to build a
house in Kingswood; and after many foreseen and unfore-
seen difficulties, in June last the foundation was laid. The
ground chosen was in the middle of the wood, between the

London and Bath roads, not far from that called Two Mile Hill, about three measured miles from Bristol.

Here a large room was begun for the school, having four small rooms at either end for the schoolmasters (and, perhaps, if it should please God, some poor children) to lodge in. Two persons are ready to teach, so soon as the house is fit to receive them, the shell of which is nearly finished; so that it is hoped the whole will be completed in spring or early in the summer.

It is true, although the masters require no pay, yet this undertaking is attended with great expense.

A sermon and a riot

1740. Tuesday April 1 (Bristol). While I was expounding the former part of the twenty-third chapter of the Acts (how wonderfully suited to the occasion! though not by my choice), the floods began to lift up their voice. Some or other of the children of Belial had laboured to disturb us several nights before: but now it seemed as if all the host of the aliens were come together with one consent. Not only the court and the alleys, but all the street, upwards and downwards, was filled with people, shouting, cursing and swearing, and ready to swallow the ground with fierceness and rage. The mayor sent order that they should disperse. But they set him at nought. The chief constable came next in person, who was, till then, sufficiently prejudiced against us. But they insulted him also in so gross a manner, as I believe fully opened his eyes. At length the mayor sent several of his officers, who took the ringleaders into custody, and did not go till all the rest were dispersed. Surely he has been to us 'the minister of God for good'.

Wednesday 2. The rioters were brought up to the court, the quarter sessions being held that day. They began to excuse themselves by saying many things of me. But the mayor cut them all short, saying, 'What Mr Wesley is, is nothing to you. I will keep the peace; I will have no rioting in this city.'

Sunday September 14 (London). As I returned home in

the evening, I had no sooner stepped out of the coach than the mob, who were gathered in great numbers about my door, quite closed me in. I rejoiced and blessed God, knowing this was the time I had long been looking for; and immediately spoke to those that were nearest me about 'righteousness, and judgement to come'. At first not many heard, the noise about us being exceeding great. But the silence spread farther and farther, till I had a quiet, attentive congregation; and when I left them, they all showed much love, and dismissed me with many blessings.

Preaching incidents

Sunday 28. I began expounding the sermon on the mount, at London. In the afternoon I described to a numerous congregation at Kennington the life of God in the soul. One person who stood on the mount made a little noise at first; but a gentleman, whom I knew not, walked up to him, and without saying one word, mildly took him by the hand and led him down. From that time he was quiet till he went away.

Tuesday 30. As I was expounding the twelfth chapter of Acts, a young man, with some others, rushed in cursing and swearing vehemently; and so disturbed all near him that, after a time, they put him out. I observed it, and called to let him come in, that our Lord might bid his chains fall off. As soon as the sermon was over, he came and declared before us all that he was a smuggler then carrying on that work, as his disguise, and the great bag he had with him, showed. But he said, he must never do this any more; for he was now resolved to have the Lord for his God.

Wesley's labour colony

Tuesday November 25 (London). After several methods proposed for employing those who were out of work, we determined to try something which several of our brethren recommended to us. Our aim was, with as little expense as possible, to keep them at once from need and from idleness, in order to which, we took twelve of the poorest, and a teacher, into the Society room, where they were employed for four months, till spring came on, in carding and spinning of cotton. And the plan worked: they were employed and maintained with very little more than the produce of their own labour.

Friday 28. A gentleman came to me full of good-will, to exhort me not to leave the church; or (which was the same thing in his account) to use extemporary prayer; which, said he, 'I will prove to a demonstration to be no prayer at all. For you cannot do two things at once. But thinking how to pray, and praying, are two things. Therefore, you cannot both think and pray at once.' Now, may it not be proved by the self-same demonstration, that praying by a set form is no prayer at all? For example: 'You cannot do two things at once. But reading and praying are two things. Therefore, you cannot both read and pray at once.' Q.E.D.

1741. Sunday February 1. A private letter, written to me by Mr Whitefield, having been printed without either his leave or mine, great numbers of copies were given to our people, both at the door and in the Foundery itself. Having procured one of them, I related (after preaching) the naked fact to the congregation, and told them, 'I will do just what I believe Mr Whitefield would, were he here himself'—upon which I tore it in pieces before them all. Everyone who had received it did the same, so that in two minutes there was not a whole copy left.

Dispute with Whitefield

Saturday March 28. Having heard much of Mr Whitefield's unkind behaviour since his return from Georgia, I went to him to hear him speak for himself, that I might know how to judge. I much approved of his plainness of speech. He told me that he and I preached two different gospels; and therefore he not only would not join with me, or give me the right hand of fellowship, but resolved publicly to preach against me and my brother, wherever he preached at all. Mr Hall (who went with me) reminded him of the promise he had made but a few days before, that whatever his private opinion was he would never publicly preach against us. He said, that promise was only an effect of human weakness, and he was now of another mind.

Monday April 6. I had a long conversation with Peter Böhler. I marvel how I refrain from joining these men. I scarcely ever see any of them but my heart burns within me. I long to be with them; and yet I am kept from them.

Thursday May 7. I reminded the United Society that many of our brethren and sisters lacked the food they needed; many were destitute of convenient clothing; many were out of work, and that not by their own fault; and many sick and ready to perish: that I had done what I could to feed the hungry, to clothe the naked, to employ the poor, and to visit the sick; but was not, alone, sufficient for these things; and therefore desired all whose hearts were as my heart:

1. To bring what clothes each could spare to be distributed among those that most needed them.

2. To give weekly a penny, or what they could afford, for the relief of the poor and sick.

My plan, I told them, is to employ for the present all the women who are out of work, and desire it, in knitting.

To these we will first give the normal price for what work they do; and then add, according as they need.

Twelve persons are appointed to inspect these, and to visit and provide things needful for the sick.

Each of these is to visit all the sick within their district every other day; and to meet on Tuesday evening, to give an account of what they have done, and consult what can be done farther.

Monday June 8. I set out from Enfield Chase for Leicester-shire. In the evening we came to Northampton: and the next afternoon to Mr Ellis's at Markfield, five or six miles beyond Leicester.

For these two days I had made an experiment which I had been so often and earnestly pressed to do—speaking to none concerning the things of God, unless my heart was free to it. And what was the result? Why, 1. That I spoke to none at all for eighty miles together; no, not even to him that travelled with me in the chaise, unless a few words at first setting out. 2. That I had no cross either to bear or to take up, and commonly, in an hour or two, fell fast asleep. 3. That I had much respect shown me wherever I came; everyone behaving to me as to a civil, good-natured gentle-man. O how pleasing is all this to flesh and blood! Do you need to 'travel over sea and land' to make 'one convert' to this?

Wesley at Nottingham

Sunday 14. I rode to Nottingham, and at eight preached at the market-place, to an immense multitude of people, on 'The dead shall hear the voice of the Son of God; and those who hear will live.' I saw only one or two who behaved lightly, whom I immediately reproved. Yet, soon after, a man behind me began aloud to contradict and blaspheme; but upon my turning to him, he stepped behind a pillar, and in a few minutes disappeared.

Monday 15. I set out for London, and on the way read over that celebrated book, Martin Luther's *Commentary on the Epistle to the Galatians*. I was utterly ashamed. How have I esteemed this book, only because I heard it so com-mended by others; or, at best, because I had read some excellent sentences occasionally quoted from it! But what shall I say, now I judge for myself, now I see with my own eyes? Why, not only that the author makes nothing out, clears up not one considerable difficulty; that he is quite shallow in his remarks on many passages, and muddy and confused almost on all; but that he is deeply tinctured with mysticism throughout, and hence often dangerously wrong.

An ox in the congregation

Friday July 10. I rode to London, and preached at Short's Gardens on 'the name of Jesus Christ of Nazareth'.

Sunday 12. While I was showing, at Charles Square, what it is 'to act justly and to love mercy and to walk humbly with our God', a great shout began. Many of the rabble had brought an ox, which they were vehemently labouring to drive in among the people. But their labour was in vain; for in spite of them all, he ran round and round, one way and the other, and at length broke through the midst of them clear away, leaving us calmly rejoicing and praising God.

Wesley at Cardiff

Thursday October 1. We set out for Wales; but missing our passage over the Severn in the morning, it was sunset before we could get to Newport. We inquired there if we could hire a guide to Cardiff; but there was none to be had. A lad coming in quickly after, who was going (he said) to Lanissan, a little village two miles to the right of Cardiff, we resolved to go there. At seven we set out: it rained pretty fast, and there being neither moon nor stars, we could neither see any road, nor one another, nor our own horses' heads; but the promise of God did not fail; he gave his angels charge over us; and soon after ten we came safe to Mr Williams's house at Lanissan.

Friday 2. We rode to Fonmon castle. We found Mr Jones's daughter ill of the smallpox; but he could cheerfully leave her and all the rest in the hands of him in whom he now believed. In the evening I preached at Cardiff, in the shire-hall, a large and convenient place, on

'God has given us eternal life, and this life is in his Son.'
There having been a feast in the town that day, I believed
it needful to add a few words on intemperance: and while
I was saying, 'As for you, drunkards, you abide in death;
you choose death and hell,' a man cried out vehemently,
'I am one; and I am going there.' But I trust God at that
hour began to show him and others 'a more excellent
way'.

Sunday November 22 (Bristol). Being not allowed to go to
church as yet [after a serious fever], I took communion at
home. I was advised to stay at home some time longer; but
I could not see it was necessary; and therefore, on *Monday
23,* went to the new room, where we praised God for all his
mercies. And I expounded, for about an hour (without
any faintness or weariness) on: 'How can I repay the Lord
for all his goodness to me? I will lift up the cup of salvation
and call on the name of the Lord.'

I preached once every day this week, and found no
inconvenience by it.

Sunday 29 I thought I might go a little farther. So I
preached both at Kingswood and at Bristol; and afterwards spent about an hour with the Society, and about two
hours at the love-feast. But my body could not yet keep
pace with my mind. I had another fit of my fever the next
day; but it lasted not long, and I continued slowly to regain
my strength.

Wesley's congregation stoned

1742. Monday January 25 (London). While I was explaining
at Long Lane, 'He who commits sin is of the devil,' his servants were above measure enraged: they not only made all
possible noise (although, as I had desired before, no man
stirred from his place, or answered them a word); but violently thrust many persons to and fro, struck others, and
broke down part of the house. At length they began throwing large stones upon the house, which, forcing their way

wherever they came, fell down, together with the tiles, among the people, so that they were in danger of their lives. I then told them: 'You must not go on thus; I am ordered by the magistrate, who is, in this respect, to us the minister of God, to inform him of those who break the laws of God and the king: and I must do it if you persist in this; otherwise I am a partaker of your sin.'

When I ceased speaking they were more outrageous than before. Upon this I said, 'Let three or four calm men take hold of the foremost, and charge a constable with him, that the law may take its course.' They did so, and brought him into the house, cursing and blaspheming in a dreadful manner. I desired five or six to go with him to Justice Copeland, to whom they nakedly related the fact. The justice immediately bound him over to the next sessions at Guildford.

I observed when the man was brought into the house, that many of his companions were loudly crying out, 'Richard Smith, Richard Smith!' who, as it afterwards appeared, was one of their stoutest champions. But Richard Smith answered not; he was fallen into the hands of one higher than they. God had struck him to the heart; as also a woman who was speaking words not fit to be repeated, and throwing whatever came to hand, whom he overtook in the very act. She came into the house with Richard Smith, fell upon her knees before us all, and strongly exhorted him never to turn back, never to forget the mercy which God had shown to his soul. From this time we had never any considerable interruption or disturbance at Long Lane; although we withdrew our prosecution, upon the offender's submission and promise of better behaviour.

Monday February 15. Many met together to consult on a proper method for discharging the public debt; and it was at length agreed, 1. That every member of the Society who was able should contribute a penny a week. 2. That the whole Society should be divided into little companies or classes—about twelve in each class. And 3. That one person in each class should receive the contribution of the rest, and bring it in to the Stewards, weekly.

A bull in the congregation

Friday March 10. I rode once more to Pensford at the earnest request of several serious people. The place where they desired me to preach was a little green spot, near the town. But I had no sooner begun than a great company of rabble, hired (as we afterwards found) for that purpose, came furiously upon us, bringing a bull, which they had been baiting, and now strove to drive in among the people. But the beast was wiser than his drivers; and continually ran either on one side of us or the other, while we quietly sang praise to God, and prayed for about an hour. The poor wretches, finding themselves disappointed, at length seized upon the bull, now weak and tired, after having been so long torn and beaten both by dogs and men; and, by main strength, partly dragged, and partly thrust him in among the people.

When they had forced their way to the little table on which I stood, they strove several times to throw it down, by thrusting the helpless beast against it, who, of himself, stirred no more than a log of wood. I once or twice put aside his head with my hand, that the blood might not drop upon my clothes; intending to go on as soon as the commotion should be a little over. But the table falling down, some of our friends caught me in their arms, and carried me right away on their shoulders; while the rabble wreaked their vengeance on the table, which they tore bit from bit. We went a little way off, where I finished my discourse, without any noise or interruption.

Sunday 21. In the evening I rode to Marshfield, and on *Tuesday*, in the afternoon, came to London.

Thursday 25. I appointed several earnest and sensible men to meet me, to whom I showed the great difficulty I had long found of knowing the people who desired to be under my care. After much discourse, they all agreed there could be no better way to come to a sure, thorough knowledge of each person, than to divide them into classes, like those at Bristol, under the inspection of those in whom I could most confide. This was the origin of our classes at London, for which I can never sufficiently praise God; the unspeakable usefulness of the institution having ever since been more and more manifest.

Friday April 9. We had the first watch-night in London. We commonly choose for this solemn service the Friday night nearest the full moon, either before or after, that those of the congregation who live at a distance, may have light to their different homes. The service begins at half an hour past eight, and continues till a little after midnight. We have often found a peculiar blessing at these seasons.

Sunday May 9. I preached in Charles Square to the largest congregation I have ever seen there. Many of the baser people would have interrupted, but they found after a time it was lost labour. One, who was more serious, was (as she afterwards confessed) exceedingly angry at them. But she was quickly rebuked by a stone which lighted upon her forehead and struck her down to the ground. In that moment her anger was at an end, and love only filled her heart.

Monday 17. I received a letter from Leicestershire, pressing me to come without delay and pay the last office of friendship to one whose soul was on the wing for eternity. On *Thursday 20* I set out.

Wesley was 'the better mounted'

The next afternoon I stopped a little at Newport Pagnell, and then rode on till I overtook a religious man, with whom I immediately fell into conversation.

He presently gave me to know what his opinions were: therefore I said nothing to contradict them. But that did not content him: he was quite uneasy to know whether I held the doctrine of the decrees as he did; but I told him over and over, 'We had better keep to practical things, lest we should be angry at one another.' And so we did for two miles, till he caught me unawares, and dragged me into the dispute before I knew where I was. He then grew warmer and warmer; told me I was rotten at heart, and supposed I was one of John Wesley's followers. I told him, 'No, I am John Wesley himself.' Upon which he would gladly have run away outright. But being the better mounted of the two, I kept close to his side, and endeavoured to show him his heart, till we came into the street of Northampton.

Thursday 27. We came to Newcastle about six; and, after a short refreshment, walked into the town. I was surprised: so much drunkenness, cursing, and swearing (even from the mouths of little children), do I never remember to have seen and heard before, in so small a compass of time. Surely this place is ripe for him who 'came not to call the righteous, but sinners'.

Sunday 30. At seven I walked down to Sandgate, the poorest and most contemptible part of the town; and, standing at the end of the street with John Taylor, began to sing the hundredth Psalm. Three or four people came out to see what was the matter; who soon increased to four or five hundred. I suppose there might be twelve or fifteen hundred before I had done preaching.

A big crowd at Newcastle

Observing the people, when I had done, to stand gaping and staring upon me, with the most profound astonishment, I told them, 'If you desire to know who I am, my name is John Wesley. At five in the evening, with God's help, I plan to preach here again.'

At five, the hill on which I planned to preach was covered, from the top to the bottom. I never saw so large a number of people together, either at Moorfields, or at Kennington Common. I knew it was not possible for the one half to hear, although my voice was then strong and clear; and I stood so as to have them all in view, as they were ranged on the side of the hill.

Wesley on his father's tombstone

Saturday June 5. It being many years since I had been in Epworth before, I went to an inn, in the middle of the town, not knowing whether there were any left in it now who would not be ashamed of my acquaintance. But an old servant of my father's, with two or three poor women, presently found me out. I asked her, 'Do you know any in Epworth who are in earnest to be saved?' She answered, 'I am, by the grace of God; and I know I am saved through faith.' I asked, 'Have you then the peace of God?' She replied, 'I thank God, I know it well. And many here can say the same thing.'

Sunday 6. A little before the service began, I went to Mr Romley, the curate, and offered to assist him either by preaching or reading prayers. But he did not care to accept my assistance. The church was exceedingly full in the afternoon, a rumour being spread that I was to preach. But the sermon, on 'Do not put out the Spirit's fire,' was not suitable to the expectation of many of the hearers. Mr Romley told them, one of the most dangerous ways of quenching the Spirit was by enthusiasm; and enlarged on the character of an enthusiast, in a very florid and oratorical manner. After the sermon John Taylor stood in the churchyard, and gave notice, as the people were coming out, 'Mr Wesley, not being permitted to preach in the church, plans to preach here at six o'clock.'

Accordingly at six I came, and found such a congregation as I believe Epworth never saw before. I stood near the east end of the church, upon my father's tombstone, and cried: 'The kingdom of God is not a matter of eating and drinking, but of righteousness, peace and joy in the Holy Spirit.'

'Let them convert the scolds'

Wednesday 9. I rode over to a neighbouring town, to see a justice of the peace, a man of candour and understanding; before whom (I was informed) their angry neighbours had carried a whole waggon-load of these new heretics. But when he asked what they had done, there was a deep silence; for that was a point the people who brought them had forgotten. At length one said they pretended to be better than other people; and besides, they prayed from morning to night.

Mr S. asked, 'But have they done nothing besides?'

'Yes, sir,' said an old man: 'an't please your worship, they have *convarted* my wife. Till she went among them, she had such a tongue! And now she is quiet as a lamb.'

'Take them back, take them back,' replied the justice, 'and let them convert all the scolds in the town.'

Saturday 12. I preached on the righteousness of the law and the righteousness of faith. While I was speaking, several dropped down as dead; and among the rest, such a cry was heard, of sinners groaning for the righteousness of faith, as almost drowned my voice. But many of these soon lifted up their heads with joy, and broke out into thanksgiving; being assured they now had the desire of their soul—the forgiveness of their sins.

Sunday 13. At seven I preached at Haxey, on 'What must I do to be saved?' From there I went to Wroote, of which (as well as Epworth) my father was rector for several years. Mr Whitelamb offering me the church, I preached in the morning on 'Ask, and it will be given to you'; in the afternoon, on the difference between the righteousness of the law and the righteousness of faith. But the church could not contain the people, many of whom came from far, and, I trust, not in vain.

At six I preached for the last time in Epworth church-yard (being to leave the town the next morning), to a vast multitude gathered together from all parts, on the beginning of our Lord's sermon on the mount. I continued among them for about three hours, and yet we scarcely knew how to part. O let none think his labour of love is lost because the fruit does not immediately appear! Near forty years did my father labour here; but he saw little fruit of all his labour. I took some pains among this people too; and my strength also seemed spent in vain; but now the fruit appeared. There were scarcely any in the town on whom either my father or I had taken any pains formerly but the seed, sown so long since, now sprang up, bringing forth repentance and remission of sins.

I left Bristol in the evening of *Sunday July 18* and on *Tuesday* came to London. I found my mother on the borders of eternity. But she had no doubt or fear; nor any desire but (as soon as God should call) 'to depart and be with Christ'.

Death of Wesley's mother

Friday 23. About three in the afternoon I went to my mother, and found her change was near. I sat down on the bed-side. She was in her last conflict; unable to speak, but I believe quite aware. Her look was calm and serene, and her eyes fixed upward, while we commended her soul to God. From three to four the silver cord was loosing, and the wheel breaking at the cistern; and then without any struggle, or sigh, or groan, the soul was set at liberty. We stood round the bed, and fulfilled her last request, uttered a little before she lost her speech: 'Children, as soon as I am released, sing a psalm of praise to God.'

Mrs Wesley as preacher

I cannot but further observe, that even she (as well as her father, and grandfather, her husband, and her three sons)

had been, in her measure and degree, a preacher of righteousness. This I learned from a letter, written long since to
my father; part of which I have here subjoined:

February 6, 1711–12
——As I am a woman, so I am also mistress of a large family.
And though the superior charge of the souls contained in it
lies upon you; yet, in your absence, I cannot but look upon
every soul you leave under my care, as a talent committed to
me under a trust, by the great Lord of all the families both of
heaven and earth. And if I am unfaithful to him or you in
neglecting to improve these talents, how shall I answer unto
him, when he shall command me to render an account of my
stewardship?

As these, and other such like thoughts, made me at first take
a more than ordinary care of the souls of my children and servants, so—knowing our religion requires a strict observation of
the Lord's day, and not thinking that we fully answered the end
of the institution by going to church, unless we filled up the
intermediate spaces of time by other acts of piety and devo-
tion—I thought it my duty to spend some part of the day in
reading to and instructing my family; and such time I
esteemed spent in a way more acceptable to God, than if I had
retired to my own private devotions.

This was the beginning of my present practice. Other
people's coming and joining with us was merely accidental.
Our lad told his parents: they first desired to be admitted;
then others that heard of it begged leave also: so our company
increased to about thirty; and it seldom exceeded forty last
winter.

But soon after you went to London last, I lighted on the
account of the Danish missionaries. I was, I think, never more
affected with anything; I could not forbear spending a good
part of that evening in praising and adoring the divine goodness for inspiring them with such ardent zeal for his glory. For
several days I could think or speak of little else. At last it came
into my mind that though I am not a man nor a minister, yet
if my heart were sincerely devoted to God, and I was inspired
with a true zeal for his glory, I might do somewhat more than
I do. I thought I might pray more for them, and might speak

to those with whom I converse with more warmth of affection. I resolved to begin with my own children; in which I observe the following method: I take such a proportion of time as I can spare every night to discourse with each child apart. On Monday, I talk with Molly; on Tuesday, with Hetty; Wednesday, with Nancy; Thursday, with Jacky; Friday, with Patty; Saturday, with Charles; and with Emily and Suky together on Sunday.

She speaks to two hundred

With those few neighbours that then came to me, I discoursed more freely and affectionately. I chose the best and most awakening sermons we have. And I spent somewhat more time with them in such exercises, without being careful about the success of my undertaking. Since this, our company increased every night; for I dare deny none that ask admittance.

Last Sunday I believe we had more than two hundred. And yet many went away, for lack of room to stand.

We banish all temporal concerns from our society. No one is allowed to mingle any talk about them with our reading or singing. We keep close to the business of the day; and when it is over, all go home.

I cannot conceive why any should reflect upon you because your wife endeavours to draw people to church, and to restrain them from profaning the Lord's Day, by reading to them, and other persuasions. For my part, I value no censure upon this account. I have long since shaken hands with the world. And I heartily wish I had never given them more reason to speak against me.

As to its looking peculiar, I grant it does. And so does almost anything that is serious, or that may any way advance the glory of God, or the salvation of souls.

As for your proposal, of letting some other person read: alas, you do not consider what a people these are! I do not think one man among them could read a sermon, without spelling a good part of it. Nor has any of our family a voice strong enough to be heard by such a number of people.

But there is one thing about which I am much dissatisfied;

that is, their being present at family prayers. I do not speak of any concern I am under, barely because so many are present; for those who have the honour of speaking to the great and holy God, need not be ashamed to speak before the whole world; but because of my sex. I doubt if it is proper for me to present the prayers of the people to God. Last Sunday I would have dismissed them before prayers; but they begged so earnestly to stay, I dared not deny them.

How the Wesleys were brought up

For the benefit of those who are entrusted, as she was, with the care of a numerous family, I cannot but add one letter more, which I received many years ago:

July 24, 1732

Dear Son,—According to your desire, I have collected the principal rules I observed in educating my family; which I now send you as they occurred to my mind, and you may (if you think they can be of use to any) dispose of them in what order you please.

The children were always put into a regular method of living, in such things as they were capable of, from their birth; as in dressing, undressing, changing their linen, etc. The first quarter commonly passes in sleep. After that, they were, if possible, laid into their cradles rocking, till it was time for them to awake. This was done to bring them to a regular course of sleeping; which at first was three hours in the morning, and three in the afternoon: afterward two hours, till they needed none at all.

When turned a year old (and some before), they were taught to fear the rod, and to cry softly; by which means they escaped abundance of correction they might otherwise have had; and that most odious noise of the crying of children was rarely heard in the house; but the family usually lived in as much quietness as if there had not been a child among them.

As soon as they were grown pretty strong, they were confined to three meals a day. At dinner their little table and chairs were set by ours, where they could be overlooked; and they were allowed to eat and drink (small beer) as much as they wanted; but not to call for anything. If they wanted anything, they used to whisper to the maid which attended them, who came and spoke to me; and as soon as they could handle a knife and fork, they were set to our table. They were never allowed to choose their meat, but always made to eat such things as were provided for the family.

Mornings they had always spoon-meat; sometimes at nights. But whatever they had, they were never permitted to eat, at those meals, of more than one thing; and of that sparingly enough. Drinking or eating between meals was never allowed, unless in case of sickness; which seldom happened. Nor were they allowed to go into the kitchen to ask anything of the servants, when they were at meat: if it was known they did, they were certainly beaten, and the servants severely reprimanded.

At six, as soon as family prayers were over, they had their supper; at seven, the maid washed them; and, beginning at the youngest, she undressed and got them all to bed by eight; at which time she left them in their several rooms awake; for there was no such thing allowed of in our house, as sitting by a child till it fell asleep.

'Conquer the child's will'

They were so constantly used to eat and drink what was given them, that when any of them was ill, there was no difficulty in making them take the most unpleasant medicine: for they dared not refuse it, though some of them would presently throw it up. This I mention to show that a person may be taught to take anything, though it be never so much against his stomach.

In order to form the minds of children, the first thing to be done is to conquer their will, and bring them to an obedient temper. To inform the understanding is a work of time, and must with children proceed by slow degrees as they are able to bear it: but the subjecting the will is a thing which must be done at once; and the sooner the better. For by neglecting timely correction, they will contract a stubbornness and obstinacy which is hardly ever after conquered; and never, without using such severity as would be as painful to me as to the child. In the esteem of the world they pass for kind and indulgent, whom I call cruel, parents, who permit their children to get habits which they know must be afterwards broken. Nay, some are so stupid and foolish as to teach their children to do things in play which, in a while after, they have severely beaten them for doing.

Whenever a child is corrected, it must be conquered; and this will be no hard matter to do, if it be not grown headstrong by too much indulgence. And when the will of a child is totally subdued, and it is brought to revere and stand in awe of the parents, then a great many childish follies and inadvertences may be passed by. Some should be overlooked and taken no notice of, and others mildly reproved; but no wilful transgression ought ever to be forgiven children, without chastisement, less or more as the nature and circumstances of the offence require.

I insist upon conquering the will of children early, because this is the only strong and rational foundation of a religious education; without which both precept and example will be ineffectual. But when this is thoroughly done, then a child is capable of being governed by the reason and piety of its parents, till its own understanding comes to maturity, and the principles of religion have taken root in the mind.

They had nothing they cried for

I cannot yet dismiss this subject. As self-will is the root of all sin and misery, so whatever cherishes this in children ensures their after-wretchedness and irreligion; whatever checks and mortifies it promotes their future happiness and piety. This is still more evident, if we farther consider that religion is nothing else than the doing the will of God, and not our own: that the one grand impediment to our temporal and eternal happiness being this self-will, no indulgences of it can be trivial, no denial unprofitable. Heaven or hell depend on this alone. So that the parent who studies to subdue it in his child works together with God in the renewing and saving a soul. The parent who indulges it does the devil's work, makes religion impracticable, salvation unattainable; and does all that in him lies to damn his child, soul and body for ever.

The children of this family were taught, as soon as they

could speak, the Lord's Prayer, which they were made to say at rising and bed-time constantly; to which, as they grew bigger, were added a short prayer for their parents, and some collects; a short catechism, and some portion of scripture, as their memories could bear.

They were very early made to distinguish the sabbath from the other days; before they could well speak or walk. They were as soon taught to be still at family prayers, and to ask a blessing immediately after, which they used to do by signs, before they could kneel or speak.

They were quickly made to understand they might have nothing they cried for, and instructed to speak handsomely for what they wanted. They were not allowed to ask even the lowest servant for anything without saying, 'Pray give me such a thing'; and the servant was told off if she ever let them omit that word. Taking God's name in vain, cursing and swearing, profaneness, obscenity, rude, ill-bred names, were never heard among them. Nor were they ever permitted to call each other by their proper names without the addition of brother or sister.

None of them were taught to read till five years old, except Kezzy, in whose case I was overruled; and she was more years learning than any of the rest had been months. The way of teaching was this: The day before a child began to learn, the house was set in order, everyone's work appointed them, and a charge given that none should come into the room from nine till twelve, or from two till five; which, you know, were our school hours. One day was allowed the child in which to learn its letters; and each of them did in that time know all its letters, great and small, except Molly and Nancy, who were a day and a half before they knew them perfectly; for which I then thought them very dull; but since I have observed how long many children are learning the horn-book, I have changed my opinion.

But the reason why I thought them so then was because the rest learned so readily; and your brother Samuel, who was the first child I ever taught, learned the alphabet in a few hours. He was five years old on February 10; the next day he began to learn, and as soon as he knew the letters, began at the first chapter of Genesis. He was taught to spell the first verse, then to read it over and over, till he could read it offhand without any hesitation, so on to the second, etc., till he took ten verses for a lesson, which he quickly did. Easter fell late that year, and by Whitsuntide he could read a chapter very well; for he read continually, and had such a prodigious memory that I cannot remember ever to have told him the same word twice.

What was yet stranger, any word he had learned in his lesson, he knew, wherever he saw it, either in his Bible, or any other book; by which means he learned very soon to read any English author well.

The same method was observed with them all. As soon as they knew the letters, they were put first to spell, and read one line, then a verse; never leaving till perfect in their lesson, were it shorter or longer. So one or other continued reading at school-time, without any intermission; and before we left school, each child read what he had learned that morning; and ere we parted in the afternoon, what they had learned that day.

Keeping the Wesley children in order

There was no such thing as loud talking or playing allowed; but everyone was kept close to their business, for the six hours of school: and it is almost incredible what a child may be taught in a quarter of a year, by a vigorous application, if it have but a tolerable capacity, and good health. Every one of these, Kezzy excepted, could read better in that time than most women can do as long as they live.

Rising out of their places, or going out of the room, was not permitted, unless for good cause; and running into the yard, garden, or street, without leave, was always esteemed a capital offence.

For some years we went on very well. Never were children in better order. Never were children better disposed to piety, or in more subjection to their parents; till that fatal dispersion of them, after the fire, into several families. In those they were left at full liberty to converse with servants, which before they had always been restrained from; and to run abroad, and play with any children, good or bad. They soon learned to neglect a strict observance of the Sabbath, and got knowledge of several songs and bad things, which before they had no notion of. The civil behaviour which made them admired, when at home, by all which saw them, was in great measure lost; and a clownish accent, and many rude ways, were learned which were not reformed without some difficulty.

When the house was rebuilt, and the children all brought home, we entered upon a strict reform; and then was begun the custom of singing psalms at beginning and leaving school, morning and evening. Then also that of a general retirement at five o'clock was entered upon; when the oldest took the youngest that could speak, and the second the next, to whom they read the Psalms for the day, and a chapter in the New Testament; as, in the morning, they were directed to read the Psalms and a chapter in the Old: after which they went to their private prayers, before they got their breakfast, or came into the family. And, I thank God, the custom is still preserved among us.

Susanna Wesley's 'by-laws'

There were several by-laws observed among us, which slipped my memory, or else they would have been inserted in their proper place; but I mention them here, because I think them useful.

1. It had been observed that cowardice and fear of punishment often lead children into lying, till they get a custom of it, which they cannot leave. To prevent this, a law was made that whoever was charged with a fault, of which they were guilty, if they would ingenuously confess it, and promise to amend, should not be beaten. This rule prevented a great deal of lying, and would have done more, if one in the family would have observed it. But he could not be prevailed upon, and therefore was often imposed on by false colours and equivocations; which none would have used (except one), had they been kindly dealt with. And some, in spite of all, would always speak truth plainly.

2. That no sinful action, such as lying, pilfering, playing at church, or on the Lord's Day, disobedience, quarrelling, etc., should ever pass unpunished.

3. That no child should ever be told off, or beaten twice for

the same fault; and that if they amended, they should never be upbraided with it afterwards.

4. That every signal act of obedience, especially when it crossed upon their own inclinations, should be always commended, and frequently rewarded, according to the merits of the cause.

5. That if ever any child performed an act of obedience, or did anything with an intention to please, though the performance was not well, yet the obedience and intention should be kindly accepted; and the child with sweetness directed how to do better for the future.

6. That propriety be inviolably preserved, and no one allowed to invade the property of anyone else in the smallest matter, though it were but the value of a farthing, or a pin; which they might not take from the owner without, much less against, his consent. This rule can never be too much inculcated on the minds of children; and from the want of parents or governors doing as they ought, proceeds that shameful neglect of justice which we may observe in the world.

7. That promises be strictly observed; and a gift once bestowed, and so the right passed away from the donor, be not resumed, but left to the disposal of him to whom it was given; unless it were conditional, and the condition of the obligation not performed.

8. That no girl be taught to work till she can read very well; and then that she be kept to her work with the same application, and for the same time, that she was held to in reading. This rule also is much to be observed; for the putting children to learn sewing before they can read perfectly is the very reason why so few women can read fit to be heard, and never to be well understood.

Mr Stephenson and Wesley

Wednesday December 1 (Newcastle). We had several places offered, on which to build a room for the Society; but none such as we wanted. And perhaps there was a providence in our not finding any as yet; for, by this means, I was kept at Newcastle, whether I would or no.

Saturday 4. I was both surprised and grieved at a genuine instance of enthusiasm. J.B., of Tunfield Leigh, who had received a sense of the love of God a few days before, came riding through the town, hallooing and shouting, and driving all the people before him; telling them, God had told him he should be a king, and should tread them all under his feet. I sent him home immediately to his work, and advised him to cry day and night to God that he might be lowly in heart; lest Satan should again get an advantage over him.

Today a gentleman called and offered me a piece of ground. On Monday an article was drawn, wherein he agreed to put me into possession on Thursday, upon payment of thirty pounds.

Tuesday 7. I was so ill in the morning that I was obliged to send Mr Williams to the room. He afterwards went to Mr Stephenson, a merchant in the town, who had a passage through the ground we intended to buy. I was willing to purchase it. Mr Stephenson told him, 'Sir, I do not want money; but if Mr Wesley wants ground, he may have a piece of my garden, adjoining to the place you mention. I am at a word. For forty pounds he shall have sixteen yards in breadth, and thirty in length.'

Wednesday 8. Mr Stephenson and I signed an article, and I took possession of the ground. But I could not fairly go back from my agreement with Mr Iddel: so I entered on his ground at the same time. The whole is about forty yards in length; in the middle of which we determined to build the house, leaving room for a small courtyard before, and a little garden behind, the building.

Newcastle's first Methodist room

Thursday 23. It being computed that such a house as was proposed could not be finished under £700, many were positive it would never be finished at all; others, that I should not live to see it covered. I was of another mind;

nothing doubting but, as it was begun for God's sake, he would provide what was needful for finishing it.

Wesley refused the sacrament at Epworth

1743. Sunday January 2 (Epworth). At five I preached on 'So it is with everyone born of the Spirit.' About eight I preached from my father's tomb on Hebrews 8:11. Many from the neighbouring towns asked if it would not be well, as it was sacrament Sunday, for them to receive it. I told them, 'By all means: but it would be more respectful first to ask Mr Romley the curate's leave.' One did so, in the name of the rest; to whom he said, 'Pray tell Mr Wesley, I shall not give him the sacrament; for he is not fit.'

Wesley in Seven Dials

Sunday May 29. I began officiating at the chapel in West Street, near the Seven Dials, of which (by a strange chain of providences) we have a lease for several years. I preached on the gospel for the day, part of the third chapter of St John; and afterwards administered the Lord's supper to some hundreds of communicants. I was a little afraid at first that my strength would not suffice for the business of the day, when a service of five hours (for it lasted from ten to three) was added to my usual employment. But God looked to that: so I must think; and they that will call it enthusiasm may. I preached at the Great Gardens at five to an immense congregation, on 'You must be born again'. Then the leaders met (who filled all the time that I was not speaking in public); and after them, the bands. At ten at night I was less weary than at six in the morning.

Sunday July 10 (Newcastle). I preached at eight on Chowden Fell, on 'Why will you die, O house of Israel?' Ever since I came to Newcastle the first time, my spirit had been moved within me at the crowds of poor wretches who were every Sunday, in the afternoon, sauntering to and fro on the Sandhill. I resolved, if possible, to find them something better to do; and so soon as the service at All Saints was over, walked straight from the church to the Sandhill, and gave out a verse of a psalm. In a few minutes I had company enough; thousands upon thousands crowding together. But the prince of this world fought with all his might lest his kingdom should be overthrown. Indeed, the very mob of Newcastle, in the height of their rudeness, have commonly some humanity left. I scarcely observed that they threw anything at all; neither did I receive the least personal hurt: but they continued thrusting one another to and fro, and making such a noise, that my voice could not be heard: so that, after spending about an hour in singing and prayer, I thought it best to adjourn to our own house.

Wesley's horses give trouble

Monday 18. I set out from Newcastle with John Downes, of Horsley. We were four hours riding to Ferry Hill, about twenty measured miles. After resting there an hour we rode softly on; and at two o'clock, came to Darlington. I thought my horse was not well; he thought the same of his; though they were both young, and very well the day before. We ordered the ostler to fetch a farrier, which he did without delay; but, before the men could determine what was the matter, both the horses lay down and died.

I hired a horse to Sandhutton, and rode on, desiring John Downes to follow me. From there I rode to Borough Bridge on *Tuesday* morning, and then walked on to Leeds.

Monday August 22 (London). After a few of us had joined in prayer, about four I set out and rode softly to Snow Hill; where, the saddle slipping quite upon my mare's neck, I fell over her head, and she ran back into Smithfield. Some boys caught her and brought her to me again, cursing and swearing all the way. I spoke plainly to them, and they promised to amend. I was setting forward, when a man cried, 'Sir, you have lost your saddle-cloth.' Two or three more would needs help me to put it on; but these, too, swore at almost every word. I turned to one and another, and spoke in love. They all took it well, and thanked me much. I gave them two or three little books, which they promised to read over carefully.

Before I reached Kennington, I found my mare had lost a shoe. This gave me an opportunity of talking privately, for about half an hour, both to the smith and his servant. I mention these little circumstances to show how easy it is to make use of every fragment of time (if I may so speak), when we feel any love to those souls for which Christ died.

Wesley goes to Cornwall

Friday 26. I set out for Cornwall. In the evening I preached at the cross in Taunton, on 'The kingdom of God is not a matter of eating and drinking, but of righteousness, peace and joy in the Holy Spirit.' A poor man had posted himself behind, in order to make some disturbance: but the time was not come; the zealous wretches who 'deny the Lord that bought them' had not yet stirred up the people. Many cried out, 'Throw down that rascal there; knock him down; beat out his brains': so that I was obliged to entreat for him more than once, or he would have been roughly handled.

Saturday 27. I reached Exeter in the afternoon; but as no one knew of my coming, I did not preach that night, only to one poor sinner at the inn; who, after listening to our conversation for a while, looked earnestly at me, and asked whether it was possible for one who had in some measure known 'the power of the world to come' and was 'fallen away' (which she said was her own case) to be 're-newed again to repentance'. We besought God on her behalf, and left her sorrowing; and yet not without hope.

Sunday 28. I preached at seven to a handful of people.

The sermon we heard at church was quite innocent of meaning: what that in the afternoon was, I know not, for I could not hear a single sentence.

From church I went to the castle; where were gathered together (as some imagined) half the grown persons in the city. It was an awe-inspiring sight. So vast a congregation in that solemn amphitheatre! And all silent and still, while I explained at large, and enforced, that glorious truth, 'Blessed are they whose transgressions are forgiven, whose sins are covered.'

Tuesday 30. In the evening we reached St Ives. At seven I invited all guilty, helpless sinners who were conscious that they 'had nothing to pay', to accept free forgiveness. The room was crowded both within and without; but all were quiet and attentive.

Wednesday 31. I spoke separately with those of the Society, who were about one hundred and twenty. About a hundred of these had found peace with God: such is the blessing of being persecuted for righteousness' sake! As we were going to church at eleven, a large group at the market-place welcomed us with a loud cry: wit as harmless as the ditty sung under my window (composed, someone assured me, by a gentlewoman of their own town),

> Charles Wesley is come to town,
> To try if he can pull the churches down.

The Cornish tinners

Saturday September 3. I rode to the Three-cornered Down (so called), nine or ten miles east of St Ives, where we found two or three hundred tinners, who had been waiting some time for us. They all appeared quite pleased and unconcerned; and many of them ran after us to Gwennap (two miles east), where their number was quickly increased to four or five hundred. I had much comfort here, in applying these words, 'He has anointed me to preach the gospel to the poor.' One who lived near invited us to lodge at his house, and conducted us back to the Green in the morning. We came there just as the day dawned.

I strongly applied those gracious words, 'I will heal their backsliding, I will love them freely,' to five or six hundred serious people. At Trezuthan Downs, five miles nearer St Ives, we found seven or eight hundred people, to whom I cried aloud, 'Rid yourselves of all the offences you have committed. . . . Why will you die, O house of Israel?' After dinner I preached again to about a thousand people, on him whom 'God exalted as Prince and Saviour'. It was here first I observed a little impression made on two or three of the hearers; the rest, as usual, showing huge approbation, and absolute unconcern.

Sunday 11. We went afterwards down, as far as we could go safely, toward the point of the rocks at the Land's End. It was an awesome sight! But how will these melt away, when God shall arise to judgement! The sea between does indeed 'churn like a boiling cauldron'. 'One would think the deep had white hair.' But 'though they swell, yet can they not prevail. He has set their bounds, which they cannot pass.'

In the Scilly Isles

Monday 12. I had had for some time a great desire to go and publish the love of God our saviour, if it were but for one day, in the Isles of Scilly; and I had occasionally mentioned it to several people. This evening three of our brethren came and offered to take me there, if I could procure the mayor's boat, which, they said, was the best sailer of any in the town. I sent, and he lent it me immediately. So the next morning, *Tuesday 13,* John Nelson, Mr Shepherd, and I, with three men and a pilot, sailed from St Ives. About half an hour after one, we landed on St Mary's, the chief of the inhabited islands.

We immediately went to see the Governor, with the

usual present, namely a newspaper. I desired him, likewise, to accept *An Earnest Appeal*. The minister not being willing I should preach in the church, I preached, at six, in the streets, to almost all the town, and many soldiers, sailors, and workmen, on 'Why will you die, O house of Israel?' It was a blessed time, so that I scarcely knew how to conclude. After the sermon I gave them some little books and hymns, which they were so eager to receive that they were ready to tear both them and me to pieces.

For what political reason such a number of workmen were gathered together, and employed at so large an expense, to fortify a few barren rocks, which whoever took deserves to have them for his pains, I could not possibly imagine: but a providential reason was easy to be discovered. God might call them together to hear the gospel, which perhaps otherwise they might never have thought of.

At five in the morning I preached again, on, 'I will heal their backsliding, I will love them dearly.' And between nine and ten, having talked with many in private, and distributed both to them and others between two and three hundred hymns and little books, we left this barren, dreary place, and set sail for St Ives, though the wind was strong, and blew directly in our teeth. Our pilot said we should have good luck if we reached the land; but he knew not him whom the winds and seas obey. Soon after three we were even with the Land's End, and about nine we reached St Ives.

Remarkable service at Gwennap

Tuesday 20. At Trezuthan Downs I preached to two or three thousand people, on the 'highway' of the Lord, the way of holiness. We reached Gwennap a little before six, and found the plain covered from end to end. It was supposed there were ten thousand people; to whom I preached Christ our 'wisdom from God—that is, our

righteousness, holiness and redemption'. I could not conclude till it was so dark we could scarcely see one another.
And there was on all sides the deepest attention; none
speaking, stirring, or scarce looking aside. Surely here,
though in a temple not made with hands, was God wor-
shipped in 'the beauty of holiness'.

A mob at Wednesbury

Thursday October 20. After preaching to a small, attentive
congregation (at Birmingham), I rode to Wednesbury. I
was writing at Francis Ward's, in the afternoon, when the
cry arose that the mob had beset the house. We prayed
that God would disperse them; and it was so: one went this
way, and another that; so that, in half an hour, not a man
was left. I told our brethren, 'Now is the time for us to go,'
but they pressed me exceedingly to stay. So, that I might
not offend them, I sat down, though I foresaw what would
follow. Before five the mob surrounded the house again,
in greater numbers than ever. The cry of one and all was,
'Bring out the minister; we will have the minister.'

I desired one to take their captain by the hand, and
bring him into the house. After a few sentences exchanged
between us, the lion became a lamb. I desired him to go
and bring one or two more of the most angry of his companions. He brought in two, who were ready to swallow
the ground with rage; but in two minutes they were as
calm as he. I then bade them make way, that I might go out
among the people.

As soon as I was in the midst of them I called for a chair,
and standing up asked, 'What do any of you want with
me?' Some said, 'We want you to go with us to the justice.'
I replied, 'That I will, with all my heart.' I then spoke a few
words, which God applied; so that they cried out, with
might and main, 'The gentleman is an honest gentleman,
and we will spill our blood in his defence.' I asked, 'Shall
we go to the justice tonight, or in the morning?' Most of

them cried, 'Tonight, tonight'; so I went before, and two or three hundred followed; the rest returning where they came from.

The night came on before we had walked a mile, together with heavy rain. However, on we went to Bentley Hall, two miles from Wednesbury. One or two ran before, to tell Mr Lane they had brought Mr Wesley before his worship. Mr Lane replied, 'What have I to do with Mr Wesley? Go and take him back again.' By this time the main body came up, and began knocking at the door. A servant told them Mr Lane was in bed. His son followed, and asked what was the matter. One replied, 'Why, an't please you, they sing psalms all day; nay, and make folks rise at five in the morning. And what would your worship advise us to do?' 'To go home,' said Mr Lane, 'and be quiet.'

Wesley in danger

Here they were all at a full stop, till one advised to go to Justice Persehouse, at Walsall. All agreed to this; so we hastened on, and about seven came to his house. But Mr P. likewise sent word that he was in bed. Now they were at a stand again; but at last they all thought it the wisest course to make the best of their way home. About fifty of them undertook to convoy me. But we had not gone a hundred yards, when the mob of Walsall came, pouring in like a flood, and bore down all before them. The Darlaston mob made what defence they could, but they were weary, as well as outnumbered, so that in a short time many being knocked down, the rest ran away and left me in their hands.

To attempt speaking was vain; for the noise on every side was like the roaring of the sea. So they dragged me along till we came to the town; where seeing the door of a large house open, I attempted to go in; but a man, catching me by the hair, pulled me back into the middle of the mob. They made no more stop till they had carried me through the main street, from one end of the town to the other. I continued speaking all the time to those within hearing, feeling no pain or weariness. At the west end of the town, seeing a door half open, I made toward it, and would have gone in, but a gentleman in the shop would not let me, saying they would pull the house down to the ground. However, I stood at the door and asked, 'Are you willing to hear me speak?' Many cried out, 'No, no! knock his brains out; down with him; kill him at once.' Others said, 'Nay, but we will hear him first.' I began asking, 'What evil have I done? Which of you all have I wronged in word or deed?' And continued speaking for more than a quarter of an hour, till my voice suddenly failed; then the floods began to lift up their voice again, many crying out 'Bring him away! Bring him away!'

In the meantime my strength and my voice returned, and I broke out aloud in prayer. And now the man who just before headed the mob, turned and said, 'Sir, I will spend my life for you: follow me, and not one soul here shall touch a hair of your head.' Two or three of his fellows confirmed his words, and got close to me immediately. At the same time, the gentleman in the shop cried out, 'For shame, for shame! Let him go.'

An honest butcher, who was a little farther off, said it was a shame they should do thus; and pulled back four or five, one after another, who were running on the most fiercely. The people then, as if it had been by common consent, fell back to the right and left; while those three or four men took me between them, and carried me through them all. But on the bridge the mob rallied again: we therefore went on one side, over the mill-dam, and thence through the meadows; till, a little before ten, God brought me safe to Wednesbury; having lost only one flap of my waistcoat, and a little skin from one of my hands.

I never saw such a chain of providence before; so many

convincing proofs that the hand of God is on every person
and thing, and overruling all as seems to him good.

His presence of mind

The poor woman of Darlaston, who had headed that mob
and sworn that no one should touch me, when she saw
her followers give way, ran into the thickets of the
throng, and knocked down three or four men, one after
another. But many assaulting her at once, she was soon
overpowered, and would probably have been killed in a
few minutes (three men keeping her down and beating
her with all their might), had not a man called to one of
them, 'Hold, Tom, hold!' 'Who is there?' said Tom: 'what,
honest Munchin? Nay, then, let her go.' So they held
their hand, and let her get up and crawl home as well as
she could.

From the beginning to the end I found the same presence of mind as if I had been sitting in my own study. But
I took no thought for one moment before another; only
once it came into my mind that if they should throw me
into the river it would spoil the papers that were in my pocket. For myself, I did not doubt but I should swim across,
having but a thin coat, and a light pair of boots.

The circumstances that follow, I thought, were particularly remarkable: 1. That many endeavoured to throw me
down while we were going down-hill on a slippery path to
the town; as well judging, that if I was once on the ground,
I should hardly rise any more. But I made no stumble at
all, nor the least slip till I was entirely out of their hands.
2. That although many strove to lay hold on my collar or
clothes, to pull me down, they could not fasten at all: only
one got fast hold of the flap of my waistcoat, which was
soon left in his hand; the other flap, in the pocket of which
was a banknote, was only half torn off. 3. That a lusty man
just behind struck at me several times with a large oak
stick, with which if he had struck me once on the back part

of my head, it would have saved him all farther trouble. But every time the blow was turned aside, I know not how; for I could not move to the right hand or left. 4. That another came rushing through the press, and raising his arm to strike, on a sudden let it drop, and only stroked my head, saying, 'What soft hair he has!' 5. That I stopped exactly at the mayor's door, as if I had known it (which the mob doubtless thought I did), and found him standing in the shop, which gave the first check to the madness of the people. 6. That the very first men whose hearts were turned were the heroes of the town, the captains of the rabble on all occasions, one of them having been a prize-fighter at the bear-garden. 7. That from first to last, I heard none give a reviling word, or call me by any opprobrious name whatever; but the cry of one and all was: 'The Preacher! The Minister!' 8. That no creature, at least within my hearing, laid anything to my charge, either true or false; having in the hurry quite forgotten to provide themselves with an accusation of any kind. And, lastly, that they were as utterly at a loss what they should do with me; none proposing any determinate thing, only, 'Away with him! Kill him at once!'

By how gentle degrees does God prepare us for his will! Two years ago a piece of brick grazed my shoulders. It was a year after that the stone struck me between the eyes. Last month I received one blow, and this evening two; one before we came into the town, and one after we were gone out; but both were as nothing: for though one man struck me on the breast with all his might, and the other on the mouth with such a force that the blood gushed out immediately, I felt no more pain from either of the blows than if they had touched me with a straw.

When the rest of the Society made all haste to escape for their lives, four only would not stir, William Sitch, Edward Slater, John Griffiths, and Joan Parks: these kept with me, resolving to live or die together; and none of them received one blow, except for William Sitch, who held me by the arm, from one end of the town to the other. He was then dragged away and knocked down; but he soon rose and got to me again. I afterwards asked him what he expected when the mob came upon us. He said, 'To die for him who had died for us': and he felt no commotion or fear; but calmly waited till God should require his soul of him.

I asked J. Parks if she was not afraid when they tore her from me. She said, 'No; no more than I am now. I could trust God for you, as well as for myself. From the beginning I had a full persuasion that God would deliver you. I knew not how; but I left that to him, and was as sure as if it were already done.' I asked, if the report was true that she had fought for me. She said, 'No; I knew God would fight for his children.'

Methodism on the stage

Wednesday November 2 (Newcastle). The following advertisement was published:

FOR THE BENEFIT OF MR ESTE

By the Edinburgh Company of Comedians, on Friday November 4, will be acted a

Comedy, called

THE CONSCIOUS LOVERS;

To which will be added a Farce, called,

TRICK UPON TRICK, or METHODISM DISPLAYED

On Friday, a vast multitude of spectators were assembled in the Moot Hall to see this. It was believed there could not be less than fifteen hundred people, some hundreds of whom sat on rows of seats built upon the stage. Soon after the comedians had begun the first act of the play, on a sudden all those seats fell down at once, their supports breaking like a rotten stick. The people were thrown one upon another, about five foot forward, but not one of them hurt. After a short time the rest of the spectators were quiet, and the actors went on. In the middle of the second act, all the shilling seats gave a crack, and sank several inches down. A great noise and shrieking followed;

and as many as could readily get to the door, went out, and returned no more. Notwithstanding this, when the noise was over, the actors went on with the play.

In the beginning of the third act the entire stage suddenly sank about six inches: the players retired with great precipitation; yet in a while they began again. At the latter end of the third act, all the sixpenny seats, without any kind of notice, fell to the ground. There was now a cry on every side; it being supposed that many were crushed in pieces; but, upon inquiry, not a single person (such was the mercy of God!) was either killed or dangerously hurt. Two or three hundred remaining still in the hall, Mr Este (who was to act the Methodist) came upon the stage and told them, for all this he was resolved the farce should be acted. While he was speaking, the stage sank six inches more; on which he ran back in the utmost confusion, and the people as fast as they could out of the door, none staying to look behind him.

Which is most surprising—that those players acted this farce the next week—or that some hundreds of people came again to see it?

The first Conference

1744. Monday June 18. I left Epworth; and on *Wednesday 20*, in the afternoon, met my brother in London.

Monday 25 and the five following days we spent in conference with many of our brethren (come from several parts), who desire nothing but to save their own souls, and those who hear them. And surely, as long as they continue thus minded, their labour will not be in vain in the Lord.

The next day we endeavoured to purge the Society of all that did not walk according to the gospel. By this means we reduced the number of members to less than nineteen hundred. But number is an inconsiderable circumstance. May God increase them in faith and love!

Friday August 24 (St Bartholomew's Day). I preached, I

suppose the last time, at St Mary's [Oxford]. Be it so. I am now clear of the blood of these men. I have fully delivered my own soul.

The Beadle came to me afterwards, and told me the Vice-Chancellor had sent him for my notes. I sent them without delay, not without admiring the wise providence of God. Perhaps few men of note would have given a sermon of mine the reading, if I had put it into their hands; but by this means it came to be read, probably more than once, by every man of eminence in the university.

Wesley's Chancery bill

Thursday December 27. I called on the solicitor whom I had employed in the suit recently commenced in Chancery; and here I first saw that foul monster, a Chancery bill! A scroll it was of forty-two pages, in large folio, to tell a story which needed not to have taken up forty lines!—and stuffed with such stupid senseless, improbable lies (many of them, too, quite foreign to the question) as, I believe, would have cost the compiler his life in any heathen court of either Greece or Rome. And this is equity in a Christian country! This is the English method of redressing other grievances!

1745. Monday February 18. I set out with Richard Moss from London for Newcastle.

Sunday March 3. As I was walking up Pilgrim Street, hearing a man call after me, I stood still. He came up, and used much abusive language, intermixed with many oaths and curses. Several people came out to see what was the matter; on which he pushed me two or three times, and went away.

Wesley's effective letter

Upon enquiry, I found this man had drawn attention to himself for a long while by abusing and throwing stones at any of our family who went that way. Therefore I would not lose the opportunity, but on *Monday 4* sent him the following note:

> Robert Young,—I expect to see you, between now and Friday, and to hear from you, that you are aware of your fault; otherwise, in pity to your soul, I shall be obliged to inform the magistrates of your assaulting me yesterday in the street.

Within two or three hours, Robert Young came and promised a quite different behaviour. So did this gentle reproof, if not save a soul from death, yet prevent a multitude of sins.

Press-gang and Methodists

Wednesday June 19 (Redruth). Being informed here of what had befallen Mr Maxfield, we turned aside toward Crowan church-town. But on the way we received information that he had been removed from there the night before. It seems the valiant constables who guarded him, having received timely notice that a body of five hundred Methodists were coming to take him away by force, had with great precipitation carried him two miles further, to the house of one Henry Tomkins.

Here we found him, nothing terrified by his adversaries. I desired Henry Tomkins to show me the warrant. It was directed by Dr Borlase, and his father, and Mr Eustick, to the constables and overseers of several parishes, requiring them to 'apprehend all such able-bodied men as had no lawful calling or sufficient maintenance'; and to bring them before the aforesaid gentlemen at Marazion, on *Friday 21* to be examined, whether they were proper persons to serve his Majesty in the land-service.

It was endorsed by the steward of Sir John St Aubyn with the names of seven or eight persons, most of whom were well known to have lawful callings, and a sufficient maintenance thereby. But that was all one: they were called 'Methodists'; therefore, soldiers they must be. Underneath was added, 'A person, his name unknown, who disturbs the peace of the parish.'

A word to the wise. The good men easily understood this could be none other but the Methodist Preacher; for who 'disturbs the peace of the parish' like one who tells all drunkards, whoremongers, and common swearers, 'You are on the high road to hell'?

When we came out of the house, forty or fifty myrmidons stood ready to receive us. But I turned full upon them, and their courage failed: nor did they recover till we were at some distance. Then they began blustering again, and throwing stones; one of which struck Mr Thompson's servant.

Friday 21. The justices and commissioners ordered Mr Maxfield to be immediately put on board a boat, and taken to Penzance. We were informed, they had first offered him to a captain of a man-of-war, that had just come into the harbour. But he answered, 'I have no authority to take such men as these, unless you would have me give him so much a week, to preach and pray to my people.'

Dramatic scenes at Falmouth

Thursday July 4. I rode to Falmouth. About three in the afternoon I went to see a gentlewoman who had been long indisposed. Almost as soon as I sat down, the house was beset on all sides by an innumerable multitude of people. A louder or more confused noise could hardly be at the taking of a city by storm. At first Mrs B. and her daughter endeavoured to quiet them. But it was labour lost. They might as well have attempted to still the raging of the sea. They were soon glad to shift for themselves, and leave K.E. and me to do as well as we could. The rabble roared with all their throats, 'Bring out the Canorum! Where is the Canorum?' (an unmeaning word which the Cornish generally use instead of Methodist).

No answer being given, they quickly forced open the outer door, and filled the passage. Only a wainscot-partition was between us, which was not likely to stand long. I immediately took down a large looking-glass which hung against it, supposing the whole side would fall in at once. When they began their work with abundance of bitter imprecations, poor Kitty was utterly astonished, and cried out, 'O sir, what must we do?' I said, 'We must pray.' Indeed at that time, to all appearance, our lives were not worth an hour's purchase. She asked, 'But, sir, is it not better for you to hide yourself—to get into the closet?' I answered, 'No. It is best for me to stand just where I am.' Among those outside were the crews of some privateers, which had recently come into the harbour. Some of these, being angry at the slowness of the rest, thrust them away, and coming up all together set their shoulders to the inner door and cried out, 'Avast, lads, avast!' Away went all the hinges at once, and the door fell back into the room.

I stepped forward at once into the midst of them, and said, 'Here I am. Which of you has anything to say to me? To which of you have I done any wrong? To you? Or you? Or you?' I continued speaking till I came, bareheaded as I was (for I purposely left my hat that they might all see my face), into the middle of the street, and then raising my voice said, 'Neighbours, countrymen! Do you desire to hear me speak?' They cried vehemently, 'Yes, yes. He shall speak. He shall. Nobody shall hinder him.' But having nothing to stand on, and no advantage of ground, I could be heard by few only. However, I spoke without intermission, and, as far as the sound reached, the people were still; till one or two of their captains turned about and swore not a man should touch him.

Mr Thomas, a clergyman, then came up, and asked, 'Are you not ashamed to treat a stranger thus?' He was soon seconded by two or three gentlemen of the town, and one of the aldermen; with whom I walked down the town, speaking all the time, till I came to Mrs Maddern's house. The gentlemen proposed sending for my horse to the door, and desired me to step in and rest in the meantime. But, on second thoughts, they judged it not advisable to let me go out among the people again: so they chose to send me there by water; the sea running close by the back door of the house in which we now were.

I never saw before, no, not at Walsall itself, the hand of God so plainly shown as here. There I had many companions who were willing to die with me: here, not a friend, but one simple girl, who likewise was hurried away from me in an instant, as soon as ever she came out of Mrs B.'s door. There I received some blows, lost part of my clothes, and was covered over with dirt: here, although the hands of perhaps some hundreds of people were lifted up to strike or throw, yet they were one and all stopped in the act; so that not a man touched me with one of his fingers; neither was anything thrown from first to last; so that I had not even a speck of dirt on my clothes. Who can deny that God hears the prayer, or that he has all power in heaven and earth?

I took boat at about half an hour past five. Many of the mob waited at the end of the town, who, seeing me escaped out of their hands, could only revenge themselves with their tongues. But a few of the fiercest ran along the shore, to receive me at my landing. I walked up the steep narrow passage from the sea, at the top of which the foremost man stood. I looked him in the face, and said, 'I wish you a good night.' He spoke not, nor moved hand or foot till I was on horseback. Then he said, 'I wish you was in hell,' and turned back to his companions.

Riot Act and a sermon

Wednesday 10. In the evening I began to expound (at Trevonan, in Morva), 'Come, all you who are thirsty, come to the waters.' In less than a quarter of an hour, the constable and his companions came, and read the proclamation against riots. When he had done, I told him, 'We will do as you require: we will disperse within an hour'; and went on with my sermon. After preaching, I had designed to meet the Society alone. But many others also followed with such earnestness that I could not turn them back: so I exhorted them all to love their enemies, as Christ has loved us. They felt what was spoken.

Thursday 25. I came back safe, blessed be God, to Bristol. I found both my soul and body much refreshed in this peaceful place.

Thursday August 1 and the following days we had our second Conference, with as many of our brethren that labour in the word as could be present.

Pelted by the mob at Leeds

Monday, September 9. I left London, and the next morning called on Dr Doddridge, at Northampton. It was about the hour when he was accustomed to expound a portion of scripture to young gentlemen under his care. He desired me to take his place. It may be the seed was not altogether sown in vain.

Thursday 12. I came to Leeds, preached at five, and at eight met the Society; after which the mob pelted us with dirt and stones great part of the way home.

Great excitement at Newcastle

Wednesday 18. About five we came to Newcastle, at an appropriate time. We found the generality of the inhabitants in the utmost consternation; news being just arrived that, the morning before, at two o'clock, the Pretender had entered Edinburgh. A great concourse of people were with us in the evening, to whom I expounded the third chapter of Jonah; insisting particularly on that verse, 'Who knows? God may yet relent and with compassion turn from his fierce anger so that we will not perish.'

Thursday 19. The mayor (Mr Ridley) summoned all the

householders of the town to meet him at the town-hall; and desired as many of them as were willing, to set their hands to a paper importing that they would, at the risk of their goods and lives, defend the town against the common enemy. Fear and darkness were now on every side; but not on those who had seen the light of God's countenance. We rejoiced together in the evening with solemn joy, while God applied those words to many hearts, 'Don't be alarmed. You are looking for Jesus the Nazarene, who was crucified.'

Friday 20. The mayor ordered the townsmen to be under arms, and to mount guard in their turns, over and above the guard of soldiers, a few companies of whom had been drawn into the town on the first alarm. Now, also, Pilgrim Street gate was ordered to be walled up. Many began to be much concerned for us, because our house stood outside the walls. Nay, but the Lord is a wall of fire to all who trust in him.

Preaching under difficulties

Sunday 22. The walls were mounted with cannon, and all things prepared for sustaining an assault. Meantime our poor neighbours, on either hand, were busy in removing their goods. And most of the best houses in our street were left without either furniture or inhabitants. Those within the walls were almost equally busy in carrying away their money and goods; and more and more of the gentry every hour rode southward as fast as they could. At eight I preached at Gateshead, in a broad part of the street, near the popish chapel, on the wisdom of God in governing the world. How do all things tend to the furtherance of the gospel!

All this week the alarms from the north continued, and the storm seemed nearer every day. Many wondered we would still stay without the walls: others told us we must remove quickly, for if the cannon began to play from the top of the gates, they would beat all the house about our ears. This made me look how the cannon on the gates were planted; and I could not but adore the providence of God, for it was obvious, 1. They were all planted in such a manner, that no shot could touch our house. 2. The cannon on New gate so secured us on one side, and those upon Pilgrim Street gate on the other, that no one could come near our house either way without being torn to pieces.

Sunday 29. Advice came that the rebels were in full march southward, so that it was supposed they would reach Newcastle by Monday evening. At eight I called on the multitude of sinners in Gateshead to seek the Lord while he might be found. Mr Ellison preached another earnest sermon, and all the people seemed to bend before the Lord. In the afternoon I expounded part of the lesson for the day—Jacob wrestling with the angel. The congregation was so moved that I began again and again, and knew not how to conclude. And we cried mightily to God to send His Majesty King George help from his holy place, and to spare a sinful land yet a little longer.

Monday November 4. I left Newcastle. Before nine we met several expresses, sent to countermand the march of the army into Scotland; and to inform them, that the rebels had passed the Tweed, and were marching southward.

1746. Sunday July 6 (London). After talking at length with both the men and women leaders, we agreed it would prevent great expense, as well of health as of time and of money, if the poorer people of our Society could be persuaded to leave off drinking tea. We resolved ourselves to begin and set the example. I expected some difficulty in breaking off a custom of twenty-six years' standing. And, accordingly, the three first days, my head ached, more or less, all day long, and I was half asleep from morning till night. The third day, on Wednesday, in the afternoon, my memory failed, almost entirely. In the evening I sought my remedy in prayer. On Thursday morning my head-ache was gone. My memory was as strong as ever, and I have found no inconvenience, but a tangible benefit in several respects, from that very day to this.

Thursday 17. I finished the little collection which I had made among my friends for a lending-stock: it did not amount to thirty pounds; which a few persons afterwards made up to fifty. And by this inconsiderable sum, more than two hundred and fifty persons were relieved in one year.

Wesley encounters severe weather

1747. Tuesday February 10 (London). My brother returned from the north, and I prepared to supply his place there.

Sunday 15. I was very weak and faint; but on *Monday 16* I rose soon after three, lively and strong, and found all my complaints were fled away like a dream.

I was wondering, the day before, at the mildness of the weather, such as seldom attends me in my journeys. But my wonder now ceased: the wind was turned full north, and blew so exceedingly hard and keen that, when we came to Hatfield, neither my companion nor I had much use of our hands or feet. After resting an hour, we bore up again through the wind and snow, which drove full in our faces. But this was only a squall. In Baldock field the storm began in earnest. The large hail drove so vehemently in our faces that we could not see, nor hardly breathe. However, before two o'clock we reached Baldock, where someone met us and conducted us safe to Potten.

About six I preached to a serious congregation.

Tuesday 17. We set out as soon as it was well light; but it was really hard work to get forward, for the frost would not well bear or break; and the untracked snow covering all the roads, we had much ado to keep our horses on their feet. Meantime the wind rose higher and higher, till it was ready to overturn both man and beast. However, after a short lunch at Bugden, we pushed on and were met in the middle of an open field with so violent a storm of rain and hail, as we had not had before. It drove through our coats, great and small, boots, and everything, and yet froze as it fell, even upon our eye-brows; so that we had scarcely either strength or motion left, when we came into our inn at Stilton.

We now gave up our hopes of reaching Grantham, the snow falling faster and faster. However, we took the advantage of a fair blast to set out, and made the best of our way to Stamford Heath. But here a new difficulty arose, from the snow lying in large drifts. Sometimes horse and man were well nigh swallowed up. Yet in less than an hour we were brought safe to Stamford. Wishing to get as far as we could, we made only a short stop here, and about sunset came, cold and weary yet well, to a little town called Brig Casterton.

Wednesday 18. Our servant came up and said, 'Sir, there is no travelling today. Such a quantity of snow has fallen in the night that the roads are quite filled up.' I told him, 'At least we can walk twenty miles a day, with our horses in our hands.' So in the name of God we set out. The north-east wind was piercing as a sword, and had driven the snow into such uneven heaps that the main road was unpassable. However, we kept on, afoot or on horseback, till we came to the White Lion at Grantham.

Preaching to the lead miners

Tuesday March 24. I rode to Blanchland, about twenty miles from Newcastle. The rough mountains round about were still white with snow. In the midst of them is a small winding valley, through which the Derwent runs. On the edge of this the little town stands, which is indeed little more than a heap of ruins. There seems to have been a large cathedral church, by the vast walls which still remain. I stood in the churchyard, under one side of the building, upon a large tombstone, round which, while I was at prayers all the congregation kneeled down on the grass.

They were gathered out of the lead-mines from all parts; many from Allandale, six miles off. A row of little children sat under the opposite wall, all quiet and still. The whole congregation drank in every word with such earnestness in their looks, I could not but hope God will make this wilderness sing for joy.

Wednesday June 24. We rode (from Bristol) to Beercrocomb, hoping to reach Tavistock the next day. So we set out at three. The rain began at four. We reached Colestock, dripping wet, before seven. The rain ceased while we were in the house, but began when we took horse, and attended us all the way to Exeter. While we stayed here to dry our clothes, I took the opportunity of writing *A Word to a Freeholder.* Soon after three we set out: but it was near eight before we could reach Oakhampton.

Friday 26. We came to Tavistock before noon; but it being market-day, I did not preach till five in the evening. The rain began almost as soon as we began singing, and drove many out of the field. After preaching (leaving Mr Swindells there) I went on to Plymouth dock.

How Wesley dealt with a mob

Within two miles of Plymouth, someone overtook us and informed us that, the night before, all the dock was in an uproar; and a constable, endeavouring to keep the peace, was beaten and much hurt. As we were entering the dock, someone met us and desired we would go the back way, 'for', said he, 'there are thousands of people waiting about Mr Hide's door.' We rode up straight into the midst of them. They greeted us with three shouts, after which I alighted, took several of them by the hand, and began to talk with them. I would gladly have passed an hour among them; and believe, if I had, there would have been an end of the riot. But the day being far spent (for it was past nine o'clock), I was persuaded to go in. The mob then recovered their spirits, and fought valiantly with the doors and windows: but about ten they were weary, and went every man to his own home.

Saturday 27. I preached at four, and then spoke separately to part of the Society. As yet I have found only one person among them who knew the love of God, before my brother came. No wonder the devil was so still; for his goods were in peace.

About six in the evening, I went to the place where I preached last year. A little before we had ended the hymn, the Lieutenant came—a famous man, with his retinue of soldiers, drummers, and mob. When the drums ceased, a gentleman barber began to speak: but his voice was quickly drowned in the shouts of the multitude, who grew fiercer and fiercer, as their numbers increased. After waiting about a quarter of an hour, perceiving the violence of the rabble still increasing, I walked down into the thickest part of them, and took the captain of the mob by the hand. He immediately said, 'Sir, I will see you safe home. Sir, no man shall touch you. Gentlemen, stand off: give back. I will knock the first man down that touches him.' We walked on in great peace; my conductor every now and then stretching out his neck (he was a very tall man) and looking round, to see if any behaved rudely, till we came to Mr Hide's door. We then parted in much love. I stayed in the street about half an hour after he was gone, talking with the people, who had now forgotten their anger, and went away in high good humour.

Wednesday July 1. I spoke separately to all those who had votes in the ensuing election. I found them such as I desired. Not one would even eat or drink at the expense of him for whom he voted. Five guineas had been given to W.C., but he returned them immediately. T.M. positively refused to accept anything. And when he heard that his mother had received money privately, he could not rest till she gave him the three guineas, which he instantly sent back.

Thursday 2 was the day of election for Parliament-men. It was begun and ended without any commotion at all. I had a large congregation in the evening, among whom two or three roared for the disquietness of their heart: as did many at the meeting which followed; particularly those who had lost their first love.

Sunday September 27 (London). I preached in Moorfields, morning and evening, and continued to do so till November. I know no church in London (that in West Street excepted) where there is so serious a congregation.

Monday 28. I talked with someone who, a little time before, was so overwhelmed with affliction that she went out one night to put an end to it all by throwing herself into the New River. As she went by the Foundery (it being a watch-night), she heard some people singing. She stopped, and went in; she listened awhile, and God spoke to her heart. She had no more desire to put an end to her life; but to die to sin, and live to God.

The bargemen and their clubs

Monday November 2. I preached at Windsor at noon, and in the afternoon rode to Reading. Mr J.R. had just sent his brother word that he had hired a mob to pull down his preaching-house that night. In the evening Mr S. Richards overtook a large group of boatmen walking towards it, whom he immediately accosted, and asked if they would go with him and hear a good sermon; telling them, 'I will make room for you, if you were as many more.' They said, they would go with all their hearts. 'But neighbours,' said he, 'would it not be as well to leave those clubs behind you? Perhaps some of the women may be frightened at them.' They threw them all away, and walked quietly with him to the house, where he set them in a pew.

In the conclusion of my sermon, one of them who used to be their captain, being the head taller than his fellows, rose up, and looking round the congregation, said, 'The gentleman says nothing but what is good; I say so; and there is not a man here that shall dare to say otherwise.'

Remarkable accident to Wesley

1748. Thursday January 28. I set out for Deverel Longbridge. About ten o'clock we were met by a loaded waggon, in a deep, hollow way. There was a narrow path between the road and the bank: I stepped into this, and John Trembath followed me. When the waggon came near, my horse began to rear, and to attempt climbing up the bank. This frighted the horse which was close behind, and made him prance and throw his head to and fro, till the bit of the bridle caught the cape of my great coat, and pulled me backward off my horse. I fell as exact on the path, between the waggon and the bank, as if one had taken me in his arms and laid me down there. Both our horses stood stock still, one just behind me, the other before; so, by the blessing of God, I rose unhurt, mounted again, and rode on.

Friday February 12. After preaching at Oakhill about noon, I rode to Shepton, and found them all under a strange consternation. A mob, they said, was hired, prepared, and made sufficiently drunk, in order to do all manner of mischief. I began preaching between four and five: none hindered or interrupted at all. We had a blessed opportunity, and the hearts of many were exceedingly comforted. I wondered what was become of the mob. But we were quickly informed: they mistook the place, imagining I should alight (as I used to do) at William Stone's house, and had summoned, by drum, all their forces together, to meet me at my coming: but Mr Swindells innocently carrying me to the other end of the town, they did not find their mistake till I had done preaching: so that the hindering this, which was one of their designs, was utterly disappointed.

A shower of stones

However, they attended us from the preaching-house to William Stone's, throwing dirt, stones, and clods, in abundance: but they could not hurt us; only Mr Swindells had a little dirt on his coat, and I a few specks on my hat.

After we had gone into the house, they began throwing great stones, in order to break the door. But perceiving this would require some time, they dropped that design for the present. They first broke all the tiles on the pent-house over the door, and then poured in a shower of stones at the windows. One of their captains, in his great zeal, had followed us into the house, and was now shut in with us. He did not like this, and wanted to get out; but it was not possible; so he kept as close to me as he could, thinking himself safe when he was near me: but, staying a little behind—when I went up two flights of stairs, and stood close on one side, where we were a little sheltered—a large stone struck him on the forehead, and the blood spouted out like a stream. He cried out, 'O sir, are we to die tonight? What must I do? What must I do?' I said, 'Pray to God. He is able to deliver you from all danger.' He took my advice, and began praying in such a manner as he had scarcely done ever since he was born.

Mr Swindells and I then went to prayer; after which I told him, 'We must not stay here; we must go down immediately.' He said, 'Sir, we cannot stir; you see how the stones fly about.' I walked straight through the room, and down the stairs; and not a stone came in, till we were at the bottom. The mob had just broken open the door when we came into the lower room; and exactly while they burst in at one door, we walked out at the other. Nor did one man take any notice of us, though we were within five yards of each other.

A horrible proposition

They filled the house at once, and proposed setting it on fire. But one of them, happening to remember that his own house was next, with much ado persuaded them not to do it. Hearing one of them cry out, 'They are gone over the grounds,' I thought the advice was good; so we went over the grounds, to the farther end of the town, where Abraham Jenkins waited, and undertook to guide us to Oakhill.

Incidents in Ireland

Saturday April 9. I preached in Connaught, a few miles from Athlone. Many heard; but, I doubt, felt nothing.

Sunday 10 (Easter Day). Never was such a congregation seen before at the sacrament in Athlone. I preached at three. Abundance of papists flocked to hear; so that the priest, seeing his command did not avail, came in person at six, and drove them away before him like a flock of sheep.

Saturday 23. I read, some hours, an extremely dull book, Sir James Ware's *Antiquities of Ireland*. By the vast number of ruins which are seen in all parts, I had always suspected what he shows at large, namely that in ancient times it was more populous, tenfold, than it is now; many that were large cities, being now ruinous heaps; many shrunk into inconsiderable villages.

I visited someone in the afternoon who was ill of a fever, and lay in a very close room. While I was near him, I found myself not well. After my return home, I felt my stomach out of order. But I imagined it was not worth any notice, and would pass off before the morning.

Wesley lives on apple tea

Sunday 24. I preached at Skinner's Alley at five; and on Oxmantown Green at eight. I was weak in body, but was greatly revived by the seriousness and earnestness of the congregation.

Monday 25. Finding my fever greatly increased, I judged it would be best to keep my bed, and to live awhile on apples and apple tea. On *Tuesday* I was quite well, and would have preached, but that Dr Rutty (who had been with me twice) insisted on my resting for a time.

I read today what is accounted the most correct history of St Patrick that is extant; and, on the maturest consideration, I was much inclined to believe, that St Patrick and St George were of one family. The whole story smells strong of romance.

Sunday May 15 (Dublin). Finding my strength greatly restored, I preached at five, and at eight on Oxmantown Green. I expected to sail as soon as I had done; but the captain putting it off (as their manner is), gave me an opportunity of declaring the gospel of peace to a still larger congregation in the evening. One of them, after listening some time, cried out, shaking his head, 'Ay, he is a Jesuit; that's plain.' To which a popish priest, who happened to be near, replied aloud, 'No, he is not; I would to God he was.'

Wednesday 18. We took ship. The wind was small in the afternoon, but exceedingly high towards night. About eight I lay down on the quarter-deck. I was soon wet from head to foot, but I took no cold at all. About four in the morning we landed at Holyhead, and in the evening reached Carnarvon.

Friday August 12. In riding to Newcastle, I finished the tenth Iliad of Homer. What an amazing genius had this man! To write with such strength of thought, and beauty of expression, when he had none to go before him! And what a vein of piety runs through his whole work, in spite of his pagan prejudices! Yet one cannot but observe such improprieties intermixed, as are shocking to the last degree.

Sunday 28. I wonder at those who still talk so loud of the indecency of field-preaching. The highest indecency is in St Paul's church, when a considerable part of the congregation are asleep, or talking, or looking about, not minding a word the preacher says. On the other hand, there is the highest decency in a churchyard or field, when the whole congregation behave and look as if they saw the judge of all, and heard him speaking from heaven.

At one I went to the cross in Bolton. There was a vast number of people, but many of them utterly wild. As soon as I began speaking, they began thrusting to and fro; endeavouring to throw me down from the steps on which I stood. They did so once or twice; but I went up again, and continued my discourse.

Three remarkable shots with stones

They then began to throw stones; at the same time some got upon the cross behind me to push me down; at which I could not but observe how God overrules even the minutest circumstances. One man was bawling just at my ear when a stone struck him on the cheek, and he was still. A second was forcing his way down to me, till another stone hit him on the forehead: it bounded back, the blood ran down, and he came no farther. The third, being got close to me, stretched out his hand, and in the instant a sharp stone came upon the joints of his fingers. He shook his hand, and was very quiet till I concluded my discourse and went away.

Saturday October 22. I spent an hour in observing the various works of God in the Physic Garden at Chelsea. It would be a noble improvement of the design if some able and industrious person were to make a full and accurate inquiry into the use and virtues of all these plants: without this, what end does the heaping them thus together answer, but the gratifying an idle curiosity?

Wesley in Wales

1749. Monday April 3. In the evening, and the next morning (*Tuesday 4*), I preached at Cardiff. O what a fair prospect was here some years ago! Surely this whole town would have known God, from the least even to the greatest, had it not been for men leaning to their own understanding, instead of 'the law and the testimony'.

Thursday 6. We rode to a hard-named place on the top of a mountain. I scarcely saw any house near: however, a large number of honest, simple people soon came together; but few could understand me: so Henry Lloyd, when I had done, repeated the substance of my sermon in Welsh.

Wednesday 12. We came to Holyhead between one and two. But all the ships were on the Irish side. One came in the next day, but could not go out, the wind being quite contrary. In this journey I read over Statius's *Thebais*. I wonder one man should write so well and so ill. Sometimes he is scarcely inferior to Virgil; sometimes as low as the dullest parts of Ovid.

Saturday 15. We went on board at six, the wind then standing due east. But no sooner were we out of the harbour than it turned south-west, and blew a storm. But in the night we got back into Dublin Bay, and landed soon after three at Dunleary, about seven English miles from the city. Leaving William Tucker to follow me in a chaise, I walked straight away, and came to Skinner's Alley a little before the time of preaching. I preached on: 'Dear friends, since God so loved us, we also ought to love one another.' In the afternoon, and again in the evening (in our own garden), I preached on: 'Let us then approach the throne of grace with confidence, so that we may receive mercy and find grace to help us in our time of need.'

On Thursday and Friday I examined the classes, and was much comforted among them. I found about four hundred in the Society; and, after all the stumbling-blocks laid in the way, I left four hundred and forty-nine.

Monday 24. The cold which I had had for some days growing worse and worse, and the swelling which began in my cheek increasing greatly, and paining me much, I sent for Dr Rutty. But, in the meantime, I applied boiled nettles, which took away the pain in a moment. Afterwards I used warm treacle, which so abated the swelling that before the doctor came I was almost well. However, he advised me not to go out that day. But I had appointed to read the letters in the evening. I returned home as early as I could, and found no inconvenience.

Methodists lease an abbey

Friday May 12. Before nine we came to Nenagh. Some years ago an old abbey here was rebuilt, with a plan to have public service in it. But that plan failing, only the shell of it was finished. Of this (lying useless) the Society has taken a lease. Here I preached in the morning, *Saturday 13,* to six or seven hundred people.

14 (being Whit Sunday). Our church was more than full in the morning, many being obliged to stand outside. I hardly knew how the time went, but continued speaking till near seven o'clock. I went at eleven to the cathedral. I had been informed it was a custom here, for the gentry especially, to laugh and talk all the time of divine service; but I saw nothing of it. The whole congregation, rich and poor, behaved suitably to the occasion.

Wesley and the soldiers' class

Wednesday 17. I met the class of soldiers, eight of whom were Scottish Highlanders. Most of these were brought up well; but evil communications had corrupted good manners. They all said, from the time they entered into the army, they had grown worse and worse. But God had now given them another call.

Wednesday 24. About eight, several of us took boat for Newtown, six miles from Limerick. After dinner we took boat, in order to return. The wind was extremely high. We endeavoured to cross over to the leeward side of the river; but it was not possible. The boat being small, and overloaded, was soon deep in water; the more so because it leaked much, and the waves washed over us frequently; and there was no staying to empty it, all our men being obliged to row with all their strength. After they had toiled about an hour, the boat struck upon a rock, the point of which lay just under the water. It had four or five shocks, the wind driving us on before we could get clear. But our men wrought for life; and about six o'clock God brought us safe to Limerick.

Wednesday July 19. I finished the translation of *Martin Luther's Life.* Doubtless he was a man highly favoured of God, and a blessed instrument in his hand. But oh, what pity that he had no faithful friend! None that would at all costs rebuke him plainly and sharply for his rough, intractable spirit, and bitter zeal for opinions, so greatly obstructive of the work of God!

Thursday 20. About ten at night we embarked [from Dublin] for Bristol, in a small sloop. On Monday morning we landed at the quay in Bristol.

Tuesday 25. I rode over to Kingswood, and inquired particularly into the state of our school there. I was concerned to find that several of the rules had been habitually neglected: I judged it necessary, therefore, to lessen the family; allowing none to remain there who were not clearly satisfied with them, and determined to observe them all.

Wednesday September 6. I reached Newcastle; and after resting a day, and preaching two evenings and two mornings, with such a blessing as we have not often found, on Friday set out to visit the northern Societies. I began with that at Morpeth, where I preached at twelve, on one side of the market-place. It was feared the market would draw many people from the sermon; but it was just the contrary: they quitted their stalls, and there was no buying or selling till the sermon was concluded.

1750. Sunday January 28. I read prayers (in London), and Mr Whitefield preached. How wise is God in giving different talents to different preachers! Even the little improprieties both of his language and manner were a means of profiting many, who would not have been touched by a more correct discourse, or a more calm and regular manner of speaking.

Tuesday March 6 (Bristol). I began writing a short French Grammar. We observed *Wednesday 7*, as a day of fasting and prayer.

Wesley in Wales

Wednesday 21. We rode to Builth, where we found notice had been given that Howell Harris would preach at noon. By this means a large congregation was assembled; but Howell did not come: so, at their request, I preached. Between four and five Mr Philips set out with us for Ryader. I was much out of sorts in the morning: however, I held out to Llanidloes, and then lay down. After an hour's sleep I was much better, and rode on to Machynlleth.

Friday 23. Before we looked out, we heard the roaring of the wind, and the beating of the rain. We took horse at five. It rained incessantly all the way we rode. And when we came on the great mountain, four miles from the town (by which time I was wet from my neck to my waist), it was with great difficulty I could avoid being borne over my mare's head, the wind being ready to carry us all away: nevertheless, about ten we came safe to Dannabul, praising him who saves both man and beast.

Waiting for the Irish boat

Our horses being well tired, and ourselves thoroughly wet, we rested the remainder of the day; the rather, because several of the family understood English—an uncommon thing in these parts. We spoke privately to these; and they appeared much moved, particularly when we all joined in prayer.

Saturday 24. We set out at five, and at six came to the sands. But the tide was in, so that we could not pass: so I sat down in a little cottage for three or four hours, and translated Aldrich's *Logic*. About ten we passed, and before five came to Baldon Ferry, and found the boat ready for us: but the boatmen desired us to stay a while, saying the wind was too high and the tide too strong. The secret was, they stayed for more passengers; and it was well they did: for while we were walking to and fro, Mr Jenkin Morgan came; at whose house, near half-way between the ferry and Holyhead, I had lodged three years before. The night soon came on; but our guide, knowing all the country, brought us safe to his own door.

Sunday 25. I preached at Howell Thomas's, in Trefollwin parish, to a small, earnest congregation.

In the night there was a vehement storm. Blessed be God that we were safe on shore!

Saturday 31. I determined to wait one week longer, and, if we could not sail then, to go and wait for a ship at Bristol. At seven in the evening, just as I was going down to preach, I heard a huge noise, and took knowledge of the rabble of gentlemen. They had now strengthened themselves with drink and numbers, and placed Captain G. (as they called him) at their head. He soon burst open both the outer and the inner door, struck old Robert Griffith, our landlord, several times, kicked his wife, and with twenty full-mouthed oaths and curses, demanded, 'Where is the parson?' Robert Griffith came up, and desired me to go into another room, where he locked me in. The captain followed him quickly, broke open one or two doors, and got on a chair to look on the top of a bed: but his foot slipping (as he was not a man made for climbing), he fell down backward all his length. He rose leisurely, turned about, and with his troop walked away.

I then went down to a small group of the poor people, and spent half an hour with them in prayer. About nine, as we were preparing to go to bed, the house was beset again. The captain burst in first. Robert Griffith's daughter was standing in the passage with a pail of water, with which (whether by design or in her fright, I know not) she covered him from head to foot. He cried as well as he could, 'M—urder! Murder!' and stood very still for some moments. In the meantime Robert Griffith stepped by him and locked the door. Finding himself alone, he began to change his voice, and cry 'Let me out! Let me out!' Upon his giving his word and honour that none of the rest should come in, they opened the door, and all went away together.

Wesley interviews Mrs Pilkington

Thursday April 12 (Dublin). I breakfasted with one of the Society, and found she had a lodger I little thought of. It was the famous Mrs Pilkington, who soon made an excuse for following me up stairs. I talked with her seriously about an hour: we then sang 'Happy Magdalene'. She appeared to be exceedingly struck: how long the impression may last, God knows.

Sunday May 20 (Cork). In the afternoon, a report being spread abroad that the mayor planned to hinder my preaching on the Marsh in the evening, I desired Mr Skelton and Mr Jones to go to see him, and inquire concerning it. Mr Skelton asked if my preaching there would be disagreeable to him, adding, 'Sir, if it would, Mr Wesley will not do it.' He replied warmly, 'Sir, I'll have no mobbing.' Mr Skelton replied, 'Sir, there was none this morning.' He answered, 'There was. Are there not churches and meeting-houses enough? I will have no more mobs or riots.' Mr Skelton replied, 'Sir, neither Mr Wesley nor they that heard him made either mobs or riots.' He answered plain, 'I will have no more preaching; and if Mr Wesley attempts to preach, I am prepared for him.'

I began preaching in our own house soon after five. Mr Mayor meantime was walking in the 'Change, and giving orders to the town-drummers and to his sergeants—doubtless to go down and keep the peace! They accordingly came down to our house, with an innumerable mob attending them. They continued drumming, and I continued preaching, till I had finished my discourse. When I came out, the mob immediately closed me in. Observing one of the sergeants standing by, I desired him to keep the King's peace; but he replied, 'Sir, I have no orders to do that.' As soon as I came into the street, the rabble threw whatever came to hand; but all went by me, or flew over my head; nor do I remember that one thing touched me. I walked on straight through the midst of the rabble, looking every man before me in the face; and they opened on the right and left till I came near Dant's Bridge. God restrained the wild beasts, so that not one attempted to follow me.

But many of the congregation were more roughly handled, particularly Mr Jones, who was covered with dirt, and escaped with his life almost by miracle. The main body of the mob then went to the house, brought out all the seats and benches, tore up the floor, the door, the frames of the windows, and whatever woodwork remained; part of which they carried off for their own use, and the rest they burned in the open street.

Wesley burnt in effigy

Monday 21. I rode on to Bandon. From three in the afternoon till past seven, the mob of Cork marched in grand procession, and then burnt me in effigy near Dant's Bridge.

At an Irish funeral

Thursday 31. I rode to Rathcormuck. There being a great burying in the afternoon, to which people came from all parts, Mr Lloyd read part of the burial service in the church; after which I preached on 'The end of all things is at hand.' I was exceedingly shocked at (what I had only heard of before) the Irish howl which followed. It was not a song, as I supposed, but a dismal, inarticulate yell, set up

at the grave by four shrill-voiced women, who (we understood) were hired for that purpose. But I saw not one that
shed a tear; for that, it seems, was not in their bargain.

Wednesday June 13. I rode to Shronill again; and in the
morning, *Thursday 14,* to Clonmell. We stayed some time,
and then thought it best to go a little on our way toward
Portarlington. But the ferryman would not come over: so
that, after waiting till we were weary, we made our way
through some grounds, and over the mountain, into the
Carrick road; and went on, about five miles, to a village
where we found a quiet house. Sufficient for this day was
the labour thereof. We were on horseback, with but an
hour or two's intermission, from five in the morning till
within a quarter of eleven at night.

Wesley rides ninety miles

Friday 15. We set out at four, and reached Kilkenny, about
twenty-five old Irish miles, about noon. My horse tired in
the afternoon; so I left him behind, and borrowed that of
my companion. I came to Aymo about eleven, and would
very willingly have passed the rest of the night there; but
the good woman of the inn was not minded that I should.
For some time she would not answer: at last she opened
the door just wide enough to let out four dogs upon me. So
I rode on to Ballybrittas, expecting a rough greeting here
too, from a large dog which was in the yard. But he never
stirred, till the ostler waked and came out. About twelve I
lay down. I think this was the longest day's journey I ever
rode; being fifty old Irish, that is, about ninety English
miles.

Thursday 21. I returned to Closeland, and preached in
the evening to a little, earnest group. Oh, who should drag
me into a great city, if I did not know there is another
world! How gladly could I spend the remainder of a busy
life in solitude and retirement!

Thursday September 6. I rode to Salisbury and preached

at Winterburn in the evening; the next, at Reading; and, on *Saturday 8*, came to London.

Here I had the following account from one of our preachers:

> John Jane was never well after walking from Epworth to Hainton on an exceedingly hot day, which threw him into a fever. But he was in great peace and love, even to those who greatly lacked love to him. He was some time at Alice Shadforth's house, with whom he daily talked of the things of God. He was never without the love of God, spent much time in private prayer, and joined likewise with her in prayer several times in a day. On Friday, August 24, growing, as she thought, stronger in body, he sat in the evening by the fire-side: about six he fetched a deep sigh, and never spoke more. He was alive till the same hour on Saturday; at which, without any struggle, or any sign of pain, with a smile on his face, he passed away. His last words were, 'I find the love of God in Christ Jesus.'

He left one shilling and fourpence

> All his clothes, linen and woollen, stockings, hat, and wig, are not thought sufficient to answer his funeral expenses, which amount to one pound seventeen shillings and threepence. All the money he had was one shilling and fourpence.

Enough for any unmarried preacher of the gospel to leave for executors.

Wesley as editor

Monday 24. I left London, and, the next morning, called at what is styled the Half-way House. I reached Kingswood in the evening; and the next day selected passages of Milton for the eldest children to transcribe and repeat weekly.

Thursday 27. I went into the school, and heard half the children their lessons, and then selected passages of the *Moral and Sacred Poems*.

Friday 28. I heard the other half of the children.

Saturday 29. I was with them from four to five in the morning. I spent most of the day in revising Kennet's *Antiquities*, and marking what was worth reading in the school.

Wednesday October 3. I revised, for the use of the children, Archbishop Potter's *Grecian Antiquities*; a dry, dull, heavy book.

Thursday 4. I revised Mr Lewis's *Hebrew Antiquities*; something more entertaining than the other, and abundantly more instructive.

Saturday 6. I nearly finished the abridgement of Dr Cave's *Primitive Christianity*; a book written with as much learning, and as little judgement, as any I remember to have read in my whole life; serving the ancient Christians just as Xenophon did Socrates; relating every weak thing they ever said or did.

Thursday 11. I prepared a short *History of England*, for the use of the children; and on Friday and Saturday a short *Roman History*, as an introduction to the Latin historians.

Monday 15. I read over Mr Holme's *Latin Grammar* and extracted from it what was needful to perfect our own.

Monday December 10. I rode to Leigh, in Essex, where I found a little group seeking God; and endeavoured to encourage them in 'provoking one another to love and good works'.

Monday 17. I set upon cleansing Augeas's stable; on purging that huge work, Mr Fox's *Acts and Monuments*, from all the trash which that honest, injudicious writer has heaped together, and mingled with those venerable records which are worthy to be had in everlasting remembrance.

1751. Wednesday January 30. Having received a pressing letter from Dr Isham, then the rector of our college, to give my vote at the election for a Member of Parliament, which was to be the next day, I set out early, in a severe frost, with the north-west wind full in my face. The roads were so slippery that it was scarcely possible for our horses to keep their feet: indeed one of them could not, but fell on his head and cut it terribly. Nevertheless, about seven in the evening, God brought us safe to Oxford. A congregation was waiting for me at Mr Evans's, whom I immediately addressed in those awesome words, 'What good is it for a man to gain the whole world, yet forfeit his soul?'

Thursday 31. I went to the schools, where the Convocation was met: but I did not find the decency and order which I expected. The gentleman for whom I came to vote was not elected: yet I did not repent of my coming; I owe much more than this to that generous, friendly man, who now rests from his labours.

Wesley decides to marry

Saturday February 2. Having received a full answer from Mr P., I was clearly convinced that I ought to marry. For many years I remained single because I believed I could be more useful in a single than in a married state. And I praise God, who enabled me to do so. I now as fully believed that in my present circumstances I might be more useful in a married state; into which, upon this clear conviction, and by the advice of my friends, I entered a few days after.

Wednesday 6. I met the single men, and showed them on how many accounts it was good for those who had received that gift from God to remain 'single for the kingdom of heaven's sake'; unless where a particular case might be an exception to the general rule.

Sunday 10. After preaching at five, I was hastening to take my leave of the congregation at Snowsfields, purposing to set out in the morning for the north; when, on the middle of London Bridge, both my feet slipped on the ice, and I fell with great force, the bone of my ankle lighting on the top of a stone. However, I got on, with some help, to the chapel, being resolved not to disappoint the people. After preaching, I had my leg bound up by a surgeon, and made a shift to walk to the Seven Dials. It was with much difficulty that I got up into the pulpit; but God then comforted many of our hearts.

I went back in a coach to Mr B.'s, and from there in a chair to the Foundery; but I was not able to preach, my sprain growing worse. I removed to Threadneedle Street; where I spent the remainder of the week, partly in prayer, reading, and conversation, partly in writing a *Hebrew Grammar* and *Lessons for Children*.

Sunday 17. I was carried to the Foundery, and preached, kneeling (as I could not stand), on part of the twenty-third Psalm; my heart being enlarged, and my mouth opened to declare the wonders of God's love.

Monday March 4. Being tolerably able to ride, though not to walk, I set out for Bristol. I came there on Wednesday, thoroughly tired; though, in other respects, better than when I set out.

Tuesday 19. Having finished the business for which I came to Bristol, I set out again for London; being desired by many to spend a few days there before I entered upon my northern journey. I came to London on Thursday, and, having settled all my affairs, left it again on *Wednesday 27*. I cannot understand how a Methodist preacher can answer it to God to preach one sermon or travel one day less in a married than in a single state. In this respect surely, 'from now on those who have wives should live as though they had none'.

Wesley and his barber

Thursday April 11 (Bolton). The barber who shaved me said, 'Sir, I praise God on your behalf. When you was at Bolton last, I was one of the most eminent drunkards in all the town; but I came to listen at the window, and God struck me to the heart. I then earnestly prayed for power against drinking; and God gave me more than I asked: he took away the very desire of it. Yet I felt myself worse and worse, till, on April 5 last, I could hold out no longer. I knew I must drop into hell that moment, unless God appeared to save me: and he did appear. I knew he loved me; and felt sweet peace. Yet I did not dare to say I had faith, till, a year ago yesterday, God gave me faith; and his love has ever since filled my heart.'

Wesley's remarkable vitality

1752. Sunday March 15 (London). While I was preaching at West Street in the afternoon, there was one of the most violent storms I ever remember. In the midst of the sermon a great part of a house opposite to the chapel was blown down. We heard a huge noise, but knew not the cause; so much the more did God speak to our hearts: and great was the rejoicing of many in confidence of his protection. Between four and five I took horse, with my wife and daughter. The tiles were rattling from the houses on both sides; but they hurt not us. We reached Hayes about seven in the evening, and Oxford the next day.

Thursday April 16. I walked over to Burnham. I had no thought of preaching there, doubting if my strength would allow of preaching always three times a day, as I had done most days since I came from Evesham. But finding a house full of people, I could not refrain. Still the more I use my strength, the more I have. I am often much tired the first time I preach in a day; a little the second time; but after the third or fourth, I rarely feel either weakness or weariness.

Friday 24. We rode by a fine seat, the owner of which (not much more than eighty years old) says he desires only to live thirty years longer; ten to hunt, ten to get money (having at present but twenty thousand pounds a year), and ten years to repent. O that God may not say to him, 'You fool! This very night your life will be demanded from you'!

I went to prayers at three in the old church [in Hull]—a grand and venerable structure. Between five and six the coach called, and took me to Mighton Car, about half a mile from the town. A huge multitude, rich and poor, horse and foot, with several coaches, were soon gathered together; to whom I cried with a loud voice and a composed spirit, 'What good is it for a man to gain the whole world, yet forfeit his soul?' Some thousands of people seriously attended; but many behaved as if possessed by Moloch. Clods and stones flew about on every side; but they neither touched nor disturbed me.

A crowded coach

When I had finished my discourse, I went to take coach; but the coachman had driven clear away. We were at a loss, till a gentlewoman invited my wife and me to come into her coach. She brought some inconveniences on herself thereby; not only as there were nine of us in the coach, three on each side and three in the middle; but also as the mob closely attended us, throwing in at the windows (which we did not think it prudent to shut) whatever came next to hand. But a large gentlewoman who sat in my lap, screened me, so that nothing came near me.

Wesley sleeps in a cellar

Monday May 25. We rode to Durham, and thence, through very rough roads, and as rough weather, to Barnard Castle.

Tuesday June 9. My lodging was not such as I should have chosen; but what providence chooses is always good. My bed was considerably under ground, the room serving both for a bedroom and a cellar. The closeness was more troublesome at first than the coolness: but I let in a little fresh air, by breaking a pane of paper (put in by way of glass) in the window; and then slept sound till morning.

Monday 15. I had many little trials in this journey, of a kind I had not known before. I had borrowed a young, strong mare, when I set out from Manchester. But she fell lame before I got to Frimsby. I procured another, but was dismounted again between Newcastle and Berwick. At my return to Manchester, I took my own: but she had lamed herself in the pasture. I thought, nevertheless, to ride her four or five miles today; but she was gone out of the ground, and we could hear nothing of her. However, I comforted myself that I had another at Manchester, which I had recently bought. But when I came there, I found someone had borrowed her too, and ridden her away to Chester.

Saturday September 23. We reached Cork.

Sunday 24. In the evening I proposed to the Society the building of a preaching-house. The next day ten persons subscribed a hundred pounds; another hundred was subscribed in three or four days, and a piece of ground taken. I saw a double providence now in our not sailing last week. If we had, probably this house would never have been built; and it is most likely we should have been cast away. More than thirty ships, we were informed, have been lost on these coasts in the recent storm.

Friday October 13. I read over Pascal's *Thoughts*. What could possibly induce such a creature as Voltaire to give such an author as this a good word; unless it was because he once wrote a satire, and so his being a satirist might atone even for his being a Christian?

Wesley's forgiveness

Saturday 14. About seven we sailed into Kingroad, and happily concluded our little voyage. I now rested a week at Bristol and Kingswood, preaching only morning and evening.

I cannot but stand amazed at the goodness of God.

Others are most assaulted on the weak side of their soul; but with me it is quite otherwise; if I have any strength at all (and I have none but what I have received), it is in forgiving injuries; and on this very side am I assaulted, more frequently than on any other. Yet leave me not here one hour to myself, or I shall betray myself and you, Lord!

In the remaining part of this (October), and in the following month, I prepared the rest of the books for the 'Christian Library'; a work by which I have lost about two hundred pounds. Perhaps the next generation may know the value of it.

1753. Saturday January 20. I advised someone who had been troubled many years with a stubborn paralytic disorder, to try a new remedy. Accordingly, she was electrified, and found immediate help. By the same means I have known two persons cured of an inveterate pain in the stomach; and another of a pain in his side, which he had had ever since he was a child. Nevertheless, who can wonder that many gentlemen of the faculty, as well as their good friends, decry a medicine so shockingly cheap and easy, as much as they do quicksilver and tar-water?

Saturday February 3. I visited someone in the Marshalsea prison, a nursery of all manner of wickedness. O shame to man, that there should be such a place, such a picture of hell, upon earth! And shame to those who bear the name of Christ, that there should need any prison at all in Christendom!

Thursday 8. A proposal was made for devolving all temporal business, books and all, entirely on the Stewards; so that I might have no care upon me (in London at least) but that of the souls committed to my charge. Oh, when shall it once be! From this day?

In the afternoon I visited many of the sick; but such scenes, who could see unmoved?

Friday and Saturday I visited as many more as I could. I found some in their cells under ground; others in their garrets, half starved both with cold and hunger, added to weakness and pain. But I found not one of them unemployed, who was able to crawl about the room. So wickedly, devilishly false is that common objection, 'They are poor, only because they are idle.' If you saw these things with your own eyes, could you lay out money in ornaments or superfluities?

Thursday 15. I visited Mr S., slowly recovering from a severe illness. He expressed much love, and did not doubt, he said, inasmuch as I meant well, but that God would convince me of my great sin in writing books; seeing men ought to read no book but the Bible. I judged it quite needless to enter into a dispute with a sea captain, seventy-five years old.

Friday March 16. I returned to Bristol; and on *Monday 19* set out with my wife for the north.

Saturday 31. I preached at Boothbank, where I met Mr C., late gardener to the Earl of W. Surely it cannot be! Is it possible the earl should turn off an honest, diligent, well-tried servant, who had been in the family more than fifty years, for no other fault than hearing the Methodists?

Wesley in Glasgow

Wednesday April 18. I walked over the city, which I take to be as large as Newcastle-upon-Tyne. The university (like that of Dublin) is only one college, consisting of two small squares; I think not larger, nor at all handsomer, than those of Lincoln College, in Oxford. The dress of the students gave me surprise. They wear scarlet gowns, reaching only to their knees. Most I saw were very dirty, some very ragged, and all of very coarse cloth. The high church is a fine building. The outside is equal to that of most cathedrals in England; but it is miserably defaced within; having no form, beauty, or symmetry left.

Friday 20. Mr G. desired me to preach in his church; so I began between seven and eight. Surely with God nothing is impossible! Who would have believed, twenty-five years

ago, either that the minister would have desired it, or that
I should have consented to preach in a Scottish kirk?

Apprenticeship customs

Wednesday 25. We came to Alnwick on the day on which
those who have gone through their apprenticeship are
made free of the corporation. Sixteen or seventeen, we
were informed, were to receive their freedom today, and
for this purpose (such is the unparalleled wisdom of the
present corporation, as well as of their forefathers), to
walk through a great bog (purposely preserved for the
occasion; otherwise it might have been drained long ago),
which takes up some of them to the neck, and many of
them to the breast.

Cornish smugglers

On *Wednesday July 25*, the Stewards met at St Ives, from the
western part of Cornwall. The next day I began examining
the Society; but I was soon obliged to stop short. I found an
accursed thing among them: well-nigh one and all bought
or sold uncustomed goods. I therefore delayed speaking to
any more till I had met them all together. This I did in the
evening, and told them plain, either they must put this
abomination away, or they would see my face no more.

Friday 27. They each and all promised to do so. So I trust
this plague is stayed.

Wesley writes his epitaph

Monday November 26. Dr F. told me plain, I must not stay
in town a day longer; adding, 'If anything does you good,
it must be the country air, with rest, asses' milk and riding
daily.' So (not being able to sit on a horse) about noon I
took coach for Lewisham.

In the evening (not knowing how it might please God to

dispose of me), to prevent vile panegyric, I wrote as follows:

Here lieth the body
of
JOHN WESLEY,
A BRAND PLUCKED OUT OF THE BURNING:

WHO DIED OF A CONSUMPTION IN THE FIFTY-FIRST YEAR OF HIS AGE,

NOT LEAVING, AFTER HIS DEBTS ARE PAID,
TEN POUNDS BEHIND HIM:

PRAYING,

GOD BE MERCIFUL TO ME, AN UNPROFITABLE SERVANT!

He ordered that this, if any, inscription should be placed on his tombstone.

Wesley his own doctor

Wednesday 28. I found no change for the better, the medicines which had helped before now taking no effect. About noon (the time that some of our brethren in London had set apart for joining in prayer) a thought came into my mind to make an experiment. So I ordered some stone brimstone to be powdered, mixed with the white of an egg, and spread on brown paper, which I applied to my side. The pain ceased in five minutes, the fever in half an hour; and from this hour I began to recover strength. The next day I was able to ride, which I continued to do every day till January 1. Nor did the weather hinder me once; it being always tolerably fair (however it was before) between twelve and one o'clock.

Friday December 14. Having finished all the books which I planned to insert in the 'Christian Library', I broke through the doctor's order not to write, and began transcribing a journal for the press; and in the evening I went to prayers with the family, without finding any inconvenience.

Thursday 20. I felt a gradual increase of strength, till I took a decoction of the bark, which I do not find (such is the peculiarity of my constitution) will agree with me in any form whatever. This immediately threw me into a purging, which brought me down again a few days, and quite disappointed me in my design of going out on Christmas Day.

1754. Tuesday January 1. I returned once more to London.

On *Wednesday 2* I set out in the machine and the next afternoon came to Chippenham. Here I took a post-chaise, in which I reached Bristol about eight in the evening.

Friday 4. I began drinking the water at the Hot Well, having a lodging at a small distance from it; and on *Sunday 6* I began writing *Notes on the New Testament*; a work which I should scarcely ever have attempted, had I not been so ill as not to be able to travel or preach, and yet so well as to be able to read and write.

Thursday 31. My wife desiring to pay the last office to her poor dying child, set out for London, and came a few days before he went home, rejoicing and praising God.

Tuesday March 19 (Bristol). Having finished the rough draft, I began transcribing the *Notes on the Gospels*.

Tuesday 26. I preached for the first time, after an intermission of four months. What reason have I to praise God that he does not take the word of his truth utterly out of my mouth!

Wesley retires to Paddington

Monday April 1. We set out in the machine, and the next evening reached the Foundery.

Wednesday 3. I settled all the business I could, and the next morning retired to Paddington. Here I spent some weeks in writing; only going to town on Saturday evenings, and leaving it again on Monday morning.

In my hours of walking I read Dr Calamy's *Abridgement of Mr Baxter's Life*. What a scene is opened here! In spite of all the prejudice of education, I could not but see that the poor Nonconformists had been treated without either justice or mercy; and that many of the Protestant bishops of King Charles had neither more religion, nor humanity, than the popish bishops of Queen Mary.

Monday 29. I preached at Sadler's Wells, in what was formerly a play-house. I am glad when it pleases God to take possession of what Satan esteemed his own ground. The place, though large, was extremely crowded; and deep attention sat on every face.

Wednesday May 22. Our Conference began; and the spirit of peace and love was in the midst of us. Before we parted, we all willingly signed an agreement not to act independently of each other: so that the breach recently made has only united us more closely together than ever.

Wesley's prescriptions

1755. Monday April 7 (Wednesbury). I was advised to take the Derbyshire road to Manchester. We lunched at a house six miles beyond Lichfield. Observing a woman sitting in the kitchen, I asked, 'Are you not well?' and found she had just been taken ill (being on her journey), with all the symptoms of an approaching pleurisy. She was glad to hear of an easy, cheap, and (almost) infallible remedy—a handful of nettles, boiled a few minutes, and applied warm to the side. While I was speaking to her, an elderly man, pretty well dressed, came in. Upon inquiry, he told us he was travelling as he could towards his home near Hounslow, in hopes of agreeing with his creditors, to whom he had surrendered his all. But how to get on he knew not, as he had no money, and had caught a tertian ague. I hope a wise providence directed this wanderer also, that he might have a remedy for both his maladies.

Monday 14. I rode by Manchester (where I preached about twelve) to Warrington. At six in the morning, *Tuesday 15*, I preached to a large and serious congregation; and then went on to Liverpool, one of the neatest, best-built towns I have seen in England: I think it is full twice as large as Chester; most of the streets are quite straight. Two thirds of the town, we were informed, have been added within these forty years. If it continue to increase in the same proportion, in forty years more it will nearly equal Bristol. The people in general are the most mild and courteous I ever saw in a seaport town; as indeed appears by their friendly behaviour, not only to the Jews and papists who live among them, but even to the Methodists (so called).

Tuesday May 6. Our Conference began at Leeds. The point on which we desired all the preachers to speak their minds at large was whether we ought to separate from the church. Whatever was advanced on one side or the other was seriously and calmly considered; and on the third day we were all fully agreed in that general conclusion —that (whether it was lawful or not) it was no ways expedient.

Thursday June 19. I reached London. From a deep sense of the amazing work which God has in recent years wrought in England, I preached in the evening on those words (Psalm 147:20): 'He has done this for no other nation'; no, not even with Scotland or New England. In both these God has indeed made bare his arm; yet not in so astonishing a manner as among us. This must appear to all who impartially consider:- 1. The numbers of persons on whom God has wrought. 2. The swiftness of his work in many, both convinced and truly converted in a few days. 3. The depth of it in most of these, changing the heart, as well as the whole conversation. 4. The clearness of it, enabling them boldly to say, 'You have loved me; you have given yourself for me'. 5. The continuance of it.

Tuesday 24 (London). Observing in that valuable book, Mr Gillies's *Historical Collections*, the custom of Christian congregations in all ages to set apart seasons of solemn thanksgivings, I was amazed and ashamed that we had never done this, after all the blessings we had received:

and many to whom I mentioned it gladly agreed to set apart a day for that purpose.

'This is no mazed man'

About noon on *Friday September 5*, I called on W. Row, in Breage, on my way to Newlyn. 'Twelve years ago,' he said, 'I was going over Gulval Downs, and I saw many people together; and I asked what was the matter; and they told me a man was going to preach: and I said, "To be sure it is some mazed man": but when I saw you, I said, "Nay, this is no mazed man": and you preached on God's raising the dry bones; and from that time I could never rest till God was pleased to breathe on me, and raise my dead soul.'

Extraordinary coincidence

Saturday 13. I preached once more at St Just, on the first stone of their new Society house. In the evening, as we rode to Camborne, John Pearce, of Redruth, was mentioning a remarkable incident: While he lived at Helston, as their class was meeting one evening, one of them cried, with an uncommon tone, 'We will not stay here: we will go to' such a house, which was in a quite different part of the town. They all rose immediately, and went; though neither they nor she knew why. Presently after they were gone, a spark fell into a barrel of gunpowder, which was in the next room, and blew up the house. So did God preserve those who trusted in him, and prevent the blasphemy of the multitude.

Wednesday November 5. Mr Whitefield called upon me;—disputings are now no more; we love one another, and join hand in hand to promote the cause of our common master.

Tuesday December 23. I was in the robe-chamber, adjoining the House of Lords, when the King put on his robes. His brow was much furrowed with age, and quite clouded with care. And is this all the world can give even to a king—all the grandeur it can afford? A blanket of ermine round his shoulders, so heavy and cumbersome he can scarcely move under it! A huge heap of borrowed hair, with a few plates of gold and glittering stones upon his head! Alas, what a bauble is human greatness! And even this will not endure.

1756. Friday January 30. In returning to London, I read the life of the late Czar, Peter the Great. Undoubtedly he was a soldier, a general, and a statesman, scarcely inferior to any. But why was he called a Christian? What has Christianity to do either with deep dissimulation or savage cruelty?

Preaching to a press-gang

Thursday March 11. I rode to Pill, and preached to a large and attentive congregation. A great part of them were seafaring men. In the middle of my discourse, a press-gang landed from a man-of-war, and came up to the place: but after they had listened a while, they went quietly by, and molested nobody.

Tuesday 23. When we took horse, there was nothing to be seen but a waste of white: the snow covered both hills and vales. As we could see no path, it was not without much difficulty, as well as danger, that we went on. But between seven and eight the sun broke out, and the snow began to melt: so we thought all our difficulty was over; till, about nine, the snow fell faster than ever. In an hour it changed into hail; which, as we rode over the mountains, drove violently in our face. About twelve this turned into hard rain, followed by an impetuous wind. However, we pushed on through all, and before sunset came to Dolgelly.

Here we found everything we wanted except sleep, of which we were deprived by company of drunken, roaring sea captains, who kept possession of the room beneath us till between two and three in the morning, so we did not take horse till after six, and then we could make no great speed, the frost being exceedingly sharp, and much ice on the road. Hence we were not able to reach Tannabull till between eleven and twelve. An honest Welshman here gave us to know (though he spoke no English) that he was just going over the sands. So we hastened on with him, and by that means came in good time to Carnarvon.

Irish honesty

Wednesday 31 (Dublin). In conversing with many, I was surprised to find that all Ireland is in perfect safety. No one here has any more apprehension of an invasion, than of being swallowed up in the sea; everyone being absolutely assured that the French dare not attempt any such thing.

Thursday April 1. I bought one or two books at Mr Smith's, on the Blind Quay. I wanted change for a guinea, but he could not give it; so I borrowed some silver from my companion. The next evening a young gentleman came from Mr Smith's to tell me I had left a guinea on his counter. Such an instance of honesty I have rarely met with, either in Bristol or London.

A remarkable premonition fulfilled

Wednesday 28. I rode to Tullamore; where one of the Society, Edward Willis, gave me a very surprising account of himself. He said:

When I was about twenty years old, I went to Waterford for business. After a few weeks I resolved to leave it; and packed up my things, in order to set out the next morning. This was Sunday; but my landlord pressed me much not to go till the next day. In the afternoon we walked out together, and went into the river. After a while, leaving him near the shore, I struck out into the deep. I soon heard a cry, and, turning, saw him rising and sinking in the channel of the river. I swam back with all speed, and, seeing him sink again, dived down after him. When I was near the bottom, he clasped his arm round my neck, and held me so fast that I could not rise.

Seeing death before me, all my sins came into my mind, and I faintly called for mercy. In a while my sense went away, and I thought I was in a place full of light and glory, with abundance of people. While I was thus, he who held me died, and I floated up to the top of the water. I then immediately came to myself, and swam to the shore, where several stood who had seen us sink, and said they never knew such a deliverance before; for I had been under the water full twenty minutes. It made me more serious for two or three months. Then I returned to all my sins.

But in the midst of all, I had a voice following me everywhere, 'When an able minister of the gospel comes, it will be well with you!' Some years after I entered into the army: our troop lay at Phillipstown, when Mr W. came. I was much affected by his preaching; but not so as to leave my sins. The voice followed me still, and when Mr J.W. came, before I saw him I had an unspeakable conviction that he was the man I looked for: and soon after I found peace with God, and it was well with me indeed.

The delights of north Wales

Friday August 6. On this and the next day I finished my business in Ireland, so as to be ready to sail at an hour's warning.

Sunday 8. We were to sail, the wind being fair; but as we were going aboard it turned full east. I find it of great use to be in suspense: it is an excellent means of breaking our will. May we be ready either to stay longer on this shore, or to launch into eternity!

Friday 13. Having hired horses for Chester, we set out about seven. Before one we reached Bangor, the situation of which is delightful beyond expression. Here we saw a large and handsome cathedral, but no trace of the good old monks of Bangor; so many hundreds of whom fell a sacrifice at once to cruelty and revenge.

Wednesday 25. We rode on to Bristol.

Thursday 26. About fifty of us being met, the Rules of the Society were read over, and carefully considered one by one; but we did not find any that could be spared. So we all agreed to abide by them all, and to recommend them with our might.

We then considered at length the necessity of keeping in the church and treating the clergy with tenderness; and there was no dissenting voice. God gave us all to be of one mind and of one judgement.

Friday 27. The Rules of the Bands were read over and considered, one by one; which, after some verbal alterations, we all agreed to observe and enforce.

Saturday 28. My brother and I closed the Conference by a solemn declaration of our purpose never to separate from the church; and all our brethren concurred in this.

Monday September 6. I set out in the machine, and on Tuesday evening came to London.

Wesley's debt of £1236

Wednesday and *Thursday,* I settled my temporal business. It is now about eighteen years since I began writing and printing books; and how much in that time have I gained by printing? Why, on summing up my accounts, I found that on March 1, 1756 (the day I left London last), I had gained by printing and preaching together, a debt of twelve hundred and thirty-six pounds.

Wesley on electricity as a cure

Tuesday November 9. Having procured an apparatus on purpose, I ordered several persons to be electrified, who were ill of various disorders; some of whom found an immediate, some a gradual, cure. From this time I appointed, first some hours in every week, and afterward an hour in every day, when anyone who desired it, might try the virtue of this surprising medicine. Two or three years after, our patients were so numerous that we were obliged to divide them, so part were electrified in South-wark, part at the Foundery, others near St Paul's, and the rest near the Seven Dials: the same method we have taken ever since; and to this day, while hundreds, perhaps thousands, have received unspeakable good, I have not known one man, woman, or child, who has received any hurt by it: so that when I hear any talk of the danger of being electrified (especially if they are medical men who talk so), I cannot but impute it to great want either of sense or honesty.

1757. Tuesday May 31. I breakfasted at Dumfries, and spent an hour with a poor backslider of London, who had been for some years settled there.

Wednesday June 1. We rode on to Glasgow; a mile short of which we met Mr Gillies, riding out to meet us.

In the evening the tent (so they call a covered pulpit) was placed in the yard of the poor-house, a very large and commodious place. Facing the pulpit was the infirmary, with most of the patients at or near the windows. Adjoining to this was the hospital for lunatics: several of them gave deep attention. And cannot God give them also the spirit of a sound mind? After the sermon, they brought four children to baptise. I was at the kirk in the morning while the minister baptised several immediately after the sermon. So I was not at a loss as to their manner of baptising. I believe this removed much prejudice.

In Glasgow cathedral

Saturday 4. I walked though all parts of the old cathedral, a very large and once beautiful structure; I think, more lofty than that at Canterbury, and nearly the same length and breadth. We then went up the main steeple, which gave us a fine view, both of the city and the adjacent country. A more fruitful and better cultivated plain is scarcely to be seen in England. Indeed nothing is lacking but more trade (which would naturally bring more people), to make a great part of Scotland no way inferior to the best counties in England.

I was much pleased with the seriousness of the people in the evening; but still I prefer the English congregation. I cannot be reconciled to men sitting at prayer, or covering their heads while they are singing praise to God.

Wesley sings a Scotch psalm

At six William Coward and I went to the market-house. We stayed some time, and neither man, woman, nor child came near us. At length I began singing a Scotch psalm, and fifteen or twenty people came within hearing; but with great circumspection, keeping their distance, as though they knew not what might follow. But while I prayed, their number increased; so that in a few minutes there was a pretty large congregation. I suppose the chief men of the town were there; and I spared neither rich nor poor. I almost wondered at myself, it not being usual with me to use so keen and cutting expressions: and I believe many felt that, for all their form, they were but heathens still.

Monday 13. I proclaimed the love of Christ to sinners, in the market-place at Morpeth. From there we rode to Placey. The Society of colliers here may be a pattern to all the Societies in England. No person ever misses his band or class: they have no conflict of any kind among them; but with one heart and one mind 'provoke one another to love and to good works'.

Thursday 16. In the evening I preached at Sunderland. I then met the Society, and told them plain, none could stay with us unless he would part with all sin; particularly, robbing the king, selling or buying smuggled goods; which I could no more allow than robbing on the highway. This I enforced on every member the next day. A few would not promise to refrain: so these I was forced to cut off. About two hundred and fifty were of a better mind.

Wednesday 22. In the evening and the following morning I preached at Chester-le-Street. Observing some very fine, but not very modest pictures, in the parlour where we supped, I desired my companion, when the company was gone, to put them where they could do no hurt. He piled them in a heap in a corner of the room, and they have not appeared since.

Wesley at Charterhouse

Monday August 8 (London). I took a walk in the Charterhouse. I wondered that all the squares and buildings, and especially the schoolboys, looked so little. I was little myself when I was at school, and measured all about me by myself. Accordingly, the upper boys being then bigger than myself, seemed to me very big and tall; quite contrary to what they appear now when I am taller and bigger than them. I question if this is not the real ground of the common imagination that our forefathers, and in general men in past ages, were much larger than now: an imagination current in the world eighteen hundred years ago. Whereas, in reality, men have been, at least ever since the deluge, very nearly the same as we find them now, both for stature and understanding.

Friday September 2. I rode to St Agnes.

Sunday 4. I.T. preached at five. I could scarcely have believed if I had not heard it, that few men of learning write so correctly as an unlearned tinner speaks extempore. Mr V. preached two such thundering sermons at church as I have scarcely heard these twenty years.

Sunday 11. I preached at St Just at nine. At one, the congregation in Morva stood on a sloping ground, rank above rank, as in a theatre. Many of them bewailed their lack of God; and many tasted how gracious he is.

At five I preached in Newlyn, to a huge multitude; and

one only seemed to be offended—a very good sort of woman, who took great pains to get away, crying aloud, 'Nay, if going to church and sacrament will not put us to heaven, I know not what will.'

Fire at Kingswood school

Tuesday October 25. A man met me near Hannam, and told me the school house at Kingswood was burned down. I felt not one moment's pain, knowing that God does all things well. When I got there, I received a fuller account: about eight on Monday evening, two or three boys went into the gallery, up two flights of stairs. One of them heard a strange crackling in the room above. Opening the staircase door, he was beaten back by smoke, on which he cried out, 'Fire! Murder! Fire!' Mr Baynes, hearing this, ran immediately down, and brought up a pail of water. But when he went into the room and saw the blaze, he had not presence of mind to go up to it, but threw the water on the floor.

Meanwhile one of the boys rang the bell; another called John Maddern from the next house, who ran up, as did James Burges quickly after, and found the room all in a flame. The deal partitions caught fire immediately, which spread to the roof of the house. Plenty of water was now brought; but they could not come near the place where it was wanted, the room being so filled with flame and smoke no one could go into it. At last a long ladder, which lay in the garden, was reared up against the wall of the house. But it was then observed that one of the sides of it was broken in two, and the other quite rotten. However, John How (a young man, who lived next door) ran up it with an axe in his hand. But he then found the ladder was so short that as he stood on the top of it he could but just lay one hand over the battlements.

How he got over to the leads none can tell: but he did so, and quickly broke through the roof, on which a vent being made, the smoke and flame issued out as from a furnace: those who were at the foot of the stairs with water, being able to go no further, then went through the smoke to the door of the leads, and poured it down through the tiling. By this means the fire was quickly quenched, having only consumed a part of the partition, with a box of clothes, and a little damaged the roof and the floor beneath.

In Norfolk

Wednesday November 23 (Norwich). I was shown Dr Taylor's new meeting-house, perhaps the most elegant one in Europe. It is octagonal, built of the finest brick, with sixteen sash-windows below, as many above, and eight skylights in the dome; which, indeed, are purely ornamental. The inside is finished in the highest taste, and is as clean as any nobleman's saloon. The communion-table is fine mahogany; the very latches of the pew-doors are polished brass. How can it be thought that the old, coarse gospel should find admission here?

1758. Wednesday January 4. I rode to Kingswood, and rejoiced over the school, which is at length what I have so long wished it to be—a blessing to all that are therein, and an honour to the whole body of Methodists.

Monday March 6 (London). I took horse about seven o'clock. The wind being east, I was pleasing myself that we should have it on our back; but in a quarter of an hour it shifted to the north-west, and blew the rain full in our face: and both increased, so that when we came to Finchley Common, it was hard work to sit our horses. The rain continued all the way to Dunstable, where we exchanged the main road for the fields; which, having been just ploughed, were deep enough. However, before three we came to Sundon.

From here, on *Thursday 9,* I rode to Bedford, and found the sermon was not to be preached till Friday. Had I known this in time, I should never have thought of preaching it; having engaged to be at Epworth on Saturday.

Another ninety-mile journey

Friday 10. The congregation at St Paul's was very large and very attentive. The judge, immediately after the sermon, sent me an invitation to dine with him. But having no time, I was obliged to send my excuse, and set out between one and two. The north-east wind was piercing cold, and, blowing exactly in our face, soon brought a heavy shower of snow, then of sleet, and afterwards of hail. However, we reached Stilton at seven, about thirty miles from Bedford.

Rest was now the more sweet, because both our horses were lame. However, resolving to reach Epworth at the time appointed, I set out in a post-chaise between four and five in the morning: but the frost made it so bad driving, that my companion came with the lame horses into Stamford as soon as me. The next stage I went on horseback; but I was then obliged to leave my mare, and take another post-chaise. I came to Bawtry about six. Some from Epworth had come to meet me, but were gone half an hour before I came. I knew no chaise could go the rest of the road; so it remained only to hire horses and a guide.

We set out about seven, but I soon found my guide knew no more of the way than myself. However, we got pretty well to Idlestop, about four miles from Bawtry, where we had just light to discern the river at our side, and the country covered with water. I had heard that one Richard Wright lived thereabouts, who knew the road over the moor perfectly well. Hearing someone speak (for we could not see him), I called 'Who is there?' He answered, 'Richard Wright.' I soon agreed with him, and he quickly mounted his horse, and rode boldly forward. The north-east wind blew full in our face; and I heard them say, 'It is very cold!' But neither my face, nor hands, nor feet were cold, till between nine and ten we came to Epworth: after travelling more than ninety miles, I was little more tired than when I rose in the morning.

Wesley's advice to travellers

Tuesday August 1. The captain with whom we were to sail was in great haste to have our things on board; but I would not send them while the wind was against us. On Wednesday he sent message after message: so in the evening we went down to the ship, near Passage; but there was nothing ready, or near ready for sailing. Hence I learned two or three rules, very needful for those who sail between England and Ireland. 1. Never pay till you set sail: 2. Go not on board till the captain goes on board: 3. Send not your baggage on board till you go yourself.

Thursday 17. I went to the Bristol cathedral to hear Mr Handel's *Messiah.* I doubt if that congregation was ever so serious at a sermon as they were during this performance. In many parts, especially several of the choruses, it exceeded my expectation.

Wesley at Norwich and Colchester

Sunday November 5 (Norwich). We went to St Peter's church, the Lord's supper being administered there. I scarcely ever remember having seen a more beautiful parish church: the more so, because its beauty results not from foreign ornaments, but from the very form and structure of it. It is very large, and of an uncommon height, and the sides are almost all window; so that it has an awesome and venerable look, and, at the same time, surprisingly cheerful.

Monday December 4. I was desired to step into the little church behind the Mansion House, commonly called St Stephen's, Walbrook. It is nothing grand; but neat and elegant beyond expression. So that I do not wonder at the speech of the famous Italian architect, who met Lord Burlington in Italy: 'My Lord, go back and see St Stephen's in London. We have not so fine a piece of architecture in Rome.'

Friday 29. Today I walked all over the famous castle (Colchester), perhaps the most ancient building in England. A considerable part of it is, without question, fourteen or fifteen hundred years old. It was mostly built with Roman bricks, each of which is about two inches thick, seven broad, and thirteen or fourteen long. Seat of ancient kings, British and Roman, once dreaded far and near! But what are they now? Is not 'a living dog better than a dead lion'? And what is it they prided themselves in, as do the present great ones of the earth?

The sands of Ravenglass

1759. Saturday May 12. Setting out early we came to Bottle about twenty-four measured miles from Fluckborough, soon after eight, having crossed the Millom sand without either guide or difficulty. Here we were informed that we could not pass at Ravenglass before one or two o'clock; whereas, had we gone on (as we afterwards found), we might have passed immediately. About eleven we were directed to a ford near Manchester Hall, which they said we might cross at noon. When we came there, they told us we could not cross; so we sat still till about one: we then found we could have crossed at noon. However, we reached Whitehaven before night. But I have taken my leave of the sand road. I believe it is ten miles shorter than the other; but there are four sands to pass, so far from each other that it is scarcely possible to pass them all in a day: especially as you have all the way to do with a generation of liars, who detain all strangers as long as they can, either for their own gain or their neighbours'. I can advise no stranger to go this way; he may go round by Kendal and Keswick, often in less time, always with less expense, and far less trial of his patience.

Useless doctors

Reflecting today on the case of a poor woman who had continual pain in her stomach, I could not but remark the inexcusable negligence of most physicians in cases of this nature. They prescribe drug after drug, without knowing a jot of the matter concerning the root of the disorder. And without knowing this, they cannot cure, though they can murder, the patient. What caused this woman's pain? She would never have told, if she had not been questioned about it. It was from fretting for the death of her son. And what availed medicines, while that fretting continued? Why then do not all physicians consider how far bodily disorders are caused or influenced by the mind; and in those cases, which are utterly out of their sphere, call in the assistance of a minister; as ministers, when they find the mind disordered by the body, call in the assistance of a physician? But why are these cases out of their sphere? Because they do not know God. It follows, no man can be a thorough physician without being a Christian in his personal experience.

Fire in a coal-pit

Thursday 17. I enquired into a signal instance of providence. When a coal-pit runs far under the ground it is customary here to build a partition wall, nearly from the shaft to within three or four yards of the end, in order to make the air circulate, which then moves down one side of the wall, turns at the end, and then moves briskly up on the other side. In a pit two miles from the town, which ran full four hundred yards under the ground, and had been long neglected, several parts of this wall were fallen down. Four men were sent down to repair it. They were about three hundred yards from the shaft, when the foul air caught fire. In a moment it tore down the wall from end to end; and, burning on till it came to the shaft, it then burst and went off like a large cannon.

The men instantly fell on their faces, or they would have been burned to death in a few moments. One of them, who once knew the love of God (Andrew English), began crying aloud for mercy. But in a very short time his breath was stopped. The other three crept on their hands and knees, till two got to the shaft and were drawn up; but one of them died in a few minutes. John M'Combe was drawn up next, burned from head to foot, but rejoicing and praising God. They then went down for Andrew, whom they found unconscious; the very circumstance which saved his life. For, losing consciousness, he lay flat on the ground, and the greatest part of the fire went over him; whereas, had he gone forward on his hands and knees, he would undoubtedly have been burned to death. But life or death was welcome; for God had restored the light of his countenance.

Newcastle as a summer resort

Monday June 4. After preaching (at Alnwick), I rode on to Newcastle. Certainly if I did not believe there was another world, I should spend all my summers here; as I know no place in Great Britain comparable to it for pleasantness. But I seek another country, and therefore am content to be a wanderer upon the earth.

Thursday 21. I preached at Nafferton at one. As I was riding away, someone stopped me on the road and said, 'Sir, do you not remember, when you was at Prudhoe, two years ago, you breakfasted at Thomas Newton's? I am his sister. You looked upon me as you was going out, and said, "Be in earnest." I knew not then what earnestness meant, nor had any thought about it; but the words sank into my heart, so that I could never rest any more till I sought and found Christ.'

Saturday 23. I spoke to each member of the Society in Sunderland. Most of the robbers, commonly called smugglers, have left us; but more than twice the number of honest people are already come in their place; and if none had come, yet should I not dare to keep those who steal here from the king or subject.

Wesley likes a soft cushion

On Monday and Tuesday evening I preached outside, near the Keelman's Hospital, to twice the people we should have had at the house. What marvel the devil does not love field-preaching? Neither do I: I love a commodious room, a soft cushion, a handsome pulpit. But where is my zeal, if I do not trample all these under foot, in order to save one more soul?

Defeating the press-gang

Wednesday July 4 (Hartlepool). Mr Jones preached at five, I at eight. Toward the close of the sermon, a queer, dirty, clumsy man, I suppose a country wit, took a deal of pains to disturb the congregation. When I had done, fearing he might hurt those who were gathered about him, I desired two or three of our brethren to go to him, one after the other, and not say much themselves, but let him talk till he weary. They did so, but without effect, as his fund of ribaldry seemed inexhaustible. W.A. then tried another way. He got into the circle close to him, and listening a while said, 'That is pretty; pray say it over again.' 'What, are you deaf?' 'No; but for the entertainment of the people. Come; we are all attention.' After repeating this twice or thrice, the wag could not stand it; but, with two or three curses, walked clear off.

In the evening I began near Stockton market-place as usual. I had hardly finished the hymn, when I observed the people in great confusion, which was occasioned by a lieutenant of a man-of-war, who had chosen that time to bring his press-gang, and ordered them to take Joseph Jones and William Alwood. Joseph Jones telling him, 'Sir, I belong to Mr Wesley,' after a few words he let him go; as he did likewise William Alwood, after a few hours, understanding he was a licensed preacher. He likewise seized upon a young man of the town; but the women rescued him by main strength. They also broke the lieutenant's head, and so stoned both him and his men, that they ran away with all speed.

Friday August 3. I preached at Gansborough, in Sir Nevil Hickman's great hall. It is just as large as the Weaver's Hall, in Bristol. At two it was filled with a rude, wild multitude (a few of a better spirit excepted). Yet all but two or three gentlemen were attentive, while I enforced our Lord's words, 'What good shall it do a man if he gains the whole world, yet forfeits his own soul?' I was walking back through a gaping, staring crowd, when Sir Nevil came and thanked me for my sermon, to the no small amazement of his neighbours, who shrank back as if they had seen a ghost.

Extraordinary trances

Monday 6 (Everton). I talked at length with Ann Thorn and two others, who had been several times in trances. What they all agreed on was, 1. That when they went away, as they termed it, it was always at the time they were fullest of the love of God. 2. That it came upon them in a moment, without any previous notice, and took away all their senses and strength. 3. That there were some exceptions, but in general, from that moment, they were in another world, knowing nothing of what was done or said by all that were round about them.

About five in the afternoon I heard them singing hymns. Soon after, Mr B. came up, and told me Alice Miller (fifteen years old) had fallen into a trance. I went down immediately, and found her sitting on a stool, and leaning against the wall, with her eyes open and fixed upwards. I made motion as if going to strike, but they continued immovable. Her face showed an unspeakable mixture of reverence and love, while silent tears stole down her cheeks. Her lips were a little open, and sometimes moved; but not enough to cause any sound.

I do not know whether I ever saw a human face look so beautiful; sometimes it was covered with a smile, as from joy, mixing with love and reverence; but the tears fell still though not so fast. Her pulse was quite regular. In about half an hour I observed her countenance change into the form of fear, pity, and distress; then she burst into a flood of tears, and cried out, 'Dear Lord; they will be damned! They will all be damned!' But in about five minutes her smiles returned, and only love and joy appeared in her face.

About half an hour after six, I observed distress take place again; and soon after she wept bitterly and cried out, 'Dear Lord, they will go to hell! The world will go to hell!' Soon after, she said, 'Cry aloud! Spare not!' And in a few moments her look was composed again, and spoke a mixture of reverence, joy, and love. Then she said aloud, 'Give God the glory.'

About seven her senses returned. I asked, 'Where have you been?'

'I have been with my saviour.'

'In heaven, or on earth?'

'I cannot tell; but I was in glory.'

'Why then did you cry?'

'Not for myself, but for the world; for I saw they were on the brink of hell.'

'Whom did you desire to give the glory to God?'

'Ministers that cry aloud to the world: else they will be proud; and then God will leave them, and they will lose their own souls.'

Wesley rides 2400 miles in seven months

Tuesday 7. After preaching at four (because of the harvest) I took horse, and rode easily to London. Indeed I wanted a little rest; having ridden, in seven months, about twenty-four hundred miles.

Monday 13. I took a little ride to Croydon, one of the seats of the Archbishops of Canterbury. Was it one of these who ordered, many years ago (for the lettering is of old standing), that dreadful inscription to be placed just over the communion table?

> And now, ye priests, this commandment is for you. If ye will not hear, and if ye will not lay it to heart, to give glory unto my name, saith the Lord, I will even send a curse among you, and I will curse your blessings: yea, I have cursed them already, because ye do not lay it to heart. Behold, I will corrupt your seed, and spread dung upon your faces, even the dung of your solemn feasts, and one shall take you away with it.

Thursday 30. I preached at the Tabernacle in Norwich, to a large, rude, noisy congregation. I took knowledge what manner of teachers they had been accustomed to, and determined to mend them or end them. Accordingly, the next evening, after the sermon I reminded them of two things: the one, that it was not decent to begin talking aloud as soon as service was ended; and hurrying to and fro as in a bear-garden. The other, that it was a bad custom to gather into knots just after the sermon, and turn a place of worship into a coffee-house. I therefore desired that none would talk under that roof, but go quietly and silently away. And on *Sunday September 2* I had the pleasure to observe that all went as quietly away as if they had been accustomed to it for many years.

Sunday September 9. I met the Society at seven; and told them in plain terms that they were the most ignorant, self-conceited, self-willed, fickle, untractable, disorderly, disjointed Society that I knew in the three kingdoms. And

God applied it to their hearts: so that many were profited; but I do not find that one was offended.

Friday 14. I returned to London.

Saturday 15. Having left orders for the immediate repairing of West Street chapel, I went to see what they had done, and saw cause to praise God for this also. The main timbers were so rotten that in many places one might thrust his fingers into them. So that probably, had we delayed till spring, the whole building must have fallen to the ground.

Field-preaching expedient

Sunday 23. A vast majority of the immense congregation in Moorfields were deeply serious. One such hour might convince any impartial man of the expediency of field-preaching. What building, except St Paul's church, would contain such a congregation? And if it would, what human voice could have reached them there? By repeated observations I find I can command three times the number in the open air, that I can under a roof. And who can say the time for field-preaching is over, while: 1. Greater numbers than ever attend. 2. The converting, as well as convincing, power of God is eminently present with them?

Wesley clothes French prisoners

Monday October 1 (Bristol). All my leisure time, during my stay at Bristol, I employed in finishing the fourth volume of *Discourses*; probably the last which I shall publish.

Monday 15. I walked up to Knowle, a mile from Bristol, to see the French prisoners. About eleven hundred of them, we are informed, were confined in that little place, without anything to lie on but a little dirty straw, or anything to cover them but a few foul thin rags, either by day or by night, so that they died like rotten sheep. I was much moved, and preached in the evening on: 'Do not oppress an alien; you yourselves know how it feels to be aliens, because you were aliens in Egypt' (Exodus 23:9). Eighteen pounds was contributed immediately, which was made up to twenty-four the next day. With this we bought linen and woollen cloth, which were made up into shirts, waistcoats, and breeches. Some dozen of stockings were added; all which were carefully distributed, where there was the greatest need. Presently after, the Corporation of Bristol sent a large quantity of mattresses and blankets. And it was not long before contributions were set on foot at London, and in various parts of the kingdom; so that I believe from this time they were pretty well provided with all the necessaries of life.

The truth about trances

Saturday November 17 (London). I spent an hour agreeably and profitably with Lady G.H., and Sir C.H. It is well a few of the rich and noble are called. O that God would increase their number! But I should rejoice (were it the will of God), if it were done by the ministry of others. If I might choose, I should still (as I have done hitherto) preach the gospel to the poor.

Friday 23. The roads were so extremely slippery, it was with much difficulty we reached Bedford. We had a pretty large congregation; but the stench from the pigs under the room was scarcely supportable. Was ever a preaching-place over a hog-sty before? Surely they love the gospel, who come to hear it in such a place.

Sunday 25. In the afternoon God was eminently present with us, though rather to comfort than convince. But I observed a remarkable difference, since I was here (Everton) before, as to the manner of the work. None now were in trances, none cried out, none fell down or were convulsed: only some trembled exceedingly, a low murmur was heard, and many were refreshed with the multitude of peace.

The danger was, to regard extraordinary circumstances too much, such as outcries, convulsions, visions, trances; as if these were essential to the inward work, so that it could not go on without them. Perhaps the danger is, to imagine they had nothing of God in them, and were a hindrance to his work. Whereas the truth is: 1. God suddenly and strongly convinced many that they were lost sinners; the natural consequence whereof was sudden outcries and strong bodily convulsions: 2. To strengthen and encourage those who believed, and to make his work more apparent, he favoured several of them with divine dreams, others with trances and visions. 3. In some of these instances, after a time, nature mixed with grace. 4. Satan likewise mimicked this work of God in order to discredit the whole work: and yet it is not wise to give up this part any more than to give up the whole. At first, it was doubtless wholly from God. It is partly so today; and he will enable us to discern how far, in every case, the work is pure, and where it mixes or degenerates.

Wednesday 28. I returned to London; and on *Thursday 29*, the day appointed for the general thanksgiving, I preached again in the chapel near the Seven Dials, both morning and afternoon. I believe the oldest man in England has not seen a thanksgiving day so observed before. It had the solemnity of the General Fast. All the shops were shut up: the people in the streets appeared, one and all, with an air of seriousness: the prayers, lessons, and whole public service were admirably suited to the occasion. The prayer for our enemies, in particular, was extremely striking: perhaps it is the first instance of the kind in Europe. There was no noise, commotion, bonfires, fireworks in the evening; and no public entertainments. This is indeed a Christian holiday, a 'rejoicing to the Lord'. The next day came the news that Sir Edward Hawke had dispersed the French fleet.

Sunday December 9. I had for the first time a love-feast for the whole Society.

Wednesday 12. I began reading over the Greek Testament and the notes, with my brother and several others; carefully comparing the translation with the original, and correcting or enlarging the notes as we saw occasion.

The same day I spent part of the afternoon in the British Museum. There is a large library, a great number of curious manuscripts, many uncommon monuments of antiquity, and the whole collection of shells, butterflies, beetles, grasshoppers, etc., which the indefatigable Sir Hans Sloane, with such vast expense and labour, procured in a life of eighty years.

1760. Wednesday January 16. Someone came to me, as she said, with a message from the Lord, to tell me I was laying up treasures on earth, taking my ease, and minding only my eating and drinking. I told her, God knew me better; and if he had sent her, he would have sent her with a more appropriate message.

Wesley and the Irish question

Monday April 21. In riding to Rosmead, I read Sir John Davis's *Historical Relations concerning Ireland*. None who reads these can wonder that, fruitful as it is, it was always so thinly inhabited; for he makes it plain: 1. That murder was never capital among the native Irish; the murderer only paid a small fine to the chief of his sept. 2. When the English settled here, still the Irish had no benefit of the English laws. They could not so much as sue an Englishman. So the English beat, plundered, indeed murdered them, at pleasure. Hence, 3. arose continual wars between them, for three hundred and fifty years together; and by this both the English and Irish natives were kept few, as well as poor. 4. When they were multiplied during a peace of forty years, from 1600 to 1641, the general massacre, with the ensuing war, again thinned their numbers; not so few as a million men, women and children being destroyed in four years. 5. Great numbers

have ever since, year by year, left the land merely for
want of employment. 6. The gentry are continually driving away hundreds, indeed thousands, of them that
remain, by throwing such quantities of arable land into
pasture, which leaves them neither business nor food.
This it is that now depopulates many parts of Ireland, of
Connaught in particular, which, it is supposed, has
scarcely half the inhabitants today which it had eighty
years ago.

Attack on Wesley's hat

Tuesday June 10. I rode to Drumersnave, a village delightfully situated.

At noon William Ley, James Glasbrook, and I rode to
Carrick-upon-Shannon. In less than an hour, an Esquire
and Justice of the Peace came down with a drum, and what
mob he could gather. I went into the garden with the congregation, while he was making a speech to his followers in
the street. He then attacked William Ley (who stood at the
door), being armed with a halberd and long sword; and
ran at him with the halberd, but missing his thrust, he then
struck at him, and broke it short upon his wrist. Having
made his way through the house to the other door, he was
at a full stop. James Glasbrook held it fast on the other
side.

While he was endeavouring to force it open, someone
told him I was preaching in the garden. On this he quitted
the door in haste, ran round the house, and with part of
his retinue, climbed over the wall into the garden; and
with a whole volley of oaths and curses declared, 'You shall
not preach here today.' I told him, 'Sir, I do not intend it;
for I have preached already.' This made him ready to tear
the ground. Finding he was not to be reasoned with, I went
into the house. Soon after he revenged himself on James
Glasbrook (by breaking the truncheon of his halberd on
his arm), and on my hat, which he beat and kicked most

valiantly; but a gentleman rescued it out of his hands, and we rode quietly out of the town.

Saturday September 20. In the evening I took my old stand in the main street in Redruth. A multitude of people, rich and poor, calmly attended. So is the roughest become one of the quietest towns in England.

Sunday 21. I preached in the same place at eight. Mr C., of St Cubert, preached at the church both morning and afternoon, and strongly confirmed what I had spoken. At one, the day being mild and calm, we had the largest congregation of all. But it rained all the time I was preaching at Gwennap. We concluded the day with a love-feast, at which James Roberts, a tinner of St Ives, related how God had dealt with his soul.

A tinner's story

He was one of the first in the Society in St Ives, but soon relapsed into his old sin, drunkenness, and wallowed in it for two years, during which time he headed the mob who pulled down the preaching-house. Not long after, he was standing with his partner at Edward May's shop when the preacher went by. His partner said, 'I will tell him I am a Methodist.' 'Nay,' said Edward, 'your speech will betray you.' James felt the word as a sword, thinking in himself, 'So does my speech now betray me!' He turned and hastened home, fancying he heard the devil stepping after him all the way. For forty hours he never closed his eyes, nor tasted either meat or drink. He was then at his wit's end, and went to the window, expecting to drop into hell that instant, when he heard those words, 'I will forgive their wickedness and will remember their sins no more.' All his load was gone; and he has now for many years walked worthy of the gospel.

Friday October 24. I visited the French prisoners at Knowle, and found many of them almost naked again. In hopes of provoking others to jealousy, I took another

collection for them, and ordered the money to be laid out
in linen and waistcoats, which were given to those that
were most in need.

Saturday 25. King George was gathered to his fathers.
When will England have a better Prince?

Many of us agreed to observe *Friday 31* as a day of fasting and prayer for the blessing of God upon our nation,
and in particular on his present Majesty. We met at five, at
nine, at one, and at half-past eight. I expected to be a little
tired, but was more lively after twelve at night than I was
at six in the morning.

Wesley writes to the *London Chronicle*

1761. Friday January 2. I wrote the following letter:

To the Editor of the London Chronicle.

Sir,—Of all the seats of woe on this side hell, few, I suppose,
exceed or even equal Newgate. If any region of horror could
exceed it a few years ago, Newgate in Bristol did; so great was
the filth, the stench, the misery, and wickedness, which
shocked all who had a spark of humanity left.

How was I surprised then, when I was there a few weeks
ago! 1. Every part of it, above stairs and below, even the pit
wherein the felons are confined at night, is as clean and sweet
as a gentleman's house; it being now a rule, that every prisoner
wash and clean his apartment thoroughly twice a week.
2. Here is no fighting or brawling. If any thinks himself ill-
used, the cause is immediately referred to the keeper, who
hears the contending parties face to face, and decides the
affair at once. 3. The usual grounds of quarrelling are
removed. For it is very rarely that anyone cheats or wrongs
another, as being sure, if anything of this kind is discovered, to
be committed to a closer confinement. 4. Here is no drunkenness suffered, however advantageous it might be to the
keeper, as well as the tapster. 5. Nor any whoredom; the
women prisoners being narrowly observed, and kept separate
from the men: nor is any woman of the town now admitted,
no, not at any price. 6. All possible care is taken to prevent

idleness: those who are willing to work at their callings are provided with tools and materials, partly by the keeper, who gives them credit at a very moderate profit; partly by the alms occasionally given, which are divided with the utmost prudence and impartiality. Accordingly, at this time, among others, a shoemaker, a tailor, a brazier, and a coachmaker are working at their several trades.

7. Only on the Lord's day they neither work nor play, but dress themselves as clean as they can, to attend the public service in the chapel, at which every person under the roof is present. None is excused, unless sick; in which case he is provided, *gratis*, both with advice and medicines. 8. And in order to assist them in things of the greatest concern (besides a sermon every Sunday and Thursday), they have a large Bible chained on one side of the chapel, which any of the prisoners may read. By the blessing of God on these regulations the prison now has a new face: nothing offends either the eye or ear; and the whole has the appearance of a quiet, serious family. And does not the keeper of Newgate deserve to be remembered full as well as the Man of Ross? May the Lord remember him in that day! Meantime, will no one follow his example?

Saturday March 14. I rode (from Birmingham) to Wednesbury.

Sunday 15. I made a shift to preach indoors at eight in the morning; but in the afternoon I knew not what to do, having a pain in my side, and a sore throat. However, I resolved to speak as long as I could. I stood at one end of the house, and the people (supposed to be eight or ten thousand) in the field adjoining. I spoke from, 'I consider everything a loss compared to the surpassing greatness of knowing Christ Jesus my Lord.' When I had done speaking, my complaints were gone.

Monday 16. I intended to rest two or three days; but being pressed to visit Shrewsbury, and having no other time, I rode over today, though upon a miserable beast. When I came, my head ached as well as my side. I found the door of the place where I was to preach surrounded by a numerous mob. But they seemed met only to starve. Yet part of them came in; almost all that did (a large number) behaved quietly and seriously.

Wesley preaches at Aberdeen

Saturday May 2 (Aberdeen). In the afternoon I sent to the Principal and Regent to desire leave to preach in the college close. This was readily granted; but as it began to rain, I was desired to go into the hall. I suppose this is fully a hundred feet long, and seated all around. The congregation was large, notwithstanding the rain; and fully as large at five in the evening.

Monday 4. About noon I took a walk to the King's College, in Old Aberdeen. It has three sides of a square, handsomely built, not unlike Queen's College in Oxford. Going up to see the hall, we found a large group of ladies, with several gentlemen. They looked, and spoke to one another, after which one of the gentlemen took courage and came to me. He said, 'We came last night to the college close, but could not hear, and should be extremely obliged if you would give us a short discourse here.' I knew not what God might have to do; and so began without delay, on 'God was in Christ, reconciling the world to himself.' I believe the word was not lost: it fell as dew on the tender grass.

In the afternoon I was walking in the library of the Marischal College, when the Principal, and the Divinity Professor, came to me; and the latter invited me to his lodgings, where I spent an hour very agreeably. In the evening, the eagerness of the people made them ready to trample each other under foot. It was some time before they were still enough to hear; but then they devoured every word. After preaching, Sir Archibald Grant (whom business had called to town) sent and desired to speak to me. I could not then, but promised to come and see him, with God's leave, when I was returning to Edinburgh.

Tuesday 5. I accepted the Principal's invitation, and

spent an hour with him at his house. I observed no stiffness at all, but the easy good breeding of a man of sense
and learning.

Wesley's criticism of Edinburgh

Monday 11. I took my leave of Edinburgh for the present.
The situation of the city, on a hill shelving down on both
sides, as well as to the east, with the stately castle upon a
craggy rock on the west, is inexpressibly fine. And the
main street, so broad and finely paved, with the lofty
houses on either hand (many of them seven or eight
storeys high), is far beyond any in Great Britain. But how
can it be suffered, that all manner of filth should still be
thrown even into this street continually? Where are the
magistracy, the gentry, the nobility of the land? Have they
no concern for the honour of their nation? How long shall
the capital city of Scotland, indeed the chief street of it,
stink worse than a common sewer? Will no lover of his
country, or of decency and common sense, find a remedy
for this?

Holyrood House, at the entrance of Edinburgh, the
ancient palace of the Scottish kings, is a noble structure. It
was rebuilt and furnished by King Charles the Second.
One side of it is a picture-gallery, wherein are pictures of
all the Scottish kings, and an original one of the celebrated
Queen Mary: it is scarcely possible for any who looks at this
to think her such a monster as some have painted her; nor
indeed for anyone who considers the circumstances of her
death, equal to that of an ancient martyr.

Wednesday 24 (Whitby). I walked round the old abbey,
which, both with regard to its size (being, I judge, a
hundred yards long), and the workmanship of it, is one of
the finest, if not the finest, ruin in the kingdom. From here
we rode to Robin Hood's Bay, where I preached at six in
the Lower Street, near the quay. In the middle of the sermon a large cat, frightened out of a room, leaped down

upon a woman's head, and ran over the heads or shoulders of many more; but none of them moved or cried out, any more than if it had been a butterfly.

Thursday 25. I had a pleasant ride to Scarborough, the wind tempering the heat of the sun. I had planned to preach outdoors in the evening, but the thunder, lightning, and rain prevented: however, I stood on a balcony, and several hundreds of people stood below: and, notwithstanding the heavy rain, would not stir till I concluded.

A monster called a Declaration

Friday July 3. We returned to York, where I was desired to call upon a poor prisoner in the castle. I had formerly occasion to take notice of a hideous monster called a Chancery bill; I now saw the fellow to it, called a Declaration. The plain fact was this: some time ago a man who lived near Yarm assisted others in smuggling some brandy. His share was about four pounds. After he had wholly left off that bad work, and was following his own business, that of a weaver, he was arrested, and sent to York prison; and, not long after, comes down a Declaration, 'that Jac. W. had landed a vessel laded with brandy and Geneva, at the port of London, and sold them there, whereby he was indebted to His Majesty five hundred and seventy-seven pounds and upwards.' And to tell this worthy story, the lawyer takes up thirteen or fourteen sheets of treble-stamped paper.

O England, England! Will this reproach never be rolled away from you? Is there anything like this to be found, either among papists, Turks, or heathens? In the name of truth, justice, mercy, and common sense, I ask, 1. Why do men lie for lying sake? Is it only to keep their hands in? What need else, of saying it was the port of London, when everyone knew the brandy was landed above three hundred miles from there? 2. Where is the justice of swell-

ing four pounds into five hundred and seventy-seven?
3. Where is the common sense of taking up fourteen
sheets to tell a story that may be told in ten lines? 4. Where
is the mercy of thus grinding the face of the poor, thus
sucking the blood of a poor, beggared prisoner? Would
not this be execrable villainy, if the paper and writing
together were only sixpence a sheet, when they have strip-
ped him already of his little all, and not left him fourteen
groats in the world?

Sunday 5. Believing one hindrance of the work of God
in York was the neglect of field-preaching, I preached this
morning at eight, in an open place near the city walls.
Abundance of people ran together, most of whom were
deeply attentive. One or two only were angry, and threw a
few stones; but it was labour lost; for no one regarded
them.

Sunday 12. I had appointed to be at Haworth; but the
church would not contain the people who came from all
sides: however, Mr Grimshaw had provided for this by
fixing a scaffold on the outside of one of the windows,
through which I went after prayers, and the people likewise all went out into the churchyard. The afternoon congregation was larger still. What has God wrought in the
midst of those rough mountains!

Wesley at Matlock Bath and Boston

Monday 27. I preached at Staincross about eleven; about
five, at Barley Hall; the next morning, at Sheffield. In the
afternoon I rode on to Matlock Bath. The valley which
reaches from the town to the bath is pleasant beyond
expression. In the bottom of this runs a little river, close to
which a mountain rises, almost perpendicular, to an
enormous height, part covered with green, part with ragged and naked rocks. On the other side, the mountain rises
gradually with tufts of trees here and there. The brow on both
sides is fringed with trees, which seem to answer each other.

Many of our friends had come from various parts. At six I preached standing under the hollow of a rock, on one side of a small plain, on the other side of which was a tall mountain. There were many well-dressed hearers, this being the high season; and all of them behaved well. But as I walked back, a gentleman-like man asked me, 'Why do you talk like this of faith? Stuff, nonsense!' Upon inquiry, I found he was an eminent deist. What, has the plague crept into the Peak of Derbyshire?

Preaching at Deptford, Welling, and Sevenoaks, on my way, on *Thursday December 3* I came to Shoreham. There I read the celebrated *Life of St Katherine, of Genoa*. Mr Lesley calls someone 'a devil of a saint': I am sure this was a fool of a saint; that is, if it was not the folly of her historian, who has aggrandised her into a mere idiot. Indeed we seldom find a saint of God's making sainted by the Bishop of Rome.

Preaching by moonlight

1762. Monday January 4. After preaching to a large congregation at Wreslingworth, we rode on to Harston. I never preached a whole sermon by moonlight before. However, it was a solemn time; a season of holy mourning to some; to others, of joy unspeakable.

Monday March 29. I preached about twelve in the new room at Chepstow. One of the congregation was a neighbouring clergyman, who lived on the same staircase with me at Christ Church, and was then far more serious than me. Blessed be God, who has looked upon me at last! Now let me make good use of the time!

Some rough journeys

In the afternoon we had such a storm of hail as I scarcely ever saw in my life. The roads likewise were so extremely bad that we did not reach Hereford till past eight. Having been well battered both by hail, rain, and wind, I got to bed as soon as I could, but was waked many times by the clattering of the curtains. In the morning I found the casement wide open; but I was never the worse. I took horse at six, with William Crane and Francis Walker. The wind was piercing cold, and we had many showers of snow and rain; but the worst was, part of the road was scarcely passable; so that at Church Stretton, one of our horses lay down and would go no further. However, William Crane and I pushed on, and before seven reached Shrewsbury.

A large group quickly gathered together: many of them were wild enough; but the far greater part were calm and attentive, and came again at five in the morning.

Remarkable speaking statue

Monday April 26. In the evening I preached to a large congregation in the market-house at Lurgan. I now embraced the opportunity which I had long desired, of talking with Mr Miller, the contriver of that statue which was in Lurgan when I was there before. It was the figure of an old man, standing in a case, with a curtain drawn before him, over against a clock which stood on the other side of the room. Every time the clock struck, he opened the door with one hand, drew back the curtain with the other, turned his head, as if looking round on the company, and then said with a clear, loud, articulate voice, 'Past one, two, three,' and so on. But so many came to see this (the like of which all agreed was not to be seen in Europe) that Mr Miller was in danger of being ruined, not having time to attend his own business; so, as none offered to purchase it, or to reward him for his pains, he took the whole machine to pieces; nor has he any thought of ever making anything of the kind again.

Monday May 3 (Sligo). In the evening a company of players began acting in the upper part of the market-house, just as we began singing in the lower. The case of these is remarkable. The Presbyterians for a long time had their public worship here; but when the strollers came to town, they were turned out; and from that time had no public worship at all. On Tuesday evening the lower part too was occupied by buyers and sellers of oatmeal; but as soon as I began, the people quitted their sacks, and listened to business of great importance.

Sunday 16. I had observed to the Society last week that I had not seen one congregation ever in Ireland behave so ill at church as that at Athlone, laughing, and staring about during the whole service. I had added, 'This is your fault; for if you had attended the church, as you ought to have done, your presence and example would not have failed to influence the whole congregation.' And so it appeared; I saw not one today either laughing, talking or staring about; but a remarkable seriousness was spread from the one end of the church to the other.

The Irish Whiteboys

Monday June 14. I rode to Cork. Here I procured an exact account of the recent commotions. About the beginning of December last, a few men met by night near Nenagh, in the county of Limerick, and threw down the fences of some commons, which had been recently enclosed. At about the same time the others met in the county of Tipperary, of Waterford, and of Cork. As no one offered to suppress or hinder them, they increased in number continually, and called themselves Whiteboys, wearing white cockades, and white linen frocks. In February, there were five or six parties of them, two or three hundred men in each, who moved up and down, chiefly in the night; but for what end, did not appear. Only they levelled a few fences, dug up some grounds, and hamstrung some cattle, perhaps fifty or sixty in all.

One body of them came into Cloheen, of about five hundred foot, and two hundred horse. They moved as exactly as regular troops, and appeared to be thoroughly disciplined. They now sent letters to several gentlemen, threatening to pull down their houses. They compelled everyone they met to take an oath to be true to Queen Sive (whatever that meant) and the Whiteboys; not to reveal their secrets; and to join them when called upon. It was supposed that eight or ten thousand were now actually risen, many of them well armed; and that a far greater number were ready to rise whenever they should be called upon. Those who refused to swear, they threatened to bury alive. Two or three they did bury up to the neck, and left them; where they would quickly have perished if they had not been found by some people travelling by. At length, toward Easter, a body of troops, chiefly light horse, were sent against them. Many were apprehended and committed to prison; the rest of them disappeared. This is the plain, naked fact, which has been so variously represented.

Whitewashing Kilkenny marble

Saturday July 10. We rode to Kilkenny, one of the pleasantest and the most ancient cities in the kingdom; and not inferior to any at all in wickedness, or in hatred to this way.

Sunday 11. I went to the cathedral, one of the best built which I have seen in Ireland. The pillars are all of black marble; but the late Bishop ordered them to be whitewashed! Indeed, marble is so plentiful near this town that the very streets are paved with it.

Monday 26. In some respects the work of God in Dublin was more remarkable than even that in London. 1. It is far greater, in proportion to the time, and to the number of people. That Society had more than 2,700 members; this not a fifth part of the number. Six months after the flame broke out there, we had about thirty witnesses of the great salvation. In Dublin there were about forty in less than four months. 2. The work was more pure. In all this time, while they were mildly and tenderly treated, there were none of them headstrong or unteachable: in short, no whimsical or enthusiastic persons: all were calm and sober-minded.

Wesley in Cornwall

Friday August 27. I set out for the west; and having preached at Shepton and Middlesey on the way, came on Saturday to Exeter. When I began the service there, the congregation (beside ourselves) were two women and one man. Before I had done, the room was about half full. This comes of omitting field-preaching.

Sunday 29. I preached at eight on Southernay Green, to an extremely quiet congregation. At the cathedral we had a useful sermon, and the whole service was performed with great seriousness and decency. Such an organ I never saw or heard before, so large, beautiful, and so finely toned; and the music of 'Glory be to God in the highest' I think exceeded the *Messiah* itself. I was well pleased to partake of the Lord's supper with my old opponent, Bishop Lavington. O may we sit down together in the kingdom of our Father!

At five I went to Southernay Green again, and found a multitude of people; but a lewd, profane, drunken vagabond had so stirred up many of the baser sort, that there was much noise, commotion and confusion. While I was preaching, several things were thrown, and much pains taken to overturn the table; and after I concluded, many endeavoured to throw me down, but I walked through the midst, and left them.

Saturday September 4. After preaching in Grampound, I rode on to Truro. I almost expected there would be some disturbance, as it was market-day, and I stood in the street at a small distance from the market. But all was quiet. Indeed both persecution and popular tumult seem to be forgotten in Cornwall.

Wednesday 15. The more I converse with the believers in Cornwall, the more I am convinced that they have sustained great loss for want of hearing the doctrine of Christian perfection clearly and strongly enforced. I see, wherever this is not done, the believers grow dead and cold. Nor can this be prevented, but by keeping up in them an hourly expectation of being perfected in love. I say an hourly expectation; for to expect it at death, or some time hence, is much the same as not expecting it at all.

That detestable practice of cheating the king (smuggling) is no more found in our Societies. And since that accursed thing has been put away, the work of God has everywhere increased.

Monday October 25. I preached at one, in the shell of the new house at Shepton Mallet. In digging the foundation they found a quarry of stone, which was more than sufficient for the house.

Thursday 28. Someone who had adorned the gospel in life and in death, having desired that I should preach her funeral sermon, I went with a few friends to the house, and sang before the body to the room. I did this especially to show my approbation of that solemn custom, and to encourage others to follow it. As we walked, our company swiftly increased, so that we had a very numerous congregation at the room. And who can tell, but some of these may bless God from it to all eternity?

Wesley's day of Pentecost

Many years ago my brother frequently said, 'Your day of Pentecost is not fully come; but I do not doubt it will; and you will then hear of persons sanctified, as frequently as you do now of persons justified.' Any unprejudiced reader may observe that it had now fully come. And accordingly we did hear of persons sanctified, in London, and most other parts of England, and in Dublin, and many other parts of Ireland, as frequently as of persons justified;

although instances of the latter were far more frequent than they had been for twenty years before. That many of these did not retain the gift of God, is no proof that it was not given them. That many do retain it to this day, is matter of praise and thanksgiving.

Wesley in Aberdeen again

1763. Sunday May 22 (Edinburgh). I had the satisfaction of spending a little time with Mr Whitefield. Humanly speaking, he is worn out; but we have to do with him who has all power in heaven and earth.

Monday 23. I rode to Forfar, and on *Tuesday 24* rode on to Aberdeen.

Wednesday 25. At seven, the evening being fair and mild, I preached to a multitude of people, in the college close, on 'Stand at the crossroads and look; ask for the ancient paths.' But the next evening, the weather being raw and cold, I preached in the college Hall. What an amazing willingness to hear runs through this whole kingdom! It only needs a few zealous, active labourers, who desire nothing but God; and they might soon carry the gospel through all this country, even as high as the Orkneys.

Plain dealing in Scotland

Sunday 29. I preached at seven in the High School yard, Edinburgh. It being the time of the General Assembly, which drew together not the ministers only, but abundance of the nobility and gentry, many of both sorts were present; but abundantly more at five in the afternoon. I spoke as plainly as ever I did in my life. But I never knew any in Scotland offended at plain dealing. In this respect the North Britons are a pattern to all mankind.

Tuesday June 7. There is something remarkable in the manner in which God revived his work in these parts. A few months ago the generality of people in this circuit were exceedingly lifeless. Samuel Meggot, perceiving this, advised the Society at Barnard Castle to observe every Friday with fasting and prayer. The very first Friday they met together, God broke in upon them in a wonderful manner; and his work has been increasing among them ever since. The neighbouring Societies heard of this, agreed to follow the same rule, and soon experienced the same blessing. Is not the neglect of this plain duty (I mean fasting, ranked by our Lord with almsgiving and prayer) one general occasion of deadness among Christians? Can anyone willingly neglect it, and be guiltless?

The drunkard's Magnificat

Thursday 16. At five in the evening I preached at Dewsbury, and on *Friday 17,* reached Manchester. Here I received a detailed account of a remarkable incident: an eminent drunkard of Congleton used to divert himself, whenever there was preaching there, by standing over against the house, cursing and swearing at the preacher. One evening he had a fancy to step in, and hear what the man had to say. He did so: but it made him so uneasy that he could not sleep all night. In the morning he was more uneasy still; he walked in the fields, but all in vain, till it came in his mind to go to one of his merry companions, who was always ready to abuse the Methodists. He told him how he was, and asked what he should do. 'Do!' said Samuel, 'go and join the Society. I will; for I was never so uneasy in my life.' They did so without delay. But presently David cried out, 'I am sorry I joined; for I shall get drunk again, and they will turn me out.' However, he stood firm for four days; on the fifth, he was persuaded by the old companions to 'take one pint', and then another, and another, till one of them said, 'See, here is a Methodist drunk!'

David started up, and knocked him over, chair and all.

He then drove the rest out of the house, caught up the landlady, carried her out, threw her into the kennel; went back to the house, broke down the door, threw it in the street, and then ran into the fields, tore his hair, and rolled up and down on the ground. In a day or two was a love-feast; he stole in, getting behind, so that no one should see him. While Mr Furze was at prayer, he was seized with a dreadful agony, both of body and mind. This caused many to wrestle with God for him. In a while he sprang up on his feet, stretched out his hands, and cried aloud, 'All my sins are forgiven!' At the same instant, one on the other side of the room cried out, 'Jesus is mine! And he has taken away all my sins.' (This was Samuel H.) David burst through the people, caught him in his arms, and said, 'Come let us sing the Virgin Mary's song; I never could sing it before. "My soul doth magnify the Lord, and my spirit hath rejoiced in God my saviour."' And their following behaviour plainly showed the reality of their profession.

Methodists and their wealth

Saturday September 17 (Bristol). I preached on the green at Bedminster. I am apt to think many of the hearers scarcely ever heard a Methodist before, or perhaps any other preacher. What but field-preaching could reach these poor sinners? And are not their souls also precious in the sight of God?

Sunday 18. I preached in the morning in Princess Street, to a numerous congregation. Two or three gentlemen, so-called, laughed at first; but in a few minutes they were as serious as the rest. On Monday evening I gave our brethren a solemn caution not to 'love the world, neither the things of the world'. This will be their grand danger: as they are industrious and frugal, they must gain more goods. This appears already: in London, Bristol, and most other trading towns, those who are in business have increased in substance seven-fold, some of them twenty, and indeed a hundred-fold. What need, then, have these of the strongest warnings, lest they be entangled in them, and perish!

Friday 23. I preached at Bath. Riding home we saw a coffin being carried into St George's church, with many children attending it. When we came near, we found they were our own children, attending the corpse of one of their school-fellows, who had died of the smallpox; and God thereby touched many of their hearts in a manner they had never known before.

Monday 26. I preached to the prisoners in Newgate, and in the afternoon rode over to Kingswood, where I had a solemn watch-night, and an opportunity of speaking privately to the children. One is dead, two recovered, seven are ill still; and the hearts of all are like melting wax.

Saturday October 1. I returned to London, and found our house in ruins, great part of it being taken down in order to effect a thorough repair. But as much remained as I needed: six foot square suffices me by day or by night.

Thursday December 22. I spent a little time in a visit to Mr M.; twenty years ago a zealous and useful magistrate, now a picture of human nature in disgrace; feeble in body and mind; slow of speech and of understanding. Lord, let me not live to be useless!

1764. Thursday February 16. I once more took a serious walk through the tombs in Westminster Abbey. What heaps of unmeaning stone and marble! But there was one tomb which showed common sense; that beautiful figure of Mr Nightingale endeavouring to screen his lovely wife from Death. Here indeed the marble seems to speak, and the statues appear all but alive.

Friday 24. I returned to London.

Wednesday 29. I heard *Judith*, an oratorio, performed at the Lock. Some parts of it are exceedingly fine; but there are two things in all modern pieces of music, which I could never reconcile to common sense. One is, singing the same words ten times over; the other, singing different words by different persons, at one and the same time. And this, in the most solemn addresses to God, whether by way of prayer or of thanksgiving. This can never be defended by all the musicians in Europe, till reason is quite out of date.

Wesley at Birmingham and Walsall

Wednesday March 21. We had an exceedingly large congregation at Birmingham, in what was formerly the playhouse. Happy would it be if all the playhouses in the kingdom were converted to so good a use.

Monday 26. I was desired to preach at Walsall. James Jones was alarmed at the suggestion, believing there would be much disturbance. However, I decided to try it. Coming into the house, I met with a token for good. A woman was telling her neighbour why she came: 'I had a desire', said she, 'to hear this man; yet I dared not, because I heard so much ill of him; but this morning I dreamed I was praying earnestly, and I heard a voice saying, "See the eighth verse of the first chapter of St John." I woke, and got my Bible, and read, "He himself was not the light; he came only as a witness to the light." I got up, and came away with all my heart.'

The house not being capable of containing the people, about seven I began preaching outside; and there was no opposer, no, nor a trifler to be seen. All present were earnestly attentive. How is Walsall changed! How has God either tamed the wild beasts, or chained them up!

'No law for Methodists'

Saturday 31 (Rotherham). An odd circumstance occurred during the morning preaching. It was well that only reverent persons were present. An ass walked gravely in at the gate, came up to the door of the house, lifted up his head and stood stock-still, in a posture of deep attention. Might not 'the dumb beast reprove' many who have far less decency, and not much more understanding?

Monday April 2. I had a day of rest.

Tuesday 3. I preached about nine at Scotter, a town six or seven miles east of Epworth, where a sudden flame has broken out, many being convinced of sin almost at once, and many justified. But there were many adversaries stirred up by a bad man who told them, 'There is no law for Methodists.' Hence continual riots followed; till, after a while, an upright magistrate took the cause in hand, and so managed both the rioters and him who set them at work, that they have been quiet as lambs ever since.

Thursday 5. About eleven I preached at Elsham. The two persons who are the most zealous and active here are the steward and gardener of a gentleman whom the minister persuaded to turn them off unless they would leave 'this way'. He gave them a week to consider it; at the end of which they calmly answered, 'Sir, we choose rather to lack bread here, than to lack "a drop of water" hereafter.' He replied, 'Then follow your own conscience, so long as you do my business as well as formerly.'

Wesley on Holy Island

Monday May 21. I took my leave of Newcastle; and about noon preached in the market-place at Morpeth. A few of the hearers were a little ludicrous at first; but their mirth was quickly spoiled. In the evening I preached in the court house at Alnwick, where I rested the next day.

Wednesday 23. I rode over the sands to Holy Island, once the famous seat of a bishop; now the residence of a few poor families, who live chiefly by fishing. At one side of the town are the ruins of a cathedral, with an adjoining monastery. It appears to have been a lofty and elegant building, the middle aisle being almost complete. I preached in what was once the market-place, to almost all the inhabitants of the island, and distributed some little books among them, for which they were exceedingly thankful. In the evening I preached at Berwick-upon-Tweed; the next evening at Dunbar; and on *Friday 25*, about ten, at Haddington, in Provost D.'s yard, to a very elegant congregation. But I expect little good will be done here, for we begin at the wrong end: religion must not go from the greatest to the least, or the power would appear to be of men.

Wesley at the General Assembly

Monday 28. I spent some hours at the General Assembly, composed of about a hundred and fifty ministers. I was surprised to find 1. That anyone was admitted, even lads twelve or fourteen years old. 2. That the chief speakers were lawyers, six or seven on one side only. 3. That a single question took up the whole time, which, when I went away, seemed to be as far from a conclusion as ever, namely, 'Shall Mr Lindsay be removed to Kilmarnock parish or not?' The argument for it was, 'He has a large family, and this living is twice as good as his own.' The argument against it was, 'The people are resolved not to hear him, and will leave the kirk if he comes.' If then the real point in view had been, as their law directs, 'the greater good of the church', instead of taking up five hours, the debate might have been determined in five minutes.

On Monday and Tuesday I spoke to the members of the Society separately.

Thursday 31. I rode to Dundee, and, about half an hour after six, preached on the side of a meadow near the town. Poor and rich attended. Indeed, there is seldom fear of lacking a congregation in Scotland. But the misfortune is, they know everything: so they learn nothing.

Monday June 11 (Inverness). After Edinburgh, Glasgow, and Aberdeen, I think Inverness is the largest town I have seen in Scotland. The main streets are broad and straight; the houses mostly old, but not very bad, nor very good. It stands in a pleasant and fruitful country, and has all things needful for life and godliness. The people in general speak remarkably good English, and are of a friendly courteous behaviour.

A sermon and congregation to order

About eleven we took horse. While we were dining at Nairn, the inn-keeper said, 'Sir, the gentlemen of the town have read the little book you gave me on Saturday, and would be glad if you would please to give them a sermon.' Upon my consenting, the bell was immediately rung, and the congregation was quickly in the kirk. O what a difference is there between South and North Britain! Everyone here at least loves to hear the word of God; and none takes it into his head to speak one uncivil word to anybody for endeavouring to save their souls.

Tuesday 12. The whole family at our inn, eleven or twelve in number, gladly joined with us in prayer at night. Indeed, so they did at every inn where we lodged; for among all the sins they have imported from England, the Scots have not yet learned, at least not the common people, to scoff at sacred things.

Wesley and a Scottish communion

Saturday 16. We had a ready passage at Kinghorn, and in the evening I preached on the Calton Hill, to a very large congregation; but a still larger assembled at seven on Sunday morning in the High School yard. Being afterwards informed that the Lord's supper was to be administered in the west kirk, I knew not what to do; but at length I judged it best to embrace the opportunity, though I did not admire the manner of administration. After the usual morning service, the minister enumerated several sorts of sinners, whom he forbade to approach. Two long tables were set on the sides of one aisle, covered with table-cloths. On each side of them a bench was placed for the people.

Each table held thirty-four or thirty-five.

Three ministers sat at the top, behind a cross-table; one of whom made a long exhortation, closed with the words of our Lord; and, then, breaking the bread, gave it to him who sat on each side of him. A piece of bread was then given to him who sat first on each of the four benches. He broke off a little piece, and gave the bread to the next; so it went on, the deacons giving more when wanted. A cup was then given to the first person on each bench, and so by one to another. The minister continued his exhortation all the time they were receiving; then four verses of the twenty-second Psalm were sung, while new persons sat down at the tables. A second minister then prayed, consecrated, and exhorted. I was informed the service usually lasted till five in the evening. How much more simple, as well as more solemn, is the service of the Church of England!

Wesley's likes and dislikes

Monday July 2. I gave a fair hearing to two of our brethren who had proved bankrupts. Such we immediately exclude from our society, unless it plainly appears not to be their own fault. Both these were in a prosperous way till they fell into that wretched trade of bill-broking, wherein no man continues long without being wholly ruined. By this means, not being sufficiently accurate in their accounts, they ran back without being aware of it. Yet it was quite clear that I.R. is an honest man; I would hope the same concerning the other.

Tuesday 3 (Leeds). I was reflecting on an odd circumstance, which I cannot account for. I never relish a tune at first hearing, not till I have almost learned to sing it; and as I learn it more perfectly, I gradually lose my relish for it. I observe something similar in poetry; indeed, in all the objects of the imagination. I seldom relish verses at first hearing; till I have heard them over and over, they give me no pleasure; and they give me next to none when I have heard them a few times more, so as to be quite familiar. Just so a face or a picture, which does not strike me at first, becomes more pleasing as I grow more acquainted with it; but only to a certain point: for when I am too much acquainted, it is no longer pleasing. O how imperfectly do we understand even the machine which we carry about us!

Sunday November 4. I proposed to the leaders, that we should assist the Society for the Reformation of Manners with regard to their heavy debt. One of them asked, 'Ought we not to pay our own debt first?' After some consultation, it was agreed to attempt it. The general debt of the Society in London, occasioned chiefly by repairing the Foundery and chapels, and by building at Wapping and Snowsfields, was about nine hundred pounds. This I laid before the Society in the evening, and desired them all to set their shoulders to the work, either by a present contribution, or by subscribing what they could pay, on the 1st of January, February or March.

Monday 5 (London). My scraps of time this week I employed in setting down my present thoughts upon a single life, which indeed, are just the same they have been these thirty years; and the same they must be, unless I give up my Bible.

Breakfast with Mr Whitefield

1765. Monday October 28. I breakfasted with Mr Whitefield, who seemed to be an old, old man, being fairly worn out in his master's service, though he has hardly seen fifty years, and yet it pleases God that I, who am now in my sixty-third year, find no disorder, no weakness, no decay, no difference from what I was at twenty-five; only that I have fewer teeth, and more grey hairs.

Sunday November 24. I preached on those words in the lesson for the day, 'The Lord our righteousness'. I said not one thing which I have not said at least fifty times within this twelvemonth; yet it appeared to many entirely new, who much importuned me to print my sermon, supposing it would stop the mouths of all gainsayers. Alas for their simplicity! In spite of all I can print, say, or do, will not those who seek occasion of offence find occasion?

1766. Friday January 31. Mr Whitefield called upon me. He breathes nothing but peace and love. Bigotry cannot stand before him, but hides its head wherever he comes.

Wednesday February 5 (London). Someone called upon me who had been cheated out of a large fortune, and was now perishing for want of bread. I had a desire to clothe him, and send him back to his own country; but was short of money. However, I appointed him to call again in an hour. He did so; but before he came, someone from whom I expected nothing less put twenty guineas into my hand; so I ordered him to be clothed from head to foot, and sent him straightaway to Dublin.

An uncouth deed

Thursday April 10. I looked over the wonderful deed which was recently made here; on which I observed, 1. It takes up three large skins of parchment, and so could not cost less than six guineas; whereas our own deed, transcribed by a friend, would not have cost six shillings. 2. It is verbose beyond all sense and reason; and also so ambiguously worded that one passage only might find matter for a suit of ten or twelve years in Chancery. 3. It everywhere calls the house a meeting-house, a name which I particularly object to. 4. It leaves no power either to the assistant or me, so much as to place or displace a steward. 5. Neither I, nor all the Conference, have power to send the same preacher two years together. To crown all, 6. If a preacher is not appointed at the Conference, the trustees and the congregation are to choose one by most votes! And can anyone wonder I dislike this deed, which tears the Methodist discipline up by the roots?

Is it not strange, that any who have the least regard either for me or our discipline, should scruple to alter this uncouth deed?

Sunday 27. As Baildon church would not near contain the congregation, after the prayers were ended I came out into the churchyard, both morning and afternoon. The wind was extremely high, and blew in my face all the time; yet, I believe, all the people could hear. At Bradford there was so huge a multitude, and the rain so damped my voice, that many on the outskirts of the congregation could not hear distinctly. They have just built a preaching-house, fifty-four feet square, the largest octagon we have in England; and it is the first of the kind where the roof is built with common sense, rising only a third of its breadth; yet it is as firm as any in England; nor does it at all hurt the walls. Why then does any roof rise higher? Only through lack of skill, or lack of honesty, in the builder.

Tuesday 29. In the evening I preached near the preaching-house at Paddiham, and strongly insisted on communion with God, as the only religion that would avail us. At the close of the sermon came Mr M. His long, white beard showed that his present disorder was of some continuance. In all other respects, he was quite sensible; but he told me, with much concern, 'You can have no place in heaven without—a beard! Therefore, I beg, let yours grow immediately.'

Wesley secures justice for Methodists

Saturday August 30. We rode to Stallbridge, long the seat of war, by a senseless, insolent mob, encouraged by their betters, so called, to outrage their quiet neighbours. For what? Why, they were mad: they were Methodists. So, to bring them to their senses, they would beat their brains out. They broke their windows, leaving not one whole pane with glass, spoiled their goods, and assaulted their persons with dirt, and rotten eggs, and stones, whenever they appeared in the street. But no magistrate, though they applied to several, would show them either mercy or justice. At length they wrote to me. I ordered a lawyer to write to the rioters. He did so; but they set him at naught. We then moved the Court of King's Bench. By various artifices, they got the trial put off from one assizes to another for eighteen months. But it fell so much the heavier on themselves, when they were found guilty; and from that time, finding there is law for Methodists, they have allowed them to be at peace.

Monday September 1. I came to Plymouth dock, where, after heavy storms, there is now a calm. The house, notwithstanding the new galleries, was extremely crowded in the evening. I strongly exhorted the backsliders to return to God; and I believe many received 'the word of exhortation'.

Tuesday 2. Being invited to preach in the Tabernacle at Plymouth, I began about two in the afternoon. In the evening I was offered the use of Mr Whitefield's room at the dock; but, large as it is, it would not contain the congregation.

Gwennap's famous amphitheatre

Sunday 7. At eight I preached in Mousehole, a large village south-west from Newlyn. Thence I went to Buryan church, and as soon as the service was ended preached near the churchyard to a numerous congregation. Just after I began, I saw a gentleman before me, shaking his whip, and vehemently striving to say something. But he was abundantly too warm to say anything intelligibly. So, after walking a little while to and fro, he wisely took horse, and rode away.

Sunday 14. I preached in St Agnes at eight. The congregation in Redruth, at one, was the largest I ever had seen there; but small compared to that which assembled at five, in the natural amphitheatre at Gwennap; far the finest I know in the kingdom. It is a round, green hollow, gently shelving down, about fifty feet deep; but I suppose it is two hundred across one way, and near three hundred the other. I believe there were full twenty thousand people; and, the evening being calm, all could hear.

Wednesday 17. I twice stopped a violent bleeding from a cut, by applying a briar-leaf. The room at Launceston would not nearly contain the congregation in the evening, to whom I strongly applied the case of the impotent man at the pool of Bethesda. Many were much moved: but, O, how few are willing to be made whole!

Monday November 3. I rode to Brentford from London, where all was quiet both in the congregation and the Society.

Tuesday 4. I preached at Brentford, Battersea, Deptford, and Welling, and examined the different Societies.

Wesley on a country life

Wednesday 5. I rode by Shoreham to Sevenoaks. In the little journeys which I have recently taken, I have thought much on the huge encomiums which have been for many ages bestowed on a country life. But, after all, what a flat contradiction is this to universal experience! See that little house, under the wood, by the riverside! There is rural life in perfection. How happy then is the farmer that lives there? Let us take a detail of his happiness. He rises with, or before, the sun, calls his servants, sees to his pigs and cows, then to his stables and barns. He sees to the ploughing and sowing his ground, in winter or in spring. In summer and autumn he hurries and sweats among his mowers and reapers. And where is his happiness in the meantime? Which of these employments do we envy? Or do we envy the delicate repast that succeeds, which the poet so languishes for? 'O the happiness of eating beans well greased with fat bacon! Nay, and cabbage too!'—Was Horace in his senses when he talked thus, or the servile herd of his imitators? Our eyes and ears may convince us there is not a less happy body of men in all England than the country farmers. In general their life is supremely dull; and it is usually unhappy too. For of all people in the kingdom they are most discontented; seldom satisfied either with God or man.

Wesley and *The Character of a Methodist*

1767. Thursday March 5. I at last obliged Dr D. by entering the lists with him. The letter I wrote (though not published till two or three weeks after) was as follows:

To the Editor of Lloyd's Evening Post

Sir,—Many times the publisher of the *Christian Magazine* has attacked me without fear or wit. The occasion of his late attack is this: thirty-five or thirty-six years ago, I much admired the character of a perfect Christian drawn by Clemens Alexandrinus. Twenty-five or twenty-six years ago, a thought came into my mind, of drawing such a character myself, only in a more scriptural manner, and mostly in the very words of scripture: this I entitled, *The Character of a Methodist,* believing that curiosity would incite more persons to read it, and also that some prejudice might thereby be removed from candid men. But that none might imagine I intended a panegyric either on myself or my friends, I guarded against this in the very title-page, saying, both in the name of myself and them, 'Not as though I had already attained, either were already perfect.' To the same effect I speak in the conclusion, 'These are the same principles and practices of our sect; these are the marks of a true Methodist'; that is, a true Christian, as I immediately after explain myself: 'by these alone do those who are in derision so called desire to be distinguished from other men' (p.11). 'By these marks do we labour to distinguish ourselves from those whose minds or lives are not according to the gospel of Christ' (p.12).

Upon this Rusticulus, or Dr Dodd, says, 'A Methodist, according to Mr Wesley, is one who is perfect, and sinneth not in thought, word, or deed.'

Sir, have me excused. This is not 'according to Mr Wesley'. I have told all the world I am not perfect; and yet you admit I am a Methodist. I tell you flat, I have not attained the character I draw. Will you pin it upon me in spite of my teeth?

'But Mr Wesley says, the other Methodists have.' I say no such thing. What I say, after having given a scriptural account of a perfect Christian, is this: 'By these marks the Methodists desire to be distinguished from other men; by these we labour to distinguish ourselves.' And do you not yourself desire and labour after the very same thing?

But you insist, 'Mr Wesley affirms the Methodists' (that is, all Methodists) 'to be perfectly holy and righteous.' Where do I affirm this? Not in the tract before us. In the front of this I affirm just the contrary; and that I affirm it anywhere else is more than I know. Be pleased, sir, to point out the place: till this is done, all you add (bitterly enough) is mere noise; and the Methodists (so called) may still declare (without any impeachment of their sincerity), that they do not come to the holy table 'trusting in their own righteousness, but in God's manifold and great mercies.'

Friday September 25. I was desired to preach at Freshford; but the people dared not come to the house, because of the smallpox, of which Joseph Allen, 'an Israelite indeed', had died the day before. So they placed a table near the churchyard. But I had no sooner begun to speak than the bells began to ring, organised by a neighbouring gentleman. However, it was labour lost; for my voice prevailed, and the people heard me distinctly: indeed, an extremely deaf person who had not been able to hear a sermon for several years told his neighbours, with great joy, that he had heard and understood all, from the beginning to the end.

Monday November 23. I went to Canterbury. Here I met with the *Life of Mahomet*, written, I suppose, by the Count de Boulanvilliers. Whoever the author is, he is a very pert, shallow, self-conceited coxcomb, remarkable for nothing but his immense assurance and thorough contempt of Christianity. And the book is a dull, ill-digested romance, supported by no authorities at all; whereas Dean Prideaux (a writer of ten times his sense) cites his authorities for everything he advances.

Sunday December 13. Today I found a little soreness on the edge of my tongue, which the next day spread to my gums, then to my lips, which inflamed, swelled, and, the skin bursting, bled considerably. Afterward, the roof of my mouth was extremely sore, so that I could chew nothing. To this was added a continual spitting. I knew a little rest would cure all. But this was not to be had; for I had appointed to be at Sheerness on Wednesday, the 16th. Accordingly, I took horse between five and six, and got there between five and six in the evening.

Queer houses at Sheerness

At half an hour after six, I began reading prayers (the governor of the fort having given me the use of the chapel), and afterwards preached, though not without difficulty, to a large and serious congregation.

Such a town as many of these live in is scarcely to be found again in England. In the dock adjoining the fort there are six old men-of-war. These are divided into small tenements, forty, fifty, or sixty in a ship, with little chimneys and windows; and each of these contains a family. In one of them, where we called, a man and his wife and six little children lived. And yet all the ship was sweet and tolerably clean; sweeter than most sailing ships I have been in.

Saturday 19. I returned to London.

1768. Monday January 4. At my leisure hours this week, I read Dr Priestley's ingenious book on electricity. He seems to have accurately collected and well digested all that is known on that curious subject. But how little is that all! Indeed the use of it we know; at least, in some good degree. We know it is a thousand medicines in one: in particular, that it is the most efficacious medicine in nervous disorders of every kind, which has ever yet been discovered. But if we aim at theory, we know nothing.

Monday 11. This week I spent my scraps of time in reading Mr Wodrow's *History of the Sufferings of the Church of Scotland*. It would transcend belief, only the evidence is too authentic to admit of any doubt. Oh what a blessed governor was that good-natured man, so called, King Charles the Second! Bloody Queen Mary was a lamb, a mere dove, in comparison of him!

Wesley travels north

Monday March 14. I set out on my northern journey, and preached at Stroud in the evening.

Saturday 19. We rode to Birmingham. The tumults which subsisted here so many years are now wholly suppressed by a resolute magistrate. After preaching, I was pleased to see a venerable monument of antiquity, George Bridgins, in the one hundred and seventh year of his age. He can still walk to the preaching, and retains his senses and understanding tolerably well. But what a dream will even a life of a hundred years appear to him the moment he awakes in eternity!

Wednesday 30. I rode to a little town called New Mills, in the High Peak of Derbyshire. I preached at noon in their large new chapel, which (in consideration that preaching-houses have need of air) has a casement in every window, three inches square! That is the custom of the country!

Wesley instructs parents

In the evening and the following morning I brought strange things to the ears of many in Manchester, concerning the government of their families, and the education of their children. But some still made that very silly answer, 'Oh, he has no children of his own!' Neither had St Paul, nor (that we know of) any of the apostles. What then? Were they therefore unable to instruct parents? Not so. They were able to instruct everyone that had a soul to be saved.

Tuesday April 26. I came to Aberdeen.

Here I found a Society truly alive, knit together in peace and love. The congregations were large both morning and evening, and, as usual, deeply attentive. But a company of strolling players, who have at length found place here also, stole away the gay part of the hearers. Poor Scotland! Poor Aberdeen! This only was lacking to make them as completely irreligious as England.

Wesley at Scoon and Holyrood

Monday May 2. I set out early from Aberdeen, and about noon preached in Brechin. After the sermon, the provost desired to see me, and said, 'Sir, my son had epileptic fits from his infancy: Dr Ogylvie prescribed for him many times, and at length told me he could do no more. I desired Mr Blair last Monday to speak to you. On Tuesday morning my son said to his mother, he had just been dreaming that his fits were gone and he was perfectly well. Soon after I gave him the drops you advised: he is perfectly well, and has not had one fit since.'

Thursday 5. We rode through the pleasant and fruitful Carse of Gowry, a plain fifteen or sixteen miles long, between the river Tay and the mountains, very thickly inhabited, to Perth. In the afternoon we walked over to the royal palace at Scoon. It is a large old house, delightfully situated, but swiftly running to ruin. Yet there are a few good pictures, and some fine tapestry left, in what they call the Queen's and the King's chambers. And what is far more curious, there is a bed and a set of hangings in the (once) royal apartments, which was wrought by poor Queen Mary, while she was imprisoned in the Castle of Lochlevin. It is some of the finest needlework I ever saw, and plainly shows both her exquisite skill and unwearied industry.

Saturday 14. I walked once more through Holyrood House, a noble pile of building; but the greatest part of it left to itself, and so (like the palace at Scone) swiftly running to ruin. The tapestry is dirty, and quite faded; the fine ceilings dropping down; and many of the pictures in the gallery torn or cut through. This was the work of good General Hawley's soldiers (like General, like men!), who, after running away from the Scots at Falkirk, revenged themselves on the harmless canvas!

Wesley's wife ill

Sunday August 14. Hearing my wife was dangerously ill, I took chaise immediately and reached the Foundery before one in the morning. Finding the fever was turned, and the danger over, about two I set out again, and in the afternoon came (not at all tired) to Bristol.

Wednesday September 7 (Penzance). After the early preaching, the select society met; such a company of lively believers, full of faith and love, as I never found in this county before. This, and the three following days, I preached at as many places as I could, though I was at first in doubt whether I could preach eight days together, mostly in the open air, three or four times a day. But my strength was equal to my work: I hardly felt any weariness, first or last.

Sunday 11. About nine I preached at St Agnes, and again between one and two. At first I took my old stand at Gwennap, in the natural amphitheatre. I suppose no human voice could have commanded such an audience on plain ground; but the ground rising all round me gave me such an advantage that I believe all could hear distinctly.

Friday 16. I rode, through heavy rain, to Polperro. Here the room over which we were to lodge being filled with pilchards and conger-eels, the perfume was too potent for me; so that I was not sorry when one of our friends invited me to lodge at her house. Soon after I began to preach, heavy rain began; yet none went away till the whole service was ended.

Sunday 18. Our room at the dock contained the morning congregation tolerably well. Between one and two I began preaching on the quay in Plymouth. Notwithstanding the rain, abundance of people stood to hear. But one silly man talked without ceasing, till I desired the people to open to the right and left, and let me look him in the face. They did so. He pulled off his hat, and quietly went away.

Wesley and seaport towns

Wednesday November 30. I rode to Dover, and came in just before a violent storm began. It did not hinder the people. Many were obliged to go away after the house was filled. What a desire to hear runs through all the seaport towns wherever we come! Surely God is besieging this nation, and attacking it at all the entrances!

Wednesday December 14. I saw the Westminster scholars act the *Adelphi* of Terence, an entertainment not unworthy of a Christian. O how do these heathens shame us! Their very comedies contain both excellent sense, the liveliest pictures of men and manner, and so fine stories of genuine morality, as are seldom found in the writings of Christians.

1769. Monday January 9. I spent a comfortable and profitable hour with Mr Whitefield, in calling to mind the former times, and the manner wherein God prepared us for a work which it had not then entered into our hearts to conceive.

Friday February 17 (Yarmouth). I abridged Dr Watts's pretty *Treatise on the Passions.* His hundred and seventy-seven pages will make a useful tract of twenty-four. Why do persons who treat the same subjects with me, write so much larger books? Of many reasons, is not this the chief—we do not write with the same view? Their principal end is to get money; my only one, to do good.

Monday 27 (London). I had one more agreeable conversation with my old friend and fellow labourer, George Whitefield. His soul appeared to be vigorous still, but his body was sinking apace; and unless God interposes, he must soon finish his labours.

Wesley's land-shark

Thursday March 30 (Dublin). I was summoned to the Court of Conscience by a poor creature who fed my horses three or four times while I was on board. For this service he demanded ten shillings. I gave him half a crown. When I informed the Court of this, he was sharply reproved. Let all beware of these land-sharks on our sea-coasts!

Wesley opens a new church

Wednesday April 19 (Armagh). We took horse about ten, being desired to call at Kinnard (ten or eleven miles out of the way), where a little Society had recently been formed, who were much alive to God. At the town end, I was met by a messenger from Archdeacon C., who desired I would take a bed with him; and soon after by another, who told me the Archdeacon desired I would alight at his door. I did so; and found an old friend whom I had not seen for thirty-four or thirty-five years.

A forsaken beauty

Thursday May 25. I rode to Bandon. In the evening we were obliged to be in the house; but the next, *Friday 26*, I stood in the main street, and cried to a numerous congregation, 'Fear God, and keep his commandments; for this is the whole of man.' Afterwards I visited someone that a year or two ago was in high life, an eminent beauty, adored by her husband, admired and caressed by some of the first men in the nation. She was now without husband, without friend, without fortune, confined to her bed, in constant pain, and in black despair, believing herself forsaken of God, and possessed by a legion of devils! Yet I found great liberty in praying for her, and a strong hope that she will die in peace.

Tuesday June 27. [From a letter 'to a pious and sensible woman']

By Christian perfection, I mean, 1. Loving God with all our heart. Do you object to this? I mean, 2. A heart and life all devoted to God. Do you desire less? I mean, 3. Regaining the whole image of God. What objection to this? I mean, 4. Having all the mind that was in Christ. Is this going too far? I mean, 5. Walking uniformly as Christ walked. And this surely no Christian will object to. If anyone means anything more or anything else by perfection, I have no concern with it. But if this is wrong, yet what need of this heat about it, this violence, I almost said fury of opposition, carried so far as even not to lay out anything with this man, or that woman, who professes it?

Sunday July 30. At five I preached at Leeds; and on *Monday 31* prepared all things for the ensuing Conference. *Tuesday August 1* it began; and a more loving one we never had. On Thursday I mentioned the case of our brethren in New York, who had built the first Methodist preaching-house in America, and were in great want of money and much more of preachers. Two of our preachers, Richard Boardman and Joseph Pillmoor, willingly offered themselves for the service; by whom we decided to send them fifty pounds, as a token of our brotherly love.

Wesley at the Countess of Huntingdon's

Wednesday August 23. I went on to Trevecca. Here we found a concourse of people from all parts, come to celebrate the Countess of Huntingdon's birthday, and the anniversary of her school, which was opened on the twenty-fourth of August last year. I preached in the evening, to as many as her chapel could well contain; which is extremely neat, or rather, elegant; as is the dining-room, the school, and all the house. About nine Howell Harris desired me to give a short exhortation to his family. I did so; and then went back to my Lady's and lay down in peace.

Thursday 24. I administered the Lord's supper to the family. At ten the public service began. Mr Fletcher preached an exceedingly lively sermon in the courtyard, the chapel being far too small. After him, Mr William Williams preached in Welsh, till between one and two o'clock. At two we dined. Meantime, a large number of people had baskets of bread and meat carried to them in the court. At three I took my turn there, then Mr Fletcher, and, about five, the congregation was dismissed. Between seven and eight the love-feast began, at which I believe many were comforted. In the evening several of us retired into the neighbouring wood, which is exceedingly pleasantly laid out in walks; one of which leads to a little mount, raised in the midst of a meadow, that commands a delightful view. This is Howell Harris's work, who has likewise greatly enlarged and beautified his house; so that, with the gardens, orchards, walks, and pieces of water that surround it, it is a kind of little paradise.

The gentleman with rotten eggs

Friday September 8. I preached about nine at Taunton, and then rode on to Bridgewater.

Tuesday 19. Between twelve and one, I preached at Freshford; and on White's Hill, near Bradford, in the evening. By this means many had an opportunity of hearing, who would not have come to the room. I had planned to preach there again the next evening; but a gentleman in the town desired me to preach at his door. The beasts of the people were tolerably quiet till I had nearly finished my sermon. They then lifted up their voice, especially one, called a gentleman, who had filled his pocket with rotten eggs: but, a young man coming unawares, clapped his hands on each side, and mashed them all at once. In an instant he was perfume all over; though it was not so sweet as balsam.

Wesley on Rousseau

Tuesday December 26. I read the letters from our preachers in America, informing us that God had begun a glorious work there; that both in New York and Philadelphia multitudes flock to hear, and behave with the deepest seriousness; and that the Society in each place already contains more than a hundred members.

1770. Monday January 1. About eighteen hundred of us met together; it was a most solemn time. As we did openly 'acknowledge the Lord to be our God, so did he acknowledge us to be his people'.

Saturday February 3 and at my leisure moments on several of the following days, I read with much expectation a celebrated book—Rousseau *On Education.* But how was I disappointed! Sure a more consummate coxcomb never saw the sun! How amazingly full of himself! Whatever he speaks, he pronounces as an oracle. But many of his oracles are as palpably false as that 'young children never love old people'. No! Do they never love grandfathers and grandmothers? Frequently more than they do their own parents. Indeed, they love all that love them, and that with more warmth and sincerity than when they come to riper years.

But I object to his temper, more than to his judgement: he is a mere misanthrope; a cynic all over. So indeed is his brother infidel, Voltaire; and well nigh as great a coxcomb. But he hides both his doggedness and vanity a little better; whereas here it stares us in the face continually.

As to his book, it is whimsical to the last degree, grounded neither upon reason nor experience. To cite particular passages would be endless; but anyone may observe concerning the whole, the advices which are good are trite and common, only disguised under new expressions. And those which are new, which are really his own, are lighter than vanity itself. Such discoveries I always expect from those who are too wise to believe their Bibles.

Swedenborg an entertaining madman

Wednesday 28. I sat down to read and seriously consider some of the writing of Baron Swedenborg. I began with huge prejudices in his favour, knowing him to be a pious man, one of a strong understanding, of much learning, and one who thoroughly believed himself. But I could not hold out long. Any one of his visions puts his real character out of doubt. He is one of the most ingenious, lively, entertaining madmen that ever set pen to paper. But his waking dreams are so wild, so far remote both from scripture and common sense, that one might as easily swallow the stories of Tom Thumb or Jack the Giant-Killer.

Wesley and his horses

Wednesday March 21. In the following days I went on slowly, through Staffordshire and Cheshire, to Manchester. In this journey, as well as in many others, I observed a mistake that almost universally prevails; and I desire all travellers to take good notice of it, which may save them both from trouble and danger. About thirty years ago, I was thinking, 'How is it that no horse ever stumbles while I am reading?' (History, poetry, and philosophy I commonly read on horseback, having other employment at other times.) No account can possibly be given but this: because I then throw the reins on his neck. I then set myself to observe; and I aver, that in riding more than a hundred thousand miles, I scarcely ever remember any horse (except two, that would fall head over heels anyway) to fall, or make a considerable stumble while I rode with a slack rein. To fancy, therefore, that a tight rein prevents stumbling is a capital blunder. I have repeated the trial more frequently than most men in the kingdom can do. A slack rein will prevent stumbling if anything will. But in some horses nothing can.

Wesley and the turnpikes

Friday June 15. I was agreeably surprised to find the whole road from Thirsk to Stokesley, which used to be extremely bad, better than most turnpikes. The gentlemen had exerted themselves, and raised money enough to mend it effectually. So they have done for several hundred miles in Scotland, and throughout all Connaught in Ireland; and so they undoubtedly might do throughout all England, without saddling the poor people with the vile imposition of turnpikes for ever.

In the afternoon we came to Whitby. Having preached three times a day for five days, I was willing to preach in the house; but notice had been given of my preaching in the market-place; so I began at six, to a large congregation most of them deeply attentive.

Sunday 17. We had a poor sermon at church. However, I went again in the afternoon, remembering the words of Mr Philip Henry, 'If the preacher does not know his duty, I bless God that I know mine.'

Thursday 28. I can hardly believe that today I enter into my sixty-eighth year. How marvellous are the ways of God! How he has kept me even from a child! From ten to thirteen or fourteen, I had little but bread to eat, and not great plenty of that. I believe this was so far from hurting me, that it laid the foundation of lasting health. When I grew up, in consequence of reading Dr Cheyne, I chose to eat sparingly, and drink water. This was another great means of continuing my health, till I was about twenty-seven. I then began spitting of blood, which continued several years. A warm climate cured this. I was afterwards brought to the brink of death by a fever; but it left me healthier than before. Eleven years after, I was in the third stage of a consumption; in three months it pleased God to remove this also. Since that time I have known neither pain nor sickness, and am now healthier than I was forty years ago. God has done this!

Congregation of 20,000

Sunday September 2. At five in the evening I preached in the natural amphitheatre at Gwennap. The people covered a circle of about eighty yards diameter, and could not be fewer than twenty thousand. Yet, upon enquiry, I found they could all hear distinctly, it being a calm, still evening.

Wesley preaches Whitefield's funeral sermon

Saturday November 10. I returned to London, and had the melancholy news of Mr Whitefield's death confirmed by his executors, who desired me to preach his funeral sermon on Sunday, the 18th. In order to write this, I retired to Lewisham on Monday; and on Sunday following, went to the chapel in Tottenham Court Road. An immense multitude was gathered together from all corners of the town. I was at first afraid that a great part of the congregation would not be able to hear; but it pleased God so to strengthen my voice that even those at the door heard distinctly. It was an awe-inspiring time: everyone was as still as night; most appeared to be deeply affected; and an impression was made on many which one would hope will not speedily be effaced.

The time appointed for my beginning at the Tabernacle was half-hour after five; but it was quite filled at three, so I began at four. At first the noise was exceedingly great; but it ceased when I began to speak; and my voice was again so strengthened that all who were within could hear, unless an accidental noise hindered here or there for a few moments. O that all may hear the voice of him with whom are the issues of life and death; and who so loudly, by this unexpected stroke, calls all his children to love one another!

Friday 23. Being desired by the trustees of the tabernacle at Greenwich to preach Mr Whitefield's funeral sermon there, I went over today for that purpose; but neither would this house contain the congregation. Those who could not get in made some noise at first, but in a little while all were silent. Here, likewise, I trust God has given a blow to that bigotry which had prevailed for many years.

1771. Wednesday January 2. I preached in the evening, at Deptford, a kind of funeral sermon for Mr Whitefield. In every place I wish to show all possible respect to the memory of that great and good man.

Wesley's wife leaves him

Wednesday 23. For what cause I know not to this day, my wife set out for Newcastle, intending 'never to return'. 'I did not desert her: I did not send her away: I will not recall her.'

Friday 25. I revised and transcribed my will, declaring as simply, as plainly, and as briefly as I could, nothing more nor anything else but 'what I would have done with the worldly goods which I leave behind me'.

Monday December 23 and so all the following days, when I was not particularly engaged, I spent an hour in the morning with our preachers, as I used to do with my pupils at Oxford.

Monday 30. At my brother's request, I sat again for my picture. This melancholy employment always reminds me of that natural reflection—

> Behold, what frailty we in man may see!
> His shadow is less given to change than he.

1772. Tuesday January 14. I spent an agreeable hour with Dr S., the oldest acquaintance I now have. He is the greatest genius in little things that ever fell under my notice. Almost everything about him is of his own invention, either in whole or in part. Even his fire-screen, his lamps of various sorts, his ink-horn, his very save-all. I really believe, were he seriously to set about it, he could invent the best mouse-trap that ever was in the world.

Wesley as art critic

Thursday 16. I set out for London. The snow lay so deep on the road that it was not without much difficulty, and some danger, we at last reached the town. I was offered the use of the church: the frost was exceedingly sharp, and the glass was taken out of the windows. However, for the sake of the people, I accepted the offer, though I might just as well have preached in the open air. I suppose four times as many people were present as would have been at the room; and about a hundred in the morning. So I did not repent of my journey through the snow.

Friday February 7. I called on a friend at Hampton Court, who went with me through the house. It struck me more than anything of the kind I have seen in England, more than Blenheim House itself. One great difference is, everything there appears designedly grand and splendid; here everything is quite, as it were, natural, and one thinks it cannot be otherwise. If the expression may be allowed, there is a kind of stiffness runs through the one, and an easiness through the other. Of pictures I do not pretend to be a judge; but there is one by Paul Rubens which particularly struck me, both with the design and the execution of it. It is Zacharias and Elizabeth, with John the Baptist, two or three years old, coming to visit Mary, and our Lord sitting upon her knee. The passions are surprisingly expressed, even in the children; but I could not see either the decency or common sense of painting them stark naked: nothing can defend or excuse this: it is shockingly absurd, even an Indian being the judge. I allow, a man who paints thus may have a good hand, but certainly no brains.

Wesley on *A Sentimental Journey*

Tuesday 11. I casually took a volume of what is called *A Sentimental Journey through France and Italy*. Sentimental— what is that? It is not English: he might as well say 'continental'. It is not sense. It conveys no determinate idea; yet one fool makes many. And this nonsensical word (who would believe it?) is become a fashionable one! However, the book agrees full well with its title; for one is as queer as the other. For oddity, uncouthness, and unlikeness to all the world beside, I suppose, the writer is without a rival.

Wednesday 12. On my way back, I read a very different book, published by an honest Quaker, on that execrable sum of all villainies, commonly called the slave trade. I read of nothing like it in the heathen world, whether ancient or modern: and it infinitely exceeds, in every instance of barbarity, whatever Christian slaves suffer in Muhammadan countries.

Friday 14. I began to execute a plan which had long been in my thoughts, to print as accurate an edition of my works as a bookseller would do. Surely I ought to be as exact for God's sake as he would be for money.

Wesley and the boarding school

Friday 21. I met several of my friends who had begun a subscription to prevent my riding on horseback; which I cannot do quite so well since a hurt which I got some months ago. If they continue it, well; if not, I shall have strength according to my need.

Monday April 6 (Manchester). In the afternoon I drank tea at Am. O. But how was I shocked! The children that used to cling about me, and drink in every word, had been at a boarding school. There they had unlearned all religion, and even seriousness; and had learned pride, vanity, affectation, and whatever should guard them against the knowledge and love of God. Methodist parents, who would send your girls headlong to hell, send them to a fashionable boarding school!

Wednesday 15. Though it was a lone house, we had a large congregation at five in the morning. Afterwards we rode for upwards of twenty miles, through a most delightful country; the fruitful mountains rising on either hand, and the clear stream running beneath. In the afternoon we had a furious storm of rain and snow: however, we reached Selkirk safe. Here I observed a little piece of stateliness which was quite new to me: the maid came in and said, 'Sir, the lord of the stable waits to know if he should feed your horses.' We call him ostler in England. After supper all the family seemed glad to join with us in prayer.

Thursday 16. We went on through the mountains covered with snow, to Edinburgh.

Wesley at Greenock and Glasgow

Saturday 18. I set out for Glasgow. One would rather have imagined it was the middle of January than the middle of April. The snow covered the mountains on either hand, and the frost was exceedingly sharp; so I preached indoors, both this evening and on Sunday morning. But in the evening the multitude constrained me to stand in the street. My text was: 'Do not call anything impure that God has made clean.' From this I took occasion to fall upon their miserable bigotry for opinions and modes of worship. Many seemed to be not a little convinced; but how long will the impression continue?

Monday 20. I went on to Greenock, a seaport town twenty miles west of Glasgow. It is built very much like

Plymouth dock, and has a safe and spacious harbour. The trade and inhabitants, and consequently the houses, are increasing swiftly; and so is cursing, swearing, drunkenness, sabbath-breaking, and all manner of wickedness. Our room is about three times as large as that at Glasgow; but it would not nearly contain the congregation. I spoke exceedingly plainly, and not without hope that we may see some fruit, even among this hardhearted generation.

Tuesday 21. The house was very full in the morning; and they showed an excellent spirit; for after I had spoken a few words on the subject, everyone stood up at the singing. In the afternoon I preached at Port Glasgow, a large town two miles east of Greenock. Many gay people were there, careless enough; but the greater part seemed to hear with understanding. In the evening I preached at Greenock; and God gave them a loud call, whether they will hear or whether they will forbear.

Wednesday 22. About eight I preached once more in the Masons' Lodge at Port Glasgow. The house was crowded greatly; and I suppose all the gentry of the town were part of the congregation. Resolving not to shoot over their heads, as I had done the day before, I spoke strongly of death and judgement, heaven and hell. This they seemed to comprehend; and there was no more laughing among them, or talking with each other; but all were quietly and deeply attentive.

In the evening, when I began at Glasgow, the congregation being but small, I chose a subject fit for experienced Christians; but soon after, a heap of fine gay people came in: yet I could not decently break off what I was about, though they gaped and stared abundantly. I could only give a short exhortation in the close, more suited to their capacity.

Tuesday 28 (Dunkeld). We walked through the Duke of Atholl's gardens, in which was one thing I never saw before—a summerhouse in the middle of a greenhouse, by means of which one might in the depth of winter enjoy the warmth of May, and sit surrounded with greens and flowers on every side.

Sunday May 3 (Aberdeen). I went in the morning to the English church. Here, likewise, I could not but admire the exemplary decency of the congregation. This was the more remarkable because so miserable a reader I never heard before. Listening with all attention, I understood but one single word, Balak, in the first lesson; and one more, begat, was all I could possibly distinguish in the second. Is there no man of spirit belonging to this congregation? Why is such a burlesque upon public worship suffered? Would it not be far better to pay this gentleman for doing nothing, than for doing mischief; for bringing a scandal upon religion?

Saturday 23. I went on to Alnwick, and preached in the town hall. What a difference between an English and a Scottish congregation! These judge themselves rather than the preacher; and their aim is not only to know but to love and obey.

Field-preaching as Wesley's cross

Sunday September 6. I preached on the quay at Kingswood, and near King's Square. To this day field-preaching is a cross to me. But I know my commission, and see no other way of 'preaching the gospel to every creature'.

Wednesday October 14. A book was given me to write on, *The Works of Mr Thomson*, of whose poetical abilities I had always had a very low opinion; but looking into one of his tragedies, 'Edward and Eleonora', I was agreeably surprised. The sentiments are just and noble; the diction strong, smooth, and elegant; and the plot conducted with the utmost art, and wrought off in a most surprising manner. It is quite his masterpiece, and I really think might vie with any modern performances of the kind.

Wednesday December 2. I preached at the new preaching-house in the parish of Bromley. In speaking separately to the members of the Society, I was surprised at the openness and artlessness of the people. Such I should never have expected to find within ten miles of London.

Wesley's letters and friends

1773. Friday January 1. We (as usual) solemnly renewed our covenant with God.

Monday 4. I began revising my letters and papers. One of them was written more than a hundred and fifty years ago (in 1619), I suppose by my grandfather's father, to the person he was to marry in a few days. Several were written by my brothers and me when at school, many while we were at the university; abundantly testifying (if it be worth knowing) what was our aim from our youth up.

Incidents in Ireland

Wednesday 21. Some applied to the Quakers at Enniscorthy, for the use of their meeting-house. They refused: so I stood at Hugh M'Laughlin's door, and both those within and without could hear.

Thursday May 13. We went on, through a most dreary country, to Galway; where, at the recent survey, there were twenty thousand papists, and five hundred Protestants. But which of them are Christians, have the mind that was in Christ, and walk as he walked? And without this, how little does it avail whether they are called Protestants or papists! At six I preached in the court-house, to a large congregation who all behaved well.

A neglected school

Friday 14. In the evening I preached at Ballinrobe; and on Saturday went on to Castlebar. Entering the town, I was struck with the sight of the Charter school—no gate to the courtyard, a large chasm in the wall, heaps of rubbish before the house door, broken windows in abundance; the whole a picture of slothfulness, nastiness, and desolation!

I did not dream there were any inhabitants till the next day I saw about forty boys and girls walking from church. As I was just behind them, I could not but observe: 1. that there was neither master nor mistress, though it seems they were both well; 2. that both boys and girls were completely dirty; 3. that none of them seemed to have any garters on, their stockings hanging about their heels; 4. that in the heels, even of many of the girls' stockings, were holes larger than a crown-piece. I gave a plain account of these things to the trustees of the Charter school in Dublin; whether they are altered or no, I cannot tell.

Monday June 14. After preaching at Lurgan, I enquired of Mr Miller whether he had any thoughts of perfecting his speaking statue, which had so long lain by. He said he had altered his design; that he intended, if he had life and health, to make two, which would not only speak, but sing hymns alternately with an articulate voice; that he had made a trial, and it worked well. But he could not tell when he should finish it, as he had much business of other kinds, and could only give his leisure hours to this. How amazing is it that no man of fortune enables him to give all his time to the work!

I preached in the evening at Lisburn. All the time I could spare here was taken up by poor patients. I generally asked, 'What remedies have you used?' and was not a little surprised. What has fashion to do with physic? Why (in Ireland at least), almost as much as with head-dress. Blisters, for anything or nothing, were all the fashion when I was in Ireland last. Now the grand fashionable medicine for twenty diseases (who would imagine it?) is mercury sublimate! Why is it not a halter, or a pistol? They would cure a little more speedily.

Tuesday 15. When I came to Belfast, I learned the real cause of the recent insurrections in this neighbourhood. Lord Donegal, the proprietor of almost the whole country, came here to give his tenants new leases. But when they came, they found two merchants of the town had taken their farms over their heads; so that multitudes of them, with their wives and children, were turned out to the wide world. It is no wonder that, as their lives were now bitter to them, they should fly out as they did. It is rather a wonder that they did not go much farther. And if they had, who would have been most at fault? Those who were without home, without money, without food for themselves and families? Or those who drove them to this extremity?

The earthquake at Madeley

Monday July 15. About eleven we crossed the Dublin bar, and were at Hoylake the next afternoon. This was the first night I ever lay awake in my life, though I was at ease in body and mind. I believe few can say this: in seventy years I never lost one night's sleep!

I went, by moderate stages, from Liverpool to Madeley, where I arrived on *Friday August 9.* The next morning we went to see the effects of the recent earthquake: such it undoubtedly was. On Monday 27 at four in the morning, a rumbling noise was heard, accompanied with sudden gusts of wind, and wavings of the ground. Presently the earthquake followed, which not only shook the farmer's house and removed it, whole, about a yard; but carried the barn about fifteen yards, and then swallowed it up in a vast chasm; tore the ground into numberless chasms, large and small; in the large, threw up mounts fifteen or twenty feet high; carried a hedge with two oaks more than forty feet and left them in their natural position. It then moved under the bed of a river; which, making more resistance, received a ruder shock, being shattered in pieces, and heaved up about thirty feet from its foundations. By throwing this and many oaks into its channel, the Severn was quite stopped up, and constrained to flow backward till, with incredible fury, it wrought itself a new channel.

Such a scene of desolation I never saw. Will no one tremble when God thus terribly shakes the earth?

A man of seventy preaches to 30,000 people

Saturday 21. I preached in Illogan and at Redruth; *Sunday 22,* in St Agnes churchtown, at eight; about one at Redruth; and at five, in the amphitheatre at Gwennap. The people both filled it, and covered the ground round about, to a considerable distance, so that, supposing the space to be eighty yards square, and to contain five persons in a square yard, there must be more than thirty-two thousand people; the largest assembly I ever preached to. Yet I found, upon enquiry, all could hear, even to the outskirts of the congregations! Perhaps the first time that a man of seventy had been heard by thirty thousand persons at once!

1774. Friday May 20. I rode over to Mr Fraser's, at Monedie, whose mother-in-law was to be buried that day. Oh what a difference is there between the English and the Scottish method of burial! The English does honour to human nature; and even to the poor remains, that were once a temple of the Holy Spirit! But when I see in Scotland a coffin put into the earth and covered up without a word spoken, it reminds me of what was spoken concerning Jehoiakim, 'He will have the burial of a donkey'!

Wednesday June 1. I went to Edinburgh, and the next day examined the Society one by one. I was agreeably surprised. They have fairly profited since I was here last. Such a number of persons having sound Christian experience I never found in this Society before. I preached in the evening to a very elegant congregation, and yet with great enlargement of heart.

Wesley's terrible ride

Monday 20. About nine I set out from Sunderland for Horsley, with Mr Hopper and Mr Smith. I took Mrs Smith and her two little girls in the chaise with me. About two miles from the town, just on the brow of the hill, on a sudden both the horses set out, without any visible cause, and flew down the hill like an arrow out of a bow. In a minute John fell off the coach-box. The horses then went on full speed, sometimes to the edge of the ditch on the right, sometimes to the left. A cart came up against them; they avoided it as exactly as if the man had been on the box. A narrow bridge was at the foot of the hill. They went directly over the middle of it. They ran up the next hill with the same speed; many persons meeting us, but getting out of the way. Near the top of the hill was a gate, which led into a farmer's yard. It stood open. They turned short, and ran through it, without touching the gate on one side or the post on the other.

I thought, 'However, the gate which is on the other side of the yard, and is shut, will stop them': but they rushed through it as if it had been a cobweb, and galloped on through the cornfield. The little girls cried out, 'Grandpapa, save us!' I told them, 'Nothing will hurt you: do not be afraid'; feeling no more fear or care (blessed be God!) than if I had been sitting in my study. The horses ran on till they came to the edge of a steep precipice. Just then Mr Smith, who could not overtake us before, galloped in between. They stopped in a moment. Had they gone on ever so little, he and we would have gone down together!

I am persuaded both evil and good angels had a large share in this transaction: how large we do not know now; but we shall know hereafter.

Tuesday 28. This being my birthday, the first day of my seventy-second year, I was considering how it was that I find just the same strength as I did thirty years ago; that my sight is considerably better now and my nerves firmer than they were then; that I have none of the infirmities of old age, and have lost several I had in my youth. The grand cause is, the good pleasure of God, who does whatever pleases him. The chief means are: 1. My constantly rising at four, for about fifty years. 2. My generally preaching at five in the morning; one of the most healthy exercises in the world. 3. My never travelling less, by sea or land, than four thousand five hundred miles in a year.

A Methodist Isaac Newton

Monday October 31 and the following days I visited the societies near London.

Friday November 4. In the afternoon John Downes (who had preached with us many years) was saying, 'I feel such a love to the people at West Street that I could be content to die with them. I do not find myself very well; but I must be with them this evening.' He went there, and began preaching on 'Come to me, all you who are weary and burdened.' After speaking ten or twelve minutes, he sank down and spoke no more, till his spirit returned to God.

I suppose he was by nature full as great a genius as Sir Isaac Newton. I will mention but two or three instances of it. When he was at school, learning algebra, he came one day to his master and said, 'Sir, I can prove this proposition a better way than it is proved in the book.' His master thought it could not be; but upon trial, acknowledged it to be so. Some time after, his father sent him to Newcastle with a clock which was to be mended. He observed the clockmaker's tools, and the manner how he took it to pieces and put it together again; and when he came home, first made himself tools, and then made a clock which went as true as any in the town. I suppose such strength of genius as this has scarcely been known in Europe before.

Another proof of it was this. Thirty years ago, while I was shaving, he was whittling the top of a stick. I asked, 'What are you doing?' He answered, 'I am taking your face, which I intend to engrave on a copper plate.' Accordingly, without any instruction, he first made himself tools, and then engraved the plate. The second picture which he engraved was that which was prefixed to the *Notes upon the New Testament*.

For several months past, he had far deeper communion with God than ever he had had in his life; and for some days he had been frequently saying, 'I am so happy that I scarcely know how to live. I enjoy such fellowship with God as I thought could not be had on this side of heaven.'

Sunday 13. After a day of much labour, at my usual time (half-past nine), I lay down to rest. I told my servants, 'I must rise at three, the Norwich coach setting out at four.' Hearing one of them knock, though sooner than I expected, I rose and dressed myself; but afterwards, looking at my watch, I found it was but half-hour past ten. While I was considering what to do, I heard a confused sound of many voices below: and looking out at the window towards the yard, I saw it was as light as day. Meantime, many large flakes of fire were continually flying about the house; all the upper part of which was built of wood, which was nearly as dry as tinder. A large timber yard, at a very small distance from us, was all in a light fire; from which the north-west wind drove the flames directly upon the Foundery; and there was no possibility of help, for no water could be found. Perceiving I could be of no use, I took my diary and my papers, and retired to a friend's house. I had no fear; committing the matter into God's hands, and knowing that he would do whatever was best. Immediately the wind turned about from north-west to south-east, and our pump supplied the engines with abundance of water; so that in a little more than two hours, all the danger was over.

Tuesday 22. I took a solemn and affectionate leave of the Society at Norwich. About twelve we took coach. About eight on *Wednesday 23,* Mr Dancer met me with a chaise and took me to Ely. Oh what lack of common sense! Water covered the high-road for a mile and a half. I asked, 'How must pedestrians come to the town?' 'Why, they must wade through!'

Saturday December 11. I made some additions to the *Calm Address to our American Colonies.* Need anyone ask from what motive this was written? Let him look round: England is in a flame! A flame of malice and rage against the king, and almost all that are in authority under him. I labour to put out this flame. Ought not every true patriot to do the same?

Sunday 12. I was desired to preach a charity sermon in Bethnal Green church, for the widows and orphans of the soldiers that were killed in America. Knowing how many would seek occasion of offence, I wrote down my sermon.

Preaching from the stocks

1776. Tuesday April 30. In the evening I preached in a kind of square, at Colne, to a multitude of people, all drinking in the word. I scarcely ever saw a congregation wherein men, women, and children stood in such a posture: and this in the town where thirty years ago no Methodist could show his head! The first that preached here was John Jane, who was innocently riding through the town when the zealous mob pulled him off his horse and put him in the stocks. He seized the opportunity and vehemently exhorted them 'to flee from the wrath to come'.

Wednesday May 1. In travelling through Berkshire, Oxfordshire, Bristol, Gloucestershire, Worcestershire, Warwickshire, Staffordshire, Cheshire, Lancashire, Yorkshire, Westmoreland, and Cumberland, I diligently made two enquiries: the first was concerning the increase or decrease of the people; the second, concerning the increase or decrease of trade. As to the latter, it is, within these two last years, amazingly increased; in several branches in such a manner as has not been known in the memory of man: such is the fruit of the entire civil and religious liberty which all England now enjoys! And as to the former, not only in every city and large town, but in every village and hamlet, there is no decrease, but a very large and swift increase.

'A very extraordinary genius'

Monday 6. After preaching at Cockermouth and Wigton, I went on to Carlisle, and preached to a very serious congregation. Here I saw a very extraordinary genius, a man blind from four years of age who could wind worsted, weave flowered plush on an engine and loom of his own making; who wove his own name in plush, and made his own clothes, and his own tools of every sort. Some years ago, being shut up in the organ loft at church, he felt every part of it, and afterwards made an organ for himself, which judges say is an exceedingly good one. He then taught himself to play upon it psalm tunes, anthems, voluntaries, or anything which he heard. I heard him play several tunes with great accuracy, and a complex voluntary: I suppose all Europe can hardly produce such another instance. His name is Joseph Strong. But what is he the better for all this, if he is still 'without God in the world'?

Friday 17. I reached Aberdeen in good time.

Saturday 18. I read over Dr Johnson's *Tour to the Western Isles.* It is a very curious book, written with admirable sense and, I think, great fidelity; although in some respects he is thought to bear hard on the nation, which I am satisfied he never intended.

Wesley criticises the Scottish universities

Monday 27. I paid a visit to St Andrews, once the largest city in the kingdom. What is left of St Leonard's college is only a heap of ruins. Two colleges remain. One of them has a tolerable square; but all the windows are broken, like those of a brothel. We were informed that the students do this before they leave the college. Where are their blessed governors in the mean time? Are they all fast asleep? The other college is a mean building, but has a handsome library newly erected. In the two colleges, we learned, were about seventy students; near the same number as at Old Aberdeen. Those at New Aberdeen are not more numerous: neither those at Glasgow. In Edinburgh, I suppose, there are a hundred. So four universities contain three hundred and ten students! These all come to their different colleges in November, and return home in May! So they may study five months in the year, and lounge all the rest! Oh where was the common sense of those who instituted such colleges? In the English colleges, every one may reside all the year, as all my pupils did; and I should have thought myself little better than a highwayman if I had not lectured them every day in the year but Sundays.

Friday June 28. I am seventy-three years old, and far abler to preach than I was at twenty-three. What natural means has God used to produce so wonderful an effect? 1. Continual exercise and change of air, but travelling more than four thousand miles in a year. 2. Constant rising at four. 3. The ability, if ever I want, to sleep immediately. 4. The never losing a night's sleep in my life. 5. Two violent fevers and two deep consumptions. These, it is true, were rough medicines; but they were of admirable service, causing my flesh to come again as the flesh of a little child. May I add, lastly, evenness of temper? I feel and grieve; but, by the grace of God, I fret at nothing.

1777. Thursday February 2. I began expounding, in order, the book of Ecclesiastes. I never before had so clear a sight either of the meaning or the beauties of it. Neither did I imagine that the several parts of it were in so exquisite a manner connected together; all tending to prove that grand truth—that there is no happiness out of God.

In Bethnal Green hamlet

Wednesday 15. I began visiting those of our Society who lived in Bethnal Green hamlet. Many of them I found in such poverty as few can conceive without seeing it. O why do not all the rich that fear God constantly visit the poor? Can they spend part of their spare time better? Certainly not. So they will find in that day when 'every man shall receive his own reward according to his own labour'.

Such another scene I saw the next day, in visiting another part of the society. I have not found any such distress, no, not in the prison of Newgate. One poor man was just creeping out of his sick-bed, to his ragged wife and three little children; who were more than half naked, and the very picture of famine; when someone brought in a loaf of bread, and they all ran, seized upon it, and tore it in pieces in an instant. Who would not rejoice that there is another world?

City Road chapel begun

Monday April 21 was the day appointed for laying the foundation stone of the new chapel. The rain befriended us much by keeping away thousands who intended to be there. But there were still such multitudes that it was with great difficulty I got through them to lay the first stone.

Monday July 21. Having been much pressed to preach at Jatterson, a colliery six or seven miles from Pembroke, I began soon after seven. The house was presently filled, and all the space about the doors and windows; and the poor people drank in every word. I had finished my sermon, when a gentleman, violently pressing in, bade the people get home and mind their business. As he used some bad words, my driver spoke to him. He fiercely said, 'Do you think I need to be taught by a chaise boy?' The lad replying, 'Really, sir, I do think so,' the conversation ended.

Are the Methodists a fallen people?

Tuesday August 5. Our yearly Conference began. I now particularly enquired (as that report had been spread far and wide) of every assistant, 'Have you reason to believe, from your own observation, that the Methodists are a fallen people? Is there a decay or an increase in the work of God where you have been? Are the societies in general more dead, or more alive to God, than they were some years ago?' The almost universal answer was, 'If we must "know them by their fruits", there is no decay in the work of God among the people in general. The societies are not dead to God: they are as much alive as they have been for many years. And we look on this report as a mere device of Satan, to make our hands hang down.'

In most places, the Methodists are still a poor despised people, labouring under reproach and many inconveniences; therefore, wherever the power of God is not, they decrease. By this, then, you may form a sure judgement. Do the Methodists in general decrease in number? Then they decrease in grace; they are a fallen, or, at least, a falling people. But they do not decrease in number; they continually increase; therefore, they are not a fallen people.

Wesley starts a magazine

Monday November 14. Having been many times desired, for about forty years, to publish a magazine, I at length complied; and now began to collect materials for it. If it once begin, I incline to think it will end only with my life.

Wesley discusses old sermons

1778. Tuesday September 1. I went to Tiverton. I was musing here on what I heard a good man say long since—'Once in seven years I burn all my sermons; for it is a shame if I cannot write better sermons now than I could seven years ago.' Whatever others can do, I really cannot. I cannot write a better sermon on the Good Steward than I did seven years ago: I cannot write a better on the Great Assize than I did twenty years ago: I cannot write a better on the use of money than I did about thirty years ago: indeed, I do not know that I can write a better on the circumcision of the heart than I did forty-five years ago. Perhaps, indeed, I may have read five or six hundred books more than I had then, and may know a little more history, or natural philosophy, than I did: but I am not aware that this has made any essential addition to my knowledge in divinity. Forty years ago I knew and preached every Christian doctrine which I preach now.

City Road chapel opened

Sunday November 1 was the day appointed for opening the new chapel in the City Road. It is perfectly neat, but not fine; and contains far more people than the Foundery: I believe, together with the morning chapel, as many as the Tabernacle.

Thursday 5. I returned to Chatham, and the following morning set out on the stage-coach for London. At the end of Stroud, I chose to walk up the hill, leaving the coach to follow me. But it was in no great haste: it did not overtake me till I had walked over five miles. I cared not if it had been ten: the more I walk, the sounder I sleep.

Sunday 15. Having promised to preach in the evening at St Antholin's church, I had desired someone to have a coach ready at the door, when the service at the new chapel was ended. But he had forgotten; so that, after preaching and meeting the society, I was obliged to walk as fast as I could to the church.

Wesley goes north

1779. Monday March 15. I began my tour through England and Scotland.

Thursday 25. I preached in the new house which Mr Fletcher has built in Madeley Wood. The people here exactly resemble those at Kingswood; only they are more

simple and teachable. But for lack of discipline, the
immense pains which he has taken with them has not done
the good which might have been expected.

I preached at Shrewsbury in the evening, and on *Friday
26,* about noon, in the assembly room at Broseley. It was
well we were in the shade; for the sun shone as hot as it
usually does at midsummer. We walked from there to
Coalbrookdale, and looked at the bridge which is shortly to
be thrown over the Severn. It is one arch, a hundred feet
broad, fifty-two high, and eighteen wide; all of cast iron,
weighing many hundred tons. I doubt whether the Colos-
sus at Rhodes weighed much more.

Sunday May 21 (Edinburgh). The rain hindered me
from preaching at noon upon the Castle Hill. In the evening the house was well filled, and I was enabled to speak
strong words. But I am not a preacher for the people of
Edinburgh.

Wednesday 31. I went to Mr Parker's, at Shincliff, near
Durham. The congregation being far too large to get into
the house, I stood near his door. It seemed as if the whole
village were ready to receive the truth. Perhaps their
earnestness may provoke the people of Durham to
jealousy.

The Bishop of Durham's tapestry

In the afternoon we viewed the castle at Durham, the residence of the bishop. The situation is wonderfully fine, surrounded by the river, and commanding all the country;
and many of the apartments are large and stately; but the
furniture is mean beyond imagination! I know not where
I have seen such in a gentleman's house, or a man of five
hundred a year, except that of the Lord Lieutenant in
Dublin. In the largest chambers, the tapestry is quite
faded; beside that, it is coarse and ill-judged. Take but one
instance—in Jacob's vision you see, on the one side, a little
paltry ladder, and an angel climbing it, in the attitude of a

chimney-sweep; and on the other side Jacob staring at him from under a large silver-laced hat.

Wesley visits Lord George Gordon in the Tower

Saturday December 16 (London). Having a second message from Lord George Gordon, earnestly desiring to see me, I wrote a line to Lord Stormont, who on *Monday 18* sent me a warrant to see him. On *Tuesday 19* I spent an hour with him, at his apartment in the Tower. Our conversation turned upon popery and religion. He seemed to be well acquainted with the Bible; and had abundance of other books, enough to furnish a study. I was agreeably surprised to find he did not complain of any person or thing; and cannot but hope his confinement will take a right turn, and prove a blessing to him.

Friday 22. At the desire of some of my friends, I accompanied them to the British Museum. What an immense field is here for curiosity to range in! One large room is filled from top to bottom with things dug out of the ruins of Herculaneum! Seven huge apartments are filled with curious books; five with manuscripts; two with fossils of all sorts, and the rest with various animals. But what account will a man give to the Judge of living and dead for a life spent in collecting all these?

Friday 29. I saw the indictment of the Grand Jury against Lord George Gordon. I stood aghast! What a shocking insult upon truth and common sense! But it is the usual form. The more is the shame. Why will not the Parliament remove this scandal from our nation?

1781. Thursday January 25. I spent an agreeable hour at a concert of my nephews. But I was a little out of my element among lords and ladies. I love plain music and plain company best.

June 3 (being Whitsunday). I preached in the market-place [in Castleton, Isle of Man] again about nine, to a still larger congregation than before, on 'I am not ashamed of the gospel of Christ.' How few of the genteel hearers could say so!

Between six and seven I preached on the sea-shore at Peel, to the largest congregation I have seen in the island; even the society nearly filled the house. I soon found what spirit they were of. Hardly in England (unless perhaps at Bolton) have I found so plain, so earnest, so simple a people.

An ideal circuit

Thursday 7. I met our little body of preachers. They were twenty-two in all. I never saw in England so many stout, well-looking preachers together. If their spirit be answerable to their look, I know not what can stand before them. In the afternoon I rode over to Dawby, and preached to a very large and very serious congregation.

Friday 8. Having now visited the island round, east, south, north, and west, I was thoroughly convinced that we have no such circuit as this either in England, Scotland, or Ireland. It is shut up from the world; and, having little trade, is visited by scarcely any strangers. Here are no papists, no Dissenters of any kind, no Calvinists, no disputers. Here is no opposition, either from the governor (a mild, humane man), from the bishop (a good man), or from the bulk of the clergy. One or two of them did oppose for a time; but they seem now to understand better. So that we have now rather too little, than too much reproach; the scandal of the cross being, for the present, ceased. The natives are a plain, artless, simple people; unpolished, that is, unpolluted; few of them are rich or genteel; the far greater part moderately poor; and most of the strangers that settle among them are men that have seen affliction. The local preachers are men of faith and love, knit together in one mind and one judgement. They speak either Manx or English, and follow a regular plan, which the assistant gives them monthly.

The isle is supposed to have thirty thousand inhabitants. Allowing half of them to be adults, and our societies to contain two thousand one hundred or two thousand two hundred members, what a fair proportion is this! What has been seen like this, in any part either of Great Britain or Ireland?

Saturday 9. We would willingly have set sail; but the strong north-east wind prevented us.

Monday 11. It being moderate, we put to sea: but it soon died away into a calm; so I had time to read over and consider Dr Johnson's *Tour through Scotland*. I had heard that he was severe upon the whole nation; but I could find nothing of it. He simply mentions (but without any bitterness) what he approved or disapproved: and many of the reflections are extremely judicious; some of them very moving.

Tuesday 12. Having several passengers on board, I offered to give them a sermon; which they willingly accepted. And all behaved with the utmost decency, while I showed 'His commandments are not burdensome'. Soon after, a little breeze sprang up which, early in the morning, brought us to Whitehaven.

Thursday 28. I preached at eleven in the main street at Selby to a large and quiet congregation; and in the evening at Thorne. Today I entered my seventy-ninth year; and by the grace of God I feel no more of the infirmities of old age than I did at twenty-nine.

Friday 29. I preached at Crowle and Epworth. I have now preached three times a day for seven days in succession; but it is just the same as if it had been but once.

'A low, soft, solemn sound'

1782. March 29 (being Good Friday). I came to Macclesfield just time enough to assist Mr Simpson in the laborious service of the day. I preached for him morning and afternoon; and we administered the sacrament to about thirteen hundred persons. While we were administering, I heard a low, soft, solemn sound, just like that of an Æolian harp. It continued five or six minutes, and so moved many people that they could not refrain from tears. It then gradually died away. Strange that no other organist (that I know) should think of this. In the evening I preached at our room. Here was that harmony which art cannot imitate.

Tuesday May 14. Some years ago four factories for spinning and weaving were set up at Epworth. In these a large number of young women, and boys and girls, were employed. The whole conversation of these was profane and loose to the last degree. But some of these stumbling in at the prayer-meeting were suddenly cut to the heart. These never rested till they had gained their companions. The whole scene was changed. In three of the factories, no more lewdness or profaneness were found; for God had put a new song in their mouth, and blasphemies were turned to praise. Those three I visited today, and found religion had taken deep root in them. No trifling word was heard among them, and they watch over each other in love. I found it exceedingly good to be there, and we rejoiced together in the God of our salvation.

Friday 31. As I lodged with Lady Maxwell at Saughton Hall (a good old mansion house, three miles from Edinburgh), she desired me to give a short discourse to a few of her poor neighbours. I did so, at four in the afternoon, on the story of Dives and Lazarus. About seven I preached in our house at Edinburgh, and fully delivered my own soul.

Saturday June 1. I spent a little time with forty poor children whom Lady Maxwell keeps at school. They are swiftly brought forward in reading and writing, and learn the principles of religion. But I observe in them all the love of finery. Be they ever so poor, they must have a scrap of finery. Many of them have not a shoe to their foot: but the girl in rags is not without her ruffles.

Sunday July 14. I heard a sermon in the old church, at Birmingham, which the preacher uttered with great vehemence against these 'hairbrained, itinerant enthusiasts'. But he totally missed his mark; having not the least conception of the persons whom he undertook to describe.

No repose for Wesley

Wednesday 17. I went on to Leicester; *Thursday 18* to Northampton; and *Friday 19* to Hinxworth, in Hertford-shire. Adjoining Miss Harvey's house is a pleasant garden; and she has made a shady walk round the neighbouring meadows. How gladly could I repose awhile here! But repose is not for me in this world. In the evening many of the villagers flocked together, so that her great hall was well filled. I would hope some of them received the seed in good ground, and will bring forth fruit with patience.

'The tide is now turned'

1783. Wednesday January 1. May I begin to live today!

Sunday 5. We met to renew our covenant with God. We never meet on this occasion without a blessing; but I do not know that we had ever so large a congregation before.

Sunday 19. I preached at St Thomas's church in the afternoon, and at St Swithin's in the evening. The tide is now turned; so that I have more invitations to preach in churches than I can accept.

Friday February 21. At our yearly meeting for that purpose, we examined our yearly accounts, and found the money (just answering the expense) was upwards of three thousand pounds a year. But that is nothing to me: what I receive of it yearly is neither more nor less than thirty pounds.

Thursday December 18. I spent two hours with that great man, Dr Johnson, who is sinking into the grave by a gentle decay.

1784. Monday April 5. I was surprised, when I came to

Chester, to find that there also morning preaching was quite left off, for this worthy reason: 'Because the people will not come, or at least not in the winter.' If so, the Methodists are a fallen people. Here is proof. They have 'lost their first love': and they never will or can recover it till they 'do the first works'.

Wesley and early rising

As soon as I set foot in Georgia, I began preaching at five in the morning; and every communicant, that is, every serious person in the town, constantly attended throughout the year: I mean, every morning, winter and summer, unless in the case of sickness. They did so till I left the province. In the year 1738, when God began his great work in England, I began preaching at the same hour, winter and summer, and never lacked a congregation. If they will not attend now, they have lost their zeal; and then, it cannot be denied, they are a fallen people.

And, in the meantime, we are labouring to secure the preaching-houses to the next generation! In the name of God, let us if possible secure the present generation from drawing back to perdition! Let all the preachers that are still alive to God join together as one man, fast and pray, lift up their voice as a trumpet, be instant, in season, out of season, to convince them they are fallen; and exhort them instantly to repent, and 'do the first works': this in particular—rising in the morning, without which neither their souls nor bodies can long remain in health.

Twelve and a half miles in heavy rain

Monday 10. I set out for Inverness. I had sent Mr M'Allum ahead, on George Whitefield's horse, to give notice of my coming, so I had to take both George and Mrs M'Allum with me in my chaise. To ease the horses we walked forward from Nairn, ordering Richard to follow us as soon as they were fed: he did so, but there were two roads. So, as we took one and he the other, we walked about twelve miles and a half of the way, through heavy rain. We then found Richard waiting for us at a little ale-house, and drove on to Inverness. But, blessed be God, I was no more tired than when I set out from Nairn. I preached at seven to a far larger congregation than I had seen here since I preached in the kirk. And surely the labour was not in vain: for God sent a message to many hearts.

Tuesday 11. Notwithstanding the long discontinuance of morning preaching, we had a large congregation at five. I breakfasted at the first house I was invited to at Inverness.

Wesley at 81

Monday June 28 (Epworth). Today I entered on my eighty-second year, and found myself just as strong to labour, and as fit for any exercise of body or mind, as I was forty years ago. I do not impute this to second causes, but to the sovereign Lord of all. It is he who bids the sun of life stand still, so long as it pleases him.

I am as strong at eighty-one as I was at twenty-one; but abundantly more healthy, being a stranger to the head-ache, toothache, and other bodily disorders which attended me in my youth. We can only say, 'The Lord reigns!' While we live, let us live to him!

Tuesday August 31. Dr Coke, Mr Whatcoat, and Mr Vasey came down from London, in order to embark for America.

Wednesday September 1. Being now clear in my own mind, I took a step which I had long weighed in my mind, and appointed Mr Whatcoat and Mr Vasey to go and serve the desolate sheep in America.

Thursday 2. I added to them three more; which, I verily believe, will be much to the glory of God.

1785. Saturday January 1. Whether this is the last or not, may it be the best year of my life!

Tuesday 4. At this season we usually distributed coals and bread among the poor of the society. But I now thought that they wanted clothes as well as food. So on this and the four following days I walked through the town, and begged two hundred pounds in order to clothe those who needed it most. But it was hard work as most of the streets were filled with melting snow, which often lay ankle deep; so that my feet were steeped in snow water nearly from morning till evening: I held it out pretty well till Saturday evening; but I was laid up with a violent flux, which increased every hour till, at six in the morning, Dr Whitehead called upon me. His first draught made me quite easy; and three or four more perfected the cure. If he lives some years, I expect he will be one of the most eminent physicians in Europe.

Sunday 23. I preached morning and evening at West Street, and in the evening in the chapel at Knightsbridge: I think it will be the last time; for I know not that I have ever seen a worse-behaved congregation.

Tuesday 25. I spent two or three hours in the House of Lords. I had frequently heard that this was the most venerable assembly in England. But how was I disappointed! What is a lord, but a sinner, born to die!

Fifty years' growth of Methodism

Thursday March 24 (Worcester). I was now considering how strangely the grain of mustard-seed, planted about fifty years ago, had grown up. It has spread through all Great Britain and Ireland; the Isle of Wight, and the Isle of Man; then to America, from the Leeward Islands through the whole continent into Canada and Newfoundland. And the societies, in all these parts, walk by one rule, knowing religion is holy tempers; and striving to worship God, not in form only, but likewise 'in spirit and in truth'.

Tuesday June 28. By the good providence of God, I finished the eighty-second year of my age. Is anything too hard for God? It is now eleven years since I have felt any such thing as weariness: many times I speak till my voice fails, and I can speak no longer; frequently I walk till my strength fails, and I can walk no farther; yet even then I feel no sensation of weariness, but am perfectly easy from head to foot. I dare not impute this to natural causes: it is the will of God.

Wesley hears the king speak

1786. Monday January 9. At leisure hours this week, I read the *Life of Sir William Penn*, a wise and good man. But I was much surprised at what he relates concerning his first wife; who lived, I suppose, fifty years, and said a little before her death, 'I bless God, I never did anything wrong in my life!' Was she then ever convinced of sin? And if not, could she be saved on any other footing than a heathen?

Tuesday 24. I was desired to go and hear the king deliver his speech in the House of Lords. But how agreeably was I surprised! He pronounced every word with exact propriety. I much doubted whether there be any other king in Europe that is so just and natural a speaker.

Tuesday September 26. Reached London. I now applied myself in earnest to the writing of Mr Fletcher's *Life*, having procured the best materials I could. To this I dedicated all the time I could spare, till November, from five in the morning till eight at night. These are my studying hours; I cannot write longer in a day without hurting my eyes.

Sunday December 24. I was desired to preach at the Old Jewry. But the church was cold, and so was the congregation. We had a congregation of another kind the next day, Christmas Day, at four in the morning, as well as five in the evening at the new chapel, and at West Street chapel about noon.

Wesley's threat to Deptford

1787. Monday January 1. We began the service at four in the morning, to an unusually large congregation. We had another comfortable opportunity at the new chapel at the usual hour, and a third in the evening at West Street.

Tuesday 2. I went over to Deptford; but it seemed, I was got into a den of lions. Most of the leading men of the Society were mad for separating from the church. I endeavoured to reason with them, but in vain: they had neither good sense nor even good manners left. At length, after meeting the whole Society, I told them, 'If you are resolved, you may have your service in church hours; but, remember, from that time you will see my face no more.' This struck deep; and from that hour I have heard no more of separating from the church!

Monday 8 and the four following days I went begging for the poor. I hoped to be able to provide food and raiment for those of the Society who were in pressing want, yet had no weekly allowance: these were about two hundred: but I was much disappointed. Six or seven, indeed, of our brethren gave me ten pounds apiece. If forty or fifty had done this, I could have executed my plan. However, much good was done with two hundred pounds, and many sorrowful hearts made glad.

Wesley visits the Irish Parliament house

Wednesday July 4. I spent an hour at the New Dargle, a gentleman's seat four or five miles from Dublin. I have not seen so beautiful a place in the kingdom. It equals the Leasowes in Warwickshire; and it greatly exceeds them in situation; all the walks lying on the side of a mountain which commands all Dublin Bay as well as an extensive and finely variegated land view. A little river runs through it, which occasions two waterfalls, at a small distance from each other. Although many places may exceed this in grandeur, I believe none can exceed it in beauty.

Afterwards I saw the Parliament house. The House of Lords far exceeds that at Westminster; and the Lord Lieutenant's throne as far exceeds that miserable throne (so called) of the King in the English House of Lords. The House of Commons is a noble room indeed. It is an octagon, wainscoted round with Irish oak, which shames all mahogany, and galleried all round for the convenience of the ladies. The Speaker's chair is far more grand than the throne of the Lord Lieutenant. But what surprised me above all were the kitchens of the house, and the extensive equipment for good eating. Tables were placed from one end of a large hall to the other; which, it seems, while the Parliament sits, are daily covered with meat at four or five o'clock, for the accommodation of the Members.

Wesley on his old age

Saturday December 22. I yielded to the importunity of a painter, and sat an hour and a half in all for my picture. I think it was the best that was ever taken; but what is the picture of a man of more than eighty?

1788. Saturday March 1 (being Leap year). I considered, what difference do I find by an increase of years? I find, 1. Less activity; I walk slower, particularly uphill. 2. My memory is not so quick. 3. I cannot read so quick by candle-light. But I bless God that all my other powers of body and mind remain just as they were.

Saturday April 19. We went on to Bolton, where I preached in the evening in one of the most elegant houses in the kingdom, and to one of the liveliest congregations. And this I must avow, there is not such a set of singers in any of the Methodist congregations in the three kingdoms. There cannot be; for we have about a hundred such trebles, boys and girls, selected out of our Sunday schools, and accurately taught, as are not found together in any chapel, cathedral, or music-room within the four seas. Besides, the spirit with which they all sing, and the beauty of many of them, so suits the melody that I defy any to exceed it; except the singing of angels in our Father's house.

Sunday 20. At eight, and at one, the house was thoroughly filled. About three I met between nine hundred and a thousand of the children belonging to our Sunday schools. I never saw such a sight before. They were all exactly clean, as well as plain, in their apparel. All were serious and well-behaved. Many, both boys and girls, had as beautiful faces as, I believe, England or Europe can afford. When they all sang together, and none of them out of tune, the melody was beyond that of any theatre; and, what is the best of all, many of them truly fear God, and some rejoice in his salvation. These are a pattern to all the town. Their usual diversion is to visit the poor that are sick (sometimes six, or eight, or ten together), to exhort, comfort, and pray with them. Frequently ten or more of them get together to sing and pray by themselves; sometimes thirty or forty; and are so earnestly engaged, alternately singing, praying and crying, that they know not how to part. You children that hear this, why should not you go and do likewise? Is not God here as well as at Bolton? Let God arise and maintain his own cause, even 'from the lips of children and infants'!

Wesley's reasons for his long life

Saturday June 28. Today I enter on my eighty-fifth year: and what cause have I to praise God, as for a thousand spiritual blessings, so for bodily blessings also! How little have I suffered yet by 'the rush of numerous years'! It is true, I am not so agile as I was in times past. I do not run or walk so fast as I did; my sight is a little decayed; my left eye is grown dim, and hardly serves me to read; I have daily some pain in the ball of my right eye, as also in my right temple (occasioned by a blow received some months ago), and in my right shoulder and arm, which I impute partly to a sprain and partly to the rheumatism.

I find likewise some decay in my memory, with regard to names and things recently past; but not at all with regard to what I have read or heard twenty, forty, or sixty years ago; neither do I find any decay in my hearing, smell, taste, or appetite (though I want but a third of the food I did once); nor do I feel any such thing as weariness, either in travelling or preaching: and I am not conscious of any decay in writing sermons; which I do as readily, and I believe as correctly, as ever.

What is to be done?'

Sunday July 6. I came to Epworth before the church service began; and was glad to observe the seriousness with which Mr Gibson read prayers, and preached a plain useful sermon; but was sorry to see scarcely twenty communicants, half of whom came on my account. I was informed likewise, that scarcely fifty persons usually attend the Sunday service. What can be done to remedy this sore evil?

I would prevent the members here from leaving the church; but I cannot do it. As Mr G. is not a pious man, but rather an enemy to piety, who frequently preaches against the truth and those that hold and love it, I cannot with all my influence persuade them either to hear him or to attend the sacrament administered by him. If I cannot carry this point even while I live, who then can do it when I die? And the case of Epworth is the case of every church where the minister neither loves nor preaches the gospel. The Methodists will not attend his ministrations. What then is to be done?

An important Conference

I preached at the new chapel (London) every evening during the Conference, which continued nine days beginning on *Tuesday July 29* and ending on *Wednesday August 6*.

One of the most important points considered at this Conference was that of leaving the church. The sum of a long conversation was, 1. that in the course of fifty years we had neither premeditately nor willingly varied from it in one article either of doctrine or discipline; 2. that we were not yet conscious of varying from it in any point of doctrine; 3. that we have in a course of years, out of necessity, not choice, slowly and warily varied in some points of discipline, by preaching in the fields, by extemporary prayer, by employing lay preachers, by forming and regulating Societies, and by holding yearly Conferences. But we did none of these things till we were convinced we could no longer omit them, except at the peril of our souls.

Wesley sits to Romney

1789. Monday January 5. At the earnest desire of Mrs T., I once more sat for my picture. Mr Romney is a painter indeed. He struck off an exact likeness at once; and did more in one hour than Sir Joshua did in ten.

Friday 9. I left no money to anyone in my will, because I had none. But now considering that, whenever I am removed, money will soon arise by the sale of books, I added a few legacies by a codicil, to be paid as soon as may be. But I would like to do a little good while I live; for who can tell what will come after him?

Tuesday 20. I retired in order to finish my year's accounts. If possible, I must be a better economist; for instead of having anything beforehand, I am now considerably in debt: but this I do not like. I would like to settle even my accounts before I die.

Wesley explains Methodism

April 12 (Dublin) (being Easter Day). We had a solemn assembly indeed; many hundred communicants in the morning; and in the afternoon far more hearers than our room would contain, though it is now considerably enlarged. Afterwards I met the Society, and explained to them at large the original design of the Methodists, namely, not to be a distinct party, but to stir up all parties, Christians or heathens, to worship God in spirit and in truth; but the Church of England in particular, to which they belonged from the beginning. With this view I have uniformly gone on for fifty years, never varying from her discipline, of choice, but of necessity: so, in a course of years, necessity was laid upon me (as I have proved elsewhere), 1. to preach in the open air; 2. to pray extempore; 3. to form societies; 4. to accept the assistance of lay preachers: and, in a few other instances, to use such means as occurred, to prevent or remove evils that we either felt or feared.

Saturday August 8. I settled all my temporal business, and, in particular, chose a new person to prepare the *Arminian Magazine*; being obliged, however unwillingly, to drop Mr O., for only these two reasons: 1. The errata are insufferable; I have borne them for these twelve years, but can bear them no longer. 2. Several pieces are inserted without my knowledge, both in prose and verse. I must see if these things cannot be amended for the short residue of my life.

The last year of the Journal

1790. Friday January 1. I am now an old man, decayed from head to foot. My eyes are dim; my right hand shakes much; my mouth is hot and dry every morning; I have a lingering fever almost every day; my motion is weak and slow. However, blessed be God, I do not slack my labour: I can preach and write still.

Monday June 28. Today I enter into my eighty-eighth year. For more than eighty-six years, I found none of the infirmities of old age; my eyes did not grow dim, neither was my natural strength abated: but last August I found almost a sudden change. My eyes were so dim that no glasses would help me. My strength likewise quite forsook me; and probably will not return in this world. But I feel no pain from head to foot; only it seems nature is exhausted.

Sunday September 5. At ten we had a numerous congregation, and more communicants than ever I saw before. Today I cut off that vile custom, I know not when or how it began, of preaching three times a day by the same preacher to the same congregation; enough to weary out both the bodies and minds of the speaker, as well as his hearers. Surely God is returning to this Society! They are now in earnest to make their calling and election sure.

Wednesday 13. In the evening I preached at Norwich; but the house would in no wise contain the congregation. How wonderfully is the tide turned! I am become an honourable man at Norwich. God has at length made our enemies to be at peace with us; and scarcely any but antinomians open their mouth against us.

Sunday 24. I explained, to a numerous congregation in Spitalfields church, 'the whole armour of God'. St Paul's, Shadwell, was still more crowded in the afternoon, while I enforced that important truth, 'One thing is needful'; and I hope many, even then, resolved to choose the better part.

Wesley's Last Hours

[This account (condensed) was written by Betsy Ritchie, one of the saints of early Methodism. At the time she was about thirty-nine, and for the last two months of Wesley's life was his constant companion.]

On Thursday [February 24, 1791] Mr Wesley paid his last visit to that lovely place and family, Mr Wolff's, at Balaam, which I have often heard him speak of with pleasure and much affection. Here Mr Rogers said he was cheerful, and seemed nearly as well as usual, till Friday, about breakfast time, when he seemed very heavy.

About eleven o'clock Mrs Wolff brought him home: I was struck with his manner of getting out of the coach, and going into the house, but more so as he went upstairs, and when he sat down in the chair. I ran for some refreshment, but before I could get anything for him he had sent Mr R. out of the room, and desired not to be interrupted for half an hour by anyone, adding, not even if Joseph Bradford come.

Mr Bradford came a few minutes after, and as soon as the limited time was expired, went into the room; immediately after, he came out and desired me to mull some wine with spices and carry it to Mr Wesley: he drank a little and seemed sleepy. In a few minutes he was seized with sickness, threw it up, and said, 'I must lie down.' We immediately sent for Dr Whitehead: on his coming in Mr

Wesley smiled and said, 'Doctor, they are more afraid than hurt.' He lay most of the day, with a quick pulse, burning fever and extremely sleepy.

Saturday the 26th, he continued much the same; spoke but little, and if roused to answer a question or take a little refreshment (which was seldom more than a spoonful at a time) soon dozed again.

On Sunday morning, with a little of Mr Bradford's help, Mr Wesley got up, took a cup of tea, and seemed much better. Many of our friends were all hopes: yet Dr Whitehead said he was not out of danger from his present complaints.

Monday the 28th, his weakness increased apace, and his friends in general being greatly alarmed, Dr Whitehead was desirous they should call in another physician. Mr Bradford mentioned his desire to our Honoured Father, which he absolutely refused, saying, 'Dr Whitehead knows my condition better than anyone; I am perfectly satisfied and will not have anyone else.' He slept most of the day, spoke but little; yet that little testified how much his whole heart was taken up in the case of the churches, the glory of God, and the things pertaining to that kingdom to which he was hastening. Once in a low, but very distinct manner, he said, 'There is no way into the holiest but by the blood of Jesus.' Had he strength at the time, it seemed as if he would have said more.

Tuesday, March 1st, after a very restless night (though, when asked whether he was in pain, he generally answered 'No,' and never complained through his whole illness, except once, when he said that he felt a pain in his left breast, when he drew his breath), he began singing:

> All glory to God in the sky,
>   And peace upon earth be restor'd.

[Having sung two verses] his strength failed, but after lying still awhile he called on Mr Bradford to give him a pen and ink; he brought them, but the right hand had well-nigh forgotten its cunning. I replied, 'Let me write for you, sir; tell me what you would say.' 'Nothing,' returned he, 'but that God is with us.' In the forenoon he said, 'I will get up.' While his things were getting ready, he broke out in a manner which, considering his extreme weakness, astonished us all, in these blessed words:

> I'll praise my Maker while I've breath,
> And when my voice is lost in death,
>   Praise shall employ my nobler pow'rs;
> My days of praise shall ne'er be past,
> While life, and thought, and being last,
>   Or immortality endures.

Which were also the last words our Reverend and dear Father ever gave out in the City Road chapel, namely, on Tuesday evening before preaching from 'We through the Spirit wait,' etc.

When he got into his chair, we saw him change for death: but he, regardless of his dying frame, said with a weak voice, 'Lord, you give strength to those that can speak, and to those that cannot: Speak, Lord, to all our hearts, and let them know that you loosen tongues.' He then sang:

> To Father, Son, and Holy Ghost,
>   Who sweetly all agree.

Here his voice failed him, and after gasping for breath, he said, 'Now we have done—Let us all go.' We were obliged to lay him down on the bed from which he rose no more: but after lying still and sleeping a little he called me to him and said, 'Betsy, you, Mr Bradford etc. pray and praise.' We knelt down, and truly our hearts were filled with the divine presence; the room seemed to be filled with God.

The next pleasing awful scene was the great exertion he

made in order to make Mr B. (who had not left the room) understand that he fervently desired a sermon he had written on the love of God should be widely distributed, and given away to everybody.

A little after, finding we could not understand what he said, he paused a little, and then with all the remaining strength he had, cried out, 'The best of all is, God is with us'—and then, as if to assert the faithfulness of our promise-keeping Jehovah, and comfort the hearts of his weeping friends, lifting up his dying arm in token of victory, and raising his feeble voice with a holy triumph not to be expressed, again repeated the heart-reviving words, 'The best of all is, God is with us!'

Most of the night following, though he was often heard attempting to repeat the psalm before-mentioned, he could only get out,

I'll praise— I'll praise—!

On Wednesday morning we found the closing scene drew near. Mr Bradford, his faithful friend, and most affectionate son, prayed with him, and the last word he was heard to articulate was, 'Farewell!' A few minutes before ten, according to his often expressed desire, without a lingering groan, this man of God gathered up his feet in the presence of his brethren.